BLACKS
IN
SCIENCE

ancient and modern

——o——

editor

Ivan Van Sertima

Transaction Books
New Brunswick (U.S.A.) and London (U.K.)

Tenth Printing, © 1990

Library of Congress Catalog Number 83-71004
ISBN 0-87855-941-8 (paper)
Printed in the United States of America

Cover design by Jacqueline Patten-Van Sertima

Blacks in Science: Ancient and Modern

Incorporating JOURNAL OF AFRICAN CIVILIZATIONS,
April & November 1983 issues (vol. 5, nos. 1 & 2)

Contents

Foreword

This is the first book of its kind in the English-speaking world. While several books on African-American science and invention have been published (see *Bibliographical Guide*) no work has yet attempted to give serious treatment to the technologies of early Africa. This is partly due to the fact that it is only within recent years that archaeology has revealed the lineaments of a lost African science, at least in areas outside of Egypt. It is also only within recent years that the discovery of a seminal black kingdom in the Nile Valley, predating the Egyptian dynasties, has settled the question, once and for all, of the roots of classical Egyptian culture and technology (see *Journal of African Civilizations*, vol. 4, no. 2, November 1982).

Within the last decade alone, evidence has been unearthed in the field of agricultural and pastoral science, architecture, aeronautics, engineering, mathematics, mining, metallurgy and medicine, navigation and physics, that has made the whole ground, upon which conventional studies of Africa have been built, rock violently with the shock of astonishing discoveries. These are astonishing only because the nerve of the world has been deadened for centuries to the vibrations of African genius. Every new revelation has made us realize that the eyes of the anthropologist and historian have been focussing on the edge or periphery of the African world, blind to all that has lain within the heartland of its civilizations.

Anthropology has had a long love affair with the primitive and has preferred to set its tent down among the African bushmen, exploring the simplicities of tiny tribal communities rather than the complexities to be found in the primary centers of large African nations. Very partial and limited visions of the African hovering on the fringes of his vast world have come to represent the totality of his capacity and potential. Even notable African scholars, in their romantic embrace of this exotic savage, have come to the conclusion that the African invented nothing, explored nothing, but occupied some special sensory or emotional realm in his experience of the natural world.

Five centuries of these falsehoods have been exploded in just five years. These years have seen the discovery of African steel-smelting in Tanzania 1,500-2,000 years ago, an astronomical observatory in Kenya 300 years before Christ, the cultivation of cereals and other crops by Africans in the Nile Valley 7,000 years before any other civilization, the domestication of cattle in Kenya 15,000 years ago, the domestic use of fire by Africans 1,400,000 years ago (one million years before its first known use in China) the use of tetracyclene by an ancient African population fourteen centuries ago, an African glider-plane 2,300 years old, a probe by microwave beams of an American radar satellite beneath the sands of the Sahara, revealing cultures 200,000 years old and the traces of ancient rivers running from this African center. Some of these buried stream valleys seem to be "ancient connections to the Upper Nile tributaries," towards which blacks migrated, later peopling Nubia and Egypt.

A book dealing with the sciences of Africa cannot be complete without essays on the paradigms or models of African science. Writers like Hunter Adams III attempt this in his work on the Dogon but we would like to open future editions of this book to more extended ventures in this virginal field. Many pieces that now exist on this subject, unfortunately, are rich in speculative fantasy and poor in theoretical substance. It would do a great disservice to this pioneering work, however tentative and inadequate, to open its pages to too much guesswork. African science does not have to apologize for its apparent paucity for enough has already been discovered in a very short time to make it quite clear that a great deal still remains to be brought to light. Nor does it have to dwell on dubious fantasies about mysterious ways or processes of arriving at the knowledge of things, methodologies which cannot be repeated by other human beings. There are certainly other ways of knowing but, until we can state with a fair amount of certainty what these other ways are, we should not encumber this virginal field with pseudoacademic dream-models and science fiction.

We have provided in our introduction an overview of the lost sciences of Africa in areas outside of Egypt. The most recent issue of the *Journal of African Civilizations* establishes, beyond a doubt, the African claim to Egyptian civilization and science but for us to cover the ground of Egyptian science comprehensively would be a formidable task. We have contented ourselves in this volume to underlining the most significant aspects of Afro-Egyptian mathematics, physics, engineering, and astronomy, and to the great debt early European technology owes to the Egyptian.

Since several books on African-American science and invention are readily available, we have confined our survey of the black contribution to modern technology to a general overview of the most significant aspects. This overview is written by Robert C. Hayden, author of three books on African-American science and invention. The other essays in this section are original probes into the African-American contribution to nuclear physics, information technologies, and the space sciences.

Few Americans are aware of the major contributions of blacks to modern technology. In 1913 alone as many as one thousand inventions were patented by African-Americans, and those were the fortunate few who got as far as the patent office. In the nineteenth century several slaves invented labor-saving devices but were not allowed to patent them in their own names. In 1858 the Attorney General of the United States ruled that since a patent was a contract between the government and the inventor, and since a slave was not considered a United States citizen, he could not make a contract with the government.

In spite of these oppressive and inhospitable circumstances, there was no total loss of black ingenuity and technological innovation. The thread of African genius began to unravel, like light speeding through spools of the glassfibre lightguides black scientist Northover developed. Or like impulses travelling along the transatlantic cable Richardson helped to lay down, channelling voices from one continent to another, one time to another, bridging the chasm between the ancestral African and the modern black, between root and branch, seed and flower, an old heart and a new brain.

Ivan Van Sertima

THE LOST SCIENCES OF AFRICA:
AN OVERVIEW

Ivan Van Sertima

One of the marvels of Africa, which mystified many early travellers, was the way in which some of its peoples communicated information almost instantly over vast distances. Europeans often told stories of arriving in a place after many days' journey to find that the people there already knew the details of an event—a battle or a birth, a death or a disaster—which had occurred in a far part of the country from whence they had just come. This was before the telegraphic morse-code or the radio. We know today, of course, of the finely tuned instruments Africans devised to relay messages over these distances, sometimes with drum-scripts so ingenious they came close to a rhythmic mimicking of the human voice. Some of their communication devices, however, still baffle us.

Charles Breasted, son of James Henry Breasted, the most celebrated of American Egyptologists, details a method the Nubians used to transmit the human voice for a distance of nearly two miles across the Nile. ''We never ceased marvelling,'' he wrote, in a biography of his father, ''at their ability to converse with one another across great stretches of water. Again and again in places where the Nile had suddenly widened to a breadth of almost two miles so that we would have to inquire locally regarding possible inscriptions or ruins along the farther shore we would watch a man address a friend so far away on the opposite bank as to be a mere speck wholly out of earshot. He would stand at the very edges of the river, perhaps ten feet above its surface, and cupping his hands some four inches in front of his lips, would talk into the water at an angle of about 45 degrees, in a loud voice but without shouting. At intervals he would stop and listen while the distant man evidently replied in kind. But we who stood close by heard no sound. Presently the exchange would end, and he would tell us in a matter-of-fact way what he had learned . . .''

This ability to communicate information swiftly over considerable distances must have been a great boon to West Africans who, between the thirteenth and fifteenth centuries, had to administer empires as large as all the states of Western Europe put together. It did not make them any different, however, from Europeans or Asians or Americans in terms of the relatively slow spread of new techniques or technologies from the centers to the edges or peripheries of their civilizations. Thus, a skilled African surgeon could be performing delicate eye-cataract surgery in the city of Jenné in medieval Mali while a villager would be going blind with cataracts a few hundred miles away on the edges of the same empire, for lack of his fine medical instrumentation and expertise.

This phenomenon of concentration of high technology in a center (scholar or priest-caste, trading post or royal capital) and its absence or slow spread to the periphery (village or desert outpost or forest) was the same the world over, at least before the industrial revolution. Instancy of communication today—the fact that we live in a "global village" connected by radio, telephone and television—makes it less so. Thus almost everyone on the planet now can be in instant touch, theoretically, with everyone else. But something very fundamental has remain unchanged. High technologies (with their complex information networks) are still concentrated in certain primary centers and still relatively absent or disproportionately dispersed at the edges. All that has changed is that the centers of high-technology now lie in powerful industrial blocs (cities of the super-powers) while whole countries or continents, with mere scraps of that technology, perch on the periphery.

It is important to understand this if we are to understand how a science or technology may rise and fall with a civilization, why the destruction of a center could lead to the almost instant evaporation or disappearance of centuries of knowledge and technical skills. Thus a nuclear war could shatter the primary centers of twentieth-century technology in a matter of days. The survivors on the periphery, although they would remember the aeroplanes and the television sets, the robots and the computers, the space machines now circling our solar system, would not be able for centuries to reproduce that technology. Apart from the almost wholesale slaughter of the technocratic class, the interconnection between those shattered centers and the equally critical interdependency between the centers and their peripheries, would be gone forever. It would be like the strands of a web which once stretched across the world, left torn and dangling in a void.

A dark age would certainly follow. Centuries afterwards, the technological brilliance of the twentieth century would seem dream-like and unreal. Until archeology began to pick up the pieces, those of us who follow in the centuries to come will obviously doubt what had been achieved in the centuries preceding the disaster. This has happened before in the world. Not in the same way, of course, but with the same catastrophic effect. It happened in Africa.

No human disaster, with the exception of the Flood (if that biblical legend is true) can equal in dimension of destructiveness the cataclysm that shook Africa. We are all familiar with the slave trade and the traumatic effect of this on the transplanted black but few of us realize what horrors were wrought on Africa itself. Vast populations were uprooted and displaced, whole generations disappeared, European diseases descended like the plague, decimating both cattle and people, cities and towns were abandoned, family networks disintegrated, kingdoms crumbled, the threads of cultural and historical continuity were so savagely torn asunder that henceforward one would have to think of two Africas: the one *before* and the one *after* the Holocaust. Anthropologists have said that eighty per cent of traditional African culture survived. What they mean by *traditional* is the only kind of culture we have come to accept as *African*—that of the primitive on the periphery, the stunned survivor. The African genius, however, was not to remain buried forever. Five centuries later, archeologists, digging among the ruins, began to pick up some of the pieces.

Metallurgy

In 1978 anthropology professor, Peter Schmidt, and professor of engineering, Donald Avery, both of Brown University, announced to the world that, between 1,500-2,000 years ago, Africans living on the western shores of Lake Victoria, in Tanzania, had produced carbon steel.

The Africans had done this is pre-heated forced-draft furnaces, a method that was technologically more sophisticated than any developed in Europe until the mid-19th century. "We have found," said Professor Schmidt, "a technological process in the African Iron Age which is exceedingly complex . . . . To be able to say that a technologically superior culture developed in Africa more than 1,500 years ago overturns popular and scholarly ideas that technological sophistication developed in Europe but not in Africa."

There were Africans still living (the Haya people, for example) who, although they no longer produced steel, remembered, down to the last identity of detail, the machine and the process their ancestors used and were able to reconstruct the furnace and carry out a successful smelt. When Schmidt and Avery began excavating near Lake Victoria and dug up 13 Iron Age furnaces, they found that "the construction of the furnaces and the composition of the steel was essentially the same."

The temperature achieved in the blast furnace of the African steel-smelting machine was higher than any achieved in an European machine until modern times. It was roughly 1,800°C, some 200 to 400°C higher than the highest reached in European cold blast bloomeries. The record for Europe was in an experimental 2nd century Roman shaft furnace where scientists recorded a temperature in the combustion zone of 1,600°C.

The African superiority was due to the fact that they preheated the air blast by inserting blowpipes into the base of the furnace. This not only led to the extraordinarily high temperatures but also to greater fuel economy. This was important since, in the areas where the Africans produced steel, there is evidence of a severe depletion of forest resources, demanding a fuel-saving technology.

The machine they devised and the resourceful way they made use of available materials, is in itself fascinating. For example, the pit they dug beneath the furnace was lined with mud made from a termite mound. The termite mound was an excellent choice since termites make their hills of materials that won't absorb water, bits of alumina and silica piled up grain by grain. The African also introduced a process in their smelting that was very original and in advance of their time, making steel through the formation of iron crystals rather than by "the sintering of solid particles" as in European smelting. This led Professor Avery to comment: "It's a very unique process that uses a large number of sophisticated techniques. This is really semi-conductor technology—the growing of crystals—not iron-smelting technology.''

This technology was not confined to Lake Victoria. Further investigations showed that there was a widespread distribution of Early Iron Age industrial sites in West Lake and neighboring areas, such as Rwanda in Uganda. The nature of the industry also indicates that these Africans lived in densely populated centers, with an organized, highly cooperative labor force.

Astronomy—Kenya

In the same year that the African steel-machine was discovered, another team of American scientists—Lynch and Robbins of Michigan State—uncovered an astronomical observatory in Kenya. It was dated 300 years before Christ and was found on the edge of Lake Turkana. It was the ruins of an African Stonehenge, with huge pillars of basalt like the stumps of petrified trees lying at angles in the ground. The place had an awesome-sounding name, *Na-mo-ra-tu-nga*, which, in the Turkana language, means "the stone people."

Not far away the scientists had found stones like these but they were merely standing in circles around graves. They were probably just ceremonial slabs of stone marking the sites of ancestors. But the huge stone pillars at Namoratunga II were different. These—there were 19 of them—were arranged in rows and set down at such angles that the sense of an order, precise and significant, immediately struck the observers.

Lynch and Robbins knew that modern Cushites in Eastern Africa had a calendar based on the rising of certain stars and constellations. If this were true, they would have before them the keystone of the system, the prehistoric beginnings, in fact, of one of the most accurate of pre-Christian calendars.

They decided to check this out carefully, to see if the stones did line up with the rising of these stars and the location of these constellations. There was, however, one problem. The world had not remained in the same precise place since 300 B.C. There had been gradual changes in its axis of rotation since then.

They made allowances for this and found that their hunch was correct. Taking observations at various points of this ancient African observatory, they found that each stone was aligned with a star as it rose in 300 B.C. Using Stone 18 as a sighting point for example (see diagram) they could see the star Bellatrix lined up with Stone 17, the constellation Orion with Stone 16, the Star Sirius with Stone 15, Saiph with Stone 14, and so on. Every stone, except one, made it quite clear that this was no random pattern but that a definite relationship existed between the pillars at Namoratunga and the stars. The one exception was a stone too small to be a line of sight.

"This evidence," the team concluded "attests to the complexity of prehistoric cultural developments in sub-Saharan Africa. It strongly suggests that an accurate and complex calendar system based on astronomical reckoning was developed by the first millenium B.C. in eastern Africa."

Astronomy—The Dogon of Mali

Far more remarkable than the megalithic observatory found in Kenya before Christ is the discovery of extremely complex knowledge of astronomy among a people in West Africa known as the Dogon. These people live in a mountainous area of the Republic of Mali, about 200 miles from where the legendary university of Timbuctoo once lay. The astronomer-priests of the Dogon had for centuries, it seems, a very modern view of our solar system and of the universe—the rings of Saturn, the moons of Jupiter, the spiral structure of the Milky Way Galaxy, in which our planet lies. They knew a billion worlds spiralled in space like the circulation of blood within the body of God. They knew that the moon was a barren world. They said it was "dry and dead, like dried blood." They knew also of things far in advance of their time, intricate details about a star which no one can see except with the most powerful of telescopes. They not only saw it. They observed or intuited its mass and its nature. They plotted its orbit almost up until the year 2,000. And they did all this between five and seven hundred years ago.

Hunter Adams III, a scientist at the Argonne National Laboratory (Argonne I), in an article, "African Observers of the Universe: The Sirius Question," has thrown the most recent light on the scientific breakthrough of these Africans. He not only summarizes the work done by anthropologists on the Dogon but he exposes the gross prejudices of Eurocentric scientists who try to explain away what the Dogon have done, who simply would not accept that any African astronomer-priest could have developed a science of the heavens so advanced that it could yield knowledge which, until the 20th century, escaped European observation.

The Dogon were studied very closely and over a considerable period of time by two French anthropologists, Marcel Griaule and Germaine Dieterlen. From 1931 to1956—a whole generation—the two lived and worked with these people, looked at and listened to everything, wrote down all they could find out, even drew diagrams of the evocative architecture of the Dogon village, which is patterned after the form of the human body. Griaule and Dieterlen sank their roots into the people so deep that they became Dogon. They were initiated into the tribe. Griaule became so loved and trusted that, when he died, quarter of a million Africans turned up at his funeral.

And yet, in spite of this intimacy, they had to pass through stage after stage of initiation—"the word at face value"—"the word on the side"—"the word from behind" before the Dogon allowed them to enter the inner sanctum of their most secret knowledge. Their education lasted longer than the American student's passage from high school to Ph.D. Not until the sixteenth year, as Adams tells us, did the Dogon call together a conference to reveal to these Europeans the *first level* in an eight-level stage on the highest ladder of their knowledge. This stage was known as "the clear word."

Among the revelations that emerged at this stage was the Dogon's intimate knowledge of, and concern with, a star within the Sirius star system. They had a ceremony to Sirius every sixty years, when the orbits of Jupiter and Saturn converge. But the odd thing about it was that, although Sirius is the brightest star in the sky, the ceremony was not to Sirius at all but to its companion, Sirius B, a star so small, so dense, so difficult to perceive, it is truly amazing that any medieval science was aware of it. It turned out that the Dogon were not only aware of it but saw it as the basis of that star system while Sirius A, the big, bright star we know so well, was simply the point around which this unusual little star orbited. To the Dogon this dwarf was the most important star in the sky. To them, it was "the egg of the world."

The Dogon knew that this star, although invisible to the naked eye, had an elliptical orbit around Sirius A that took 50 years to complete. Modern science confirms this orbit. The Dogon drew a diagram (see illustration) showing the course and trajectory of this star up unto the year 1990. Modern astronomical projections are identical with this. The Dogon say that this tiny star is composed of a metal brighter than iron and that if all the men on earth were a single lifting force they could not budge it. Modern science confirms that this is the nature of that type of star—"a white dwarf"—a star so compacted that its mass may be many times greater than a star which appears many times larger. But the Dogon go even farther than that in their observations about this star, *beyond what we know now*. They say it has an orbit of one year around its own axis. They were so certain of this that they held a special celebration—the *bado* celebration—to honor that orbit. Modern science has not yet been able to confirm or deny that observation.

To provide such detail about something that only the most advanced observatories can detect today and to do it in advance of them, has sent, as Adams puts it "shock waves throughout the scientific world." Adams cites a number of responses from scholars which reveal the profound contempt for African scientific capabilities which still dominates world scholarship.

Kenneth Brecher of the Massachusetts Institute of Technology, for example, said quite bluntly in an article "They [the Dogon] have no business knowing any of this." Brecher suggests that perhaps a Jesuit priest told them about it. Robert Temple, a member of the Royal Astronomical Society of Great Britain, in a highly acclaimed book, *The Sirius Mystery*, speculates that space-beings from the Sirius star-system must have brought this marvelous knowledge down to the Africans. Humbled by evidence of the scientific advances of the Egyptians and the Sumerians, whom he links with the later Dogon, Temple arrogantly claims: "Civilization, as we know it, was an importation from another star in the first place . . . . The linked cultures of Egypt and Sumer in the Meditteranean area simply came out of nowhere. We knew there were lots of people but we found no traces of civilization." Carl Sagan, superstar of the TV series *Cosmos*, goes one step further. His solution to the mystery is some clever European traveller who appeared among the Dogon before the anthropologists came to study them. This scientifically literate European, proposes Sagan, exchanged his sophisticated knowledge of the stars in return for the savages' simple lore. When Griaule and Dieterlen came, the blacks merely played back what they had heard in parrot-like fashion. Sagan has not even stopped to consider that no scientifically literate European, even today, much less before 1931, can speak with the certainty of the Dogon elders of the one-year orbit of Sirius B on its own axis. Nor has it occurred to him that this obsession with that star-system expressed itself in ceremonies among the Dogon centuries ago nor that the tradition they were supposed to have imbibed from an itinerant white genius and regurgitated to the anthropologists like parrots, never surfaced until after sixteen years of continuous probing.

Recent evidence by Russian archeologists, Chinese astronomers, an American orbiting satellite, and a French film-maker, provide more rational explanations for this African breakthrough. Adams is at pains to point out that the whole approach to science by the Dogon may have been very different from the West, such a subtle blend of the empirical and the intuitive that it enabled them to arrive at this knowledge in a variety of ways, without the instruments we think are necessary. He nevertheless presents evidence that such instruments (telescopes) were available to them. Their trade with the Egyptians, even after the decline of Egyptian civilization, may be one clue. The Russians have found crystal lenses, perfectly spherical and of great precision, in ancient Egypt, during the African-dominated period. Galileo always insisted that the ancients had telescopes. "It is a short and simple step," says Adams "to place one lens in front of another to make a basic telescope, and the chances are it could have happened and many times."

He also points to aspects of this astronomical knowledge which they could have acquired by acute and sustained observations with the naked eye. For example, the rings of Saturn, the moons of Jupiter and one of the stars in the Sirius system which they show in their drawings in various states of emergence.

Corroborating this, Adams points out: First, the Chinese report sighting the moons of Jupiter with the naked eye 2000 years before Galileo. To prove that this is possible, China's Institute for the History of Natural Science of Academia Sinica conducted an experiment in 1981 in which six Chinese astronomers did in fact see Jupiter's moons with the naked eye. Second, the "Einstein" orbiting observatory recently discovered a dwarf-novae in the vicinity of Sirius B, which appears to be part of the Sirius star-system. Dwarf-nova are stars that rhythmically expand and contract and, at certain times, their luminosity is so great that they can possibly be seen with the naked eye. Jean Rouch, the French anthropologist/film-maker, who worked closely with Griaule and Dieterlen, and who has recently been in touch with Adams, reports that the Dogon elders stay up all night and watch the sky. "They watch from caves and from the roof-top terraces of their homes." Their eyes would be extremely dark-adapted. Adams contends, on the strength of a Dogon drawing, in which they show a star in the Sirius system in various states of emergence, that this star could have been the very dwarf-novae recently observed, yet the Dogon saw it at its maximum brightness and recorded the event five to seven centuries ago.

Mathematics

The tendency to deny an African astronomical science is due to the fact that such accurate observations over long periods involve the most precise record-keeping, a capacity to measure complex distances and times, to calculate orbits and azimuths and convergences. That calls for a mathematics and not just the simple handcount of one, two, many. Very few anthropological works have ever mentioned a mathematical system in Africa. At the moment only one single book exists—*Africa Counts: Number and Pattern in African Culture* by Claudia Zaslavsky—which attempts to deal with mathematics south of the Sahara.

Why is mathematics so rarely mentioned in the study of the African? One reason, of course, is the assumption that the African was incapable of developing an abstract body of thought. Another is the fact that anthropology has a love affair with the primitive and would prefer to set its tent down among the bushmen of the Kalahari than among African traders who are accustomed to dealing in large sums of currency. There is a world of difference between the mathematical thinking of a hunter and gatherer and a trader from an African city-state.

Not all Africans had mathematics, it is true, but neither did all Europeans. Most Europeans got their mathematics from the Greeks who used cumbersome letters of their alphabet for numbers. It was not until 1202 that Hindu numerals were introduced into Western Europe. These are the numerals we use today. We call them Arabic numerals because it was the Arabs who eventually got them accepted by most European traders as the Moorish hold was consolidated. The Church at first banned them. Mathematics progressed very little in Europe outside the commercial centers. The universities only taught some arithmetic and bits of Euclidean geometry, translated into Latin from the Arabic. Mathematics was viewed with general suspicion. One of the crimes for which the Spanish Inquisition inflicted death, Zaslavsky tells us, was possession of Arabic manuscripts and the study of mathematics. As late as the 17th century, the time of the persecution of Galileo, "mathematics was looked upon with fear in Europe because of the magical use of numbers."

Among the earliest evidence of the use of numbers is a find in Africa in the Congo (Zaire). These are markings—a notation count—on a bone 8,000 years old. It is known as the Ishango bone since it was found near an ancient fishing site of that name. The discoverer, Dr. de Heinzelin, says it is a numeration system. Dr. Marshack, who has examined the notches on the bone, concludes it was used as a lunar calendar. For whatever purpose the number system was used, it is the first we know of in Africa and among the first in the world.

Mathematics develops according to a need. If a situation calls for a simple count of objects a people will develop a simple set of numbers. If their cultural demands are more complex, a more complex mathematics system will evolve. Thus systems of numerations may range in Africa from a few number words among the San people, who have been pushed into the least hospitable areas of the continent, to the extensive numerical vocabulary of African nations having a history of centuries of commerce.

One such nation is the Yoruba and the related people of the city of Benin in Nigeria, who have been urbanized farmers and traders for centuries. They have a complex number system. The mathematician Conant calls it "the most peculiar number scales in existence." One has to be really bright at maths in our system to handle the Yoruba one. It is a system based on twenty, of which we find many examples in Western Africa. The unusual feature of this system is that it relies on substraction to a very high degree. To the Yoruba it seems perfectly natural and he uses it with the same ease with which we write IX (ten minus one) for nine in Roman numerals, or read the time as "Twenty (minutes) to three." Robert Armstrong, in a study of the Yoruba numerals, states that "it is a testimony to the Yoruba capacity for abstract reasoning that they could have developed and learned such a system."

But a mathematical system is not always recoverable, is not always blessed with historical continuity like that found among the Yoruba and a number of large African communities. It may be hidden in architectural design, like the Granary of the Master of Pure Earth (among the Dogon) or in abstract patterns, like that obtained from the combination of two geometric operations, translation and reflection on an axis (as in decorations on bowls and cloths of the Kuba of the Congo) or in measuring systems (like the exquisite brass weights for measuring gold dust currency among the Ashante) or in the complex network games the Shongo children play or in mathematical recreations, which are the delight of many Africans.

Zaslavsky touches on all these, but, as she herself admits, this is only a preliminary survey of a vast field, awaiting further investigation.

Architecture and Engineering

Mathematics is also needed for great engineering projects, the construction of enormous palaces or churches or ceremonial centers. Most people think that this kind of building may only be found in the north of Africa and that mud and straw and vines is the limit of materials used by the traditional African. People use what materials are available to them and where stone was available to Africans they built in stone. When less sturdy materials lay at hand, the African was still able to place the stamp of technological ingenuity upon those materials. A British engineer has cited suspension bridges built with vines by the Kikuyu which equalled in engineering skill and potential durability any comparable bridges of wood he had seen in his own country. South of the Sahara lie several architectural wonders. One of these is Great Zimbabwe, the most immense construction site found in Africa outside of the pyramids of Egypt.

Great Zimbabwe is a massive stone complex—perhaps we should call it a stone city—found seventeen miles south of Nyanda, a city in today's Zimbabwe. It is more than 800 years old but it was only two years ago, when Zimbabwe regained her independence, that any African scholars ventured to the site to study it closely. Molefi Asante and his wife, Kariamu Asante, both Fulbright scholars, have done the most recent study of this remarkable ruin.

The ancient plan of this stone city is in two parts. The king's part, the Royal Enclosure, is on the top of a hill. The other buildings—nine separate stone sites—are down in a valley. Among the buildings in the valley is the IMBA HURU, the Great Enclosure. Here the king really lived although he spent a lot of his time up on the hill. From that hill he could see the coming and going of traders and warriors along that valley for a distance of about thirty miles.

The Royal Enclosure on the hill is a fascinating and mysterious place. Secret winding passageways and stone steps approach it from the south and within the hill-top castle there are vast rooms, among these one for ritual, one for smelting, one for iron-keeping. The king kept his ironsmiths and copper craftsmen there. There was also a royal treasure-cove made by a huge granite rock.

Down in the valley, where the rest of the ancient city lies, is the largest of all the buildings—the Great Enclosure. The wall around this palace is 250 meters long. It is composed of 15,000 tons of granite blocks. Our African team, the Asantes, calculated that within a single section one meter long, from top to bottom, two meters thick, there were approximately 4,500 stone blocks. It is estimated that 10,000 people lived in that city, making it one of the largest cities of its day.

But it was not an isolated achievement at all. The Asantes point to the fact that in that area there are more than 200 stone villages. They are scattered over Zimbabwe and Mozambique. The site, Great Zimbabwe, was the seat of a civilization in the South. The same type of structural concept was spread over a very large area occupied by native Africans. The engineering skill of these Africans was not confined to architecture. Even before Great Zimbabwe became a seat of civilization, Africans in the southern part of the continent had dug the most ancient mines found in the world. Several such ancient mine works and rare minerals were discovered by the German treasure-seeker, Karl Mauch, not far from Great Zimbabwe itself.

Yet when this great stone city was found, Europeans not only began to steal the treasure but even the right of the native Africans to lay claim to their own civilization. Many books have been written, trying to prove that this architectural site, which is right in the heartland of Africa, half a thousand miles away from any seacoast, was built by Persians, Phoenicians, Portuguese, Arabs or Chinese. The fact that there are no prototypes for Zimbabwean architecture and art and ritual among any of these foreign peoples does not seem to bother the conjectural historians.

Had they stopped at stealing the claim, it would have been bad enough. But they stole everything they could put their hands on. Not just the faience and glass and celadon which the Africans imported in their overseas trade but enormous caches of ivory and gold, copper rings and necklaces and bangles and bracelets, bells and gongs, sacred birds of soapstone, divination bowls and dishes, even ritual phalli. The Asantes catalogue the thefts, part of the massive movement of ancient African treasures from their place of manufacture to the museums of the West. In 1871 a German prospector even carted away stone posts and confiscated a beautiful platter which he sold to Cecil Rhodes, after whom that area was solemnly named Rhodesia. As if that were not enough, the English Royal Horseguards attacked the Great Enclosure in 1892, gutting the inside of the building, taking everything that could be removed. When they were done, it was nothing but a shell of stone. "Even so," say the Asantes, "in its bewildering emptiness it remained an impressive example of African workmenship."

Great Zimbabwe rose in significance from the 12th century and flourished as the capital of an African empire, known as the *Munhu Mutapa* (or Monomotapa) for 300 years. The great stone city housed the emperor, his family, officials of the court, servants, and later, traders. It was the Shona people, say the Asantes, who built this center, seat of power for the southeastern interior of Africa. Like the earlier pyramids of Egypt, this structure not only "symbolized the power, permanence and authority of the ruler" but it also crystallized the science and technology of that people, place, and time.

Navigation

African engineering skill may also be seen in the skillful construction of boats. The image of jungle canoes promoted by Tarzan movies has created the popular impression of a fragile and easily capsizable dugout as the hallmark of African watercraft. The dugout, in fact, is just a basic building block, "a template," as oceanographer Stewart Malloy has shown, "for extension and expansion techniques used world-wide to make boats sea-worthy." Africans in West and Central Africa developed a variety of boats. They had a marine highway, two thousand, six hundred miles long, and on that highway—the Niger—one could find reed boats with sails, like the reed-boats of ancient Egypt and Ethiopia; log-rafts lashed together; enormous dugouts as wide-berthed, long and sturdy as Viking ships; double-canoes connected catamaran-fashion like the Polynesian; lateen-rigged dhows as used by the Arabs and the African maritime peasants on the Indian Ocean; rope-sewn plank vessels with cooking facilities in the hold and jointed boats fitted out with woven straw cabins.

Malloy has taken a new look at the watercraft of Western and Central Africa, a region which once formed part of a great interlocking trade network running from the Mediterranean to the Gulf of Guinea and from the West Coast to Lake Chad (see map). Western Africa was crisscrossed with a network of trade routes leading to the interior. These trade links between the West Coast and the Niger river existed for many centuries before the coming of the European. The nautical skills on the Atlantic coasts of Africa, which I note in my book *They Came Before Columbus*, originated largely, according to Malloy, beyond the coast, particularly on the Niger and in the neighborhood of Jenné and Timbuctoo, which were major cities in the Mali and Songhay empires.

When Mali and Songhay fell and Timbuctoo was destroyed, the trade routes leading to the interior of Africa lost much of their importance. The Niger, its tributaries, and the Senegambia region, no longer enjoyed the vast volumes of traffic and intercourse. As a result "there was a stagnation in innovative boat-building." Before this technology deteriorated, however, some travellers reported glimpses of the varied type of craft used on African rivers and seacoasts.

French traveller, Rene Caillié, describes a flotilla of eighty large boats carrying on trade between the cities of Jenné and Timbuctoo. The average vessel in this commercial fleet was of sixty to eighty tons burden, ninety to one hundred feet long, twelve to fourteen feet broad at midships, drawing six or seven feet of water. At Brasstown, above the Niger delta, Richard and John Lander found African trading vessels more than fifty feet in length, laden with several tons of cargo, ferrying sixty passengers, three sitting abreast with ease. Mungo Park, the famous explorer, cites jointed boats on the Niger. The technology of "jointing" greatly increases the potential length and width of a vessel and Henry Barth hired one of these to take three camels up the Niger. Some of these jointed boats, like those of the Djenne people, had woven straw cabins.

The most unique boat found in the interior of Africa, and using the dugout as a base, is the rope-sewn plank vessel. Malloy mentions some of these, ninety to one hundred feet long, with decks as well as berths, and cooking stoves in the hold. Dr. D.J. Muffett, O.B.E., formerly attached to the Institute of African Affairs, Duquesne University, wrote me about Kedde trading boats, which also had the dugout as a foundation base but which extended and expanded on this basic template. As a British administrator he had himself sailed on the Niger in one of these vessels.

"Dugout" would indeed be a poor way to describe such a vessel," wrote Dr. Muffett, "for, although based on a dugout in regard to its keel piece, it has a free board built up two feet six or three feet by wide planks fitted to the keel-boards and then stitched with either hemp or rawhide in a manner which Robert Rothberg has pointed out, closely resembles the technology of the Carthage-nians. These are big draught vessels able to heft ten tons or more of shifting cargo and powered by the familiar leg-o'-mutton sail."

Some dugouts resemble the lines of ancient Egyptian sea-going boats, with stem and stern upswept in curves out of the water. Their sails too look like those on these ancient types of boats. The Portuguese found African boats with sails on the Congo estuary. The sail, however, seems not to have been very common on African boats plying the inland waterways since it was not needed, whereas we find them rigged with sails on the Indian Ocean coast of Africa and in the trade-wind zones of the Atlantic Coast. In my own work I have cited African sailing boats used by the Swahili, like the model of the 70-ton *mtepe* found in the Fort Jesus museum in Mombasa, Kenya. The Chinese record Africans coming with elephants to the court of China in such ships as early as the thirteenth century, two hundred years before Columbus stumbled into the Caribbean.

Africans were found to be using nautical science in the Sahara desert. E.W. Bovill, in his famous work *The Golden Trade of the Moors*, reports the use of the compass and astronomical computations to guide the African caravans across the desert. The journey across the Sahara, in fact, is twice as long and twice as hazardous as a journey by Africans across the open sea from Africa to America (1,500 miles). Africans had to cross thousands of miles of trackless wasteland, whereas the Atlantic ocean has natural seaways (Heyerdahl calls them "marine conveyor belts") which automatically direct the seafarer, whether on an accidental or planned expedition. Africans had to solve the problems of storing grain for months while traversing the barren sands, whereas the sea is a mobile foodstore. Africans had to take huge waterjugs in their caravans to ensure supply before the next oasis, while fishjuice supplemented rainfall, however uncertain, in the trade wind zones of the Atlantic. Ignorance of their knowledge of navigation, gained on the longest commercial waterway in the world, has led many conventional anthropologists to doubt their capacity and potential for extended sea voyages.

It is not my intention here to cite evidence for the African presence in America before Columbus but there are certain facts touching on that thesis that must of necessity be noted here only because they also bear upon the African navigational knowledge as well as the diffusion of some of their plants, so critical to a discussion of their agricultural science.

Agricultural Science

Before I enter that discussion, I must note that several plants in the Sudanic agricultural complex—the bottle gourd, a species of jackbean and of yam, a strain of cultivated cotton—have been discovered in pre-Columbian strata in Middle and South America. The three main currents off the coast of Africa (off the Cape Verde, the Senegambia, and the southern African coast) which suck everything that remains afloat from Africa to America, can explain an unmanned drift voyage before Columbus of the bottle gourd. *The other plants, however, could not have come into this continent without the help of man.* This has been clearly established by botanists. They would have either submerged below the current and eventually sank or, if held up by driftwood, would have been unable to preserve their potency during a long drift. In models of African-type boats, such as we have described above, common on African waterways long before Columbus, the Atlantic journey has been successfully accomplished.

New studies of the Atlantic crossing show that African raft or reed boats could travel 60 miles per day on the currents, sailboats (and the wind is usually favorable) about a hundred miles per day. Gales seldom occur and most crossings are gentle. Thus Alain Bombard, using an African boat and fishing gear, did the journey in less time than either Columbus or Vespucci, whose sails, by the way, were lateen sails developed by the Arabs on another ocean.

The potential for plant diffusion, therefore, whether by accident or design, lay well within the range of African navigational science. But what of the science that produced the plants themselves? How could an African cultivated cotton intermarry with an American wild cotton (as the chromosomes clearly show) as early as 3,500 B.C.? Did Africans cultivate plants that early? A look at the most recent archeological discoveries in African agriculture provides the answer to that question.

The earliest technological leap from hunting and gathering activities to the scientific cultivation of crops occurred in Africa at least 7,000 years before it did on any other continent. *Science* magazine reported in 1979 the discovery by Fred Wendorf of agricultural sites near the Nile going back more than 10,000 years before the dynasties of Egypt. There, Africans were cultivating and harvesting barley and einkorn wheat. Grains of these cereals were carbon-dated at *Kubbaniya*, a site just a few miles north of Aswan, and these gave a reading of 17,850 B.C. plus or minus 200 years, which is roughly 17,500-18,000 years ago. Other sites, farther south, like *Tushka* in Nubia, indicated the same dating.

But not only were the Africans the first in crop-science but the first also in the domestication of cattle. These are the keystone elements necessary for the development of civilizations. University of Massachusetts anthropologist, Dr. Charles Nelson, announced to the *New York Times* in 1980 that his team had unearthed evidence in the Lukenya Hill district in the Kenya Highlands, about 25 miles from Nairobi, that Africans had been domesticating cattle 15,000 years ago.

Dr. Nelson said that the findings led them to conclude that pre-Iron Age Africans in that area had a relatively sophisticated society and could have spread their mores, living modes and philosophy, eventually reaching the fertile crescent of the Euphrates River Valley, which many had once thought was the cradle of civilization. African technologies, he suggested, were exported to the Middle East through trade and the cultural diffusion of information and ideas.

The possible diffusion of African agricultural technology, however, is not limited to the Nile and the Euphrates. As I mentioned earlier, some African cultivated crops (a strain of African cotton, a species of jackbean, and yam) have turned up before Columbus in the American agricultural complex, while African indigenous rice, finger millet, sorghum, pearl millet and cultivated cotton entered Western Asia surprisingly early. The questions arise: Where in Africa and how soon were these crops domesticated? How did they spread to other major agricultural complexes?

The picture in Africa is not yet complete but certain things we do know. Apart from the latest finds in Eastern Africa by Wendorf and Nelson, we have hard carbon dates for domesticated grains in the Saharan agricultural complex as early as 6,000 B.C. We know too that, as the Sahara became drier (5,020-2,500 B.C.) Africans were forced to migrate to other parts of the continent, taking their crop science with them. While, therefore, not enough work has yet been done along the Niger and hard carbon datings are few, we can link the sunset of the Saharan agricultural complex with the dawn of the Sudanic agricultural complex in the

Niger. Professor Davies has given the earliest hard carbon dating of roughly 3,000 B.C. (5,140 plus or minus 170 years) for an agricultural phase on the Niger but evidence from other disciplines suggests that this phase, known as the Tenere Neolithic, is a later phase in the development of West African agriculture. Considering that other Africans on the continent were thousands of years ahead of this, we should look very closely at the other suggestive evidence until archeology does more excavation in the region of the Niger.

The link up between the Saharan and the later Sudanic agricultural complex may be inferred by the great migration of peoples after the fertile Sahara began to turn into a desert, by the wide and early distribution of language networks and shared agricultural terms, by linked cultural and techno-complexes, by a study of plant geography. Peter Murdock, who concluded that over 25 food and fiber plants were domesticated around the Niger circa 4,500 B.C., has been violently attacked and, perhaps, with good reason, on some points of his thesis. But, as more and more has been unearthed, especially agricultural settlements 10,000 years earlier in the east of Africa, the botanists who tend towards this view are growing and are being taken more seriously.

It has been suggested that a people known as the Mande brought agriculture from the north to western Africa. The ancient Mande did have trade routes—a western one from southern Morocco toward the Upper Niger, another running from the Fezzan to the eastern side of the Niger. These routes are clearly marked by engravings of wheeled vehicles drawn by small horses. This small horse has not died out. It can still be found today in the Sahel region.

Professor Clyde Winters has placed the Mande very clearly in the Sahara at a very early date, citing their inscriptions at Oued Mertoutek, and demonstrating their movement down towards the Niger by a distribution of their habitation signs. He uses a new type of evidence, the evidence of an ancient African script in use by these Mande people.

In several articles, he has shown also the movement of Africans into Western Asia and the African origin of the Dravidians. It is the Dravidians, belonging to the C-group in Nubia, who are credited with the diffusion of several African domesticates to Asia. Winters has established many connections between the Dravidians, who are now Afro-Asiatic, with Black Africa in the far past, particularly through linguistic evidence and shared cultural traits. He also demonstrates that the crops we mentioned above, indigenous to Africa, appeared later in the Asian context in areas where these Dravidians settled.

The diffusion to America of African plants is of equal importance and I have dealt with this in considerable detail in my book *They Came Before Columbus*. Briefly, botanists have found that an African diploid cotton (*G. herbaceum*) crossed with a wild New World cotton several thousand years ago (3,500 B.C.) to form the New World tetraploid cottons (*G. hirsutum* and *G. barbadense*). They have also found that a jackbean (*canavalia sp.*) grew from an early marriage between African and New World beans. Karl Schwerin, an anthropologist attached to the University of New Mexico, has presented the case for this with great force.

He also holds that a species of yam (*dioscorea cayennensis*) which has its original home in West Africa, was the plant *ajes* cited by early Spanish explorers to America.

Africans indeed had the most intimate knowledge of plants, a fact used to great advantage not only in crop cultivation but also in the development of medicine, to which we now turn our attention.

Medicine

African plant medicine was more developed than any in the world before the disruption of its cultures. In spite of the tremendous knowledge that was lost and the fact that African medicine today does not reflect the best of what the earlier doctors knew, the fragments that survive still tell us quite a lot. Dr. Charles Finch of the Morehouse School of Medicine, writing in the *Journal of African Civilizations*, sketches in the background to African traditional medicine, not just its plant science but its psychotherapy, its approach to the diagnosis of diseases, its very early knowledge of anaesthetics, antiseptics, vaccination, and the advanced surgical techniques in use among African doctors.

African herbal medicine is extremely impressive. No one has yet done a comprehensive study of it but even the little that has been done so far reveals that several Western medicines were known to Africans before the Europeans discovered them. The Africans had their own aspirin. The Bantu-speaking peoples use the bark of *Salix capensis* to treat musculoskeletal pains and this family of plants yields salicylic acid, the active ingredient in aspirin. In Mali they had one of the most effective cures for diarrhea, using kaolin, the active ingredient in the American brand Kaopectate. Nigerian doctors have developed a herbal preparation to treat skin infections which rivals the best in the modern world. It was subjected to tests by Western-trained doctors in 1969 and found to have powerful bacteriocidal activity against gram-positive bacteria, the very organisms that cause skin infections. A breakthrough in cancer treatment may also lie in Nigerian medicine where the rootbark *Annona senegalensis* has been found to possess strong anti-cancer properties. Dr. Finch introduces us to far too many plant medicines than we can mention here—for abortion, for retarded labor, malaria fever, rheumatism, neurotoxic venoms, snakebite, intestinal parasites, skin ulcers, tumours, catarrh, convulsions, venereal disease, bronchitis, conjunctivitis, urethral stricture—all as effective as those in use in Western medicine which has borrowed African ouabain, capsicum, physostigmine, kola and calabar beans, to name just a few plant medicines. The African herbal pharmacy is staggering. The Zulus alone know the medicinal uses of 700 plants.

African doctors have also pioneered in the treatment of psychosis through herbs. There was an interesting case in 1925 of an eminent Nigerian, Finch tells us, who was suffering from severe psychotic episodes and English doctors could do nothing for him. A Nigerian traditional doctor used decoctions made from a rauwolfia root. The Rauwolfia family of plants is today the source of Reserpine, which was first used as a major tranquilizer to treat severe psychosis, and is now used against hypertension.

There is an element of ritual and magic in some African healing practices. This has been highlighted so often for sensational effect in films and books that it has obscured the serious scientific superstructure to African medicine. "Traditional medical practice is intimately acquainted with the psychic, social, and cultural naunces of the patients," Dr. Finch points out, "and the traditional African doctor is often an expert psychotherapist, achieving results with his patients that conventional Western psychotherapy cannot." The use of suggestion and hypnosis and the placebo, in addition to internal and external treatment, as the case may warrant, is becoming more and more appreciated in Western medicine. After all, many illnesses are more psychosomatic than organic. The typical African doctor did not emphasize the one at the expense of the other. Obviously, every profession has its quacks but Western-trained doctors who have studied the traditional medicine-man concede that the African doctor has a profound knowledge of the human body and anatomy. He usually gives a careful diagnosis, beginning with a history of the disease, followed by a thorough physical examination.

There were autopsies among the Banyoro of Uganda and the Likundu of Central Africa. These involved prolonged and exacting searches, the opening up and examination of a variety of organs, which contributed to an extensive knowledge of anatomy. The Africans also developed quarantine systems for contagious diseases. Finch cites the Mano of Liberia who designed a "sick bush" area to isolate patients suffering from smallpox. They developed also a smallpox vaccine centuries before Jenner, using the same principle of the later European vaccines. "During an epidemic, material from the pustule of a sick person is scratched into the skin of unaffected persons with a thorn."

Surgery also seems to be an area in which African doctors "attained a level of skill comparable with, and in some respects superior to, that of Western surgeons up unto the twentieth century." Finch cites traction methods for fractured limbs among the Mano of Liberia, inducing partial collapse of the lung to treat pleurisy and pneumoritis among the Masai, locating and removing a bullet by the use of stiff elephant hairs in the Congo, the almost miraculous replacement of intestines into an abdominal cavity ripped open by an elephant in Nigeria. These are just a few of the operations witnessed by Westerners and reported upon.

The most impressive of these is a Caesarean operation performed by Banyoro surgeons in East Africa. It was witnessed and sketched by Dr. Felkin in 1879, at a time when such operations were rare in Europe. The skill demonstrated in this operation startled readers of the Edinburgh Medical Journal where it was reported. The Africans were not only found to be doing the Caesarean section with routine skill but to be using antiseptic surgery, which Lister pioneered only two years earlier than this event, and when the universal application of his methods in the operating rooms of Europe were still years away. Not only did the African surgeon show an understanding of the sophisticated concepts of anaesthesia and antisepsis, says Dr. Finch, but he demonstrated advanced surgical technique, especially in his cautious use of the cautery iron, which without great skill can cause serious tissue damage.

As one commentator has said: "This was a skilled long-practiced surgical team at work conducting a well-tried and familiar operation with smooth efficiency and unhurried skill. . . . Lister's team in London could hardly have performed with greater smoothness."

Some of the medical practices and prescriptions, Dr. Finch tells us, were transmitted orally and since the oral tradition was subject to centuries of cultural disruption, a great deal was lost. It should be pointed out, however, that the oral tradition, especially traditions preserved by *griots* (pronounced gree-ohs) in the great African courts,were often as detailed, reliable, and enduring as written documents. British anthropologists were amazed when King Mutesa II of Uganda, fleeing the fall of the royal house, was able to recite 700 years of the history of the Baganda people, enough to fill a large volume.

Nevertheless, the question remains, why did the Africans leave no written documents? Why did they remain pre-literate while other peoples invented scripts and tried to write down what they knew for posterity to preserve and build upon?

Writing Systems

First of all, the assumption underlying these questions—that Africans did not develop writing systems—is a myth. There is evidence that probably half a dozen scripts were invented and used by Africans before the holocaust, although many of their manuscripts perished in the sack of Alexandria, the razing of Timbuctoo, and the burning of the Moorish documents in the squares of Granada on the order of Cardinal Ximenez.

Most of us have heard of the Meroitic script invented by the Nubians and partly influenced by the Egyptians. But what is far less known and far more important is the discovery, announced four years ago, that the origin of the Egyptian hieroglyphic system itself lies among black people in the Sudan. On March 1, 1979, this discovery made front-page news in the *New York Times*. Dr. Bruce Williams, a research associate of the Oriental Institute, University of Chicago, announced the discovery of a black kingdom, known as *Ta-Seti*, at a place called Qustul, which preceded the first dynasty in Egypt by twelve generations. About a dozen black kings reigned at Ta-Seti and all the major religious and political symbols of a later Egypt were found in this kingdom, the very first in the Nile Valley. On a stone incense burner dated 3,300 B.C. were carvings of the falcon-god Horus, the uniquely-shaped crown that was to adorn the later Egyptian kings, the sacred boat-litter of the pharoahs, the elaborate palace serekhs and facades—everything already in place among these royal blacks. Most important, the excavators found inscriptions—the earliest in the hieroglyphic system—in the tombs of Qustul, a system that was not only to be the mother of the Egyptian but was to have a seminal effect upon some European writing systems as well.

There were also ancient writing systems in the Saharan and Sudanic cultures — the Manding and the Akan, to mention two that have been the subject of recent discussion and debate. It must be conceded that scripts like these were used by relatively few Africans — by scholars and priests, by members of secret societies, sometimes by traders. Not many of the common people wrote and in some regions there was no writing at all. But this was no different from the situation among Europeans or Asians or native Americans. Literacy was limited to very few all over the world before the Industrial Revolution. It is so common today that we take it for granted but it was the preserve of special circles everywhere in ancient and medieval times. Many tribes in Europe were illiterate. The English, for example, never invented a script. The script we use today to write English sounds is the script introduced to these "oral" people by their Roman conquerors. The same may be said of many other European tribes. Even medieval European kings were, for the most part, illiterate. Wise men who have profoundly affected the thinking of a thousand generations, Christ and Mohammed, may also have been illiterate.

The symbols in more than one African script have been found preserved in objects more durable than paper. The Portuguese found the Akan people using certain objects for measuring gold. These objects became familiarly known, therefore, as the Akan or Ashanti gold-weights. Only a few of them were used for this purpose, in fact, and a professor from the Ivory Coast, Niangoran Bouah, has recently shown in a book *Sankofa*, that these so-called gold-weights are really a kind of encyclopedia that preserve in miniature the objects and ideas of their ancient culture.

He demonstrates that they are not merely artistic devices or memory aids or weights but preserve all the symbols of an ancient Numidian script. They are actually relics of the ancient writing of the Akan, a writing similar in some respects to scripts used in the Saharan area of northeast Africa. It is not an alphabetic script but it is a writing system in the sense that it is a representation of speech and thinking by suitable symbols. Prof. Bouah has identified 135 basic symbols in this system, establishing a basis for the full decipherment of the writing.

It would be interesting to compare this script with a script discovered recently among the blacks of Suriname, who are related to the Akan people. They appear to have brought a script with them from Africa, which Dr. Erzel, of the University of Suriname, has identified as the *Afaka* script. They escaped from the European slavers more than 300 years ago and established themselves as independent nations in the forests of Guiana. The extraordinary variety of their symbols, as it appears in their art, has been studied by many scholars but research into this aspect of their symbolism is only just beginning.

Professor Clyde-Ahmad Winters claims that the Manding (not to be confused with the medieval Mandingo, whom they precede by thousands of years) invented an ancient script, which was used by Mande tribes like the Vai, for development of a script suited to their own language, before their later use of Arabic and Roman characters. Delafosse (1899) and Hau (1973) have presented evidence even before Winters that these writing systems were invented in ancient times by the Manding but Winters has deciphered scripts in regions far apart to show the migrations of the Manding in ancient times and of other peoples using the script.

The script was used by secret societies of the Manding and even after the introduction of Arabic (which, according to the biographies of Ibn Khallikan was invented by an African, Abul Aswan) continued to be used. The Manding have long held paramount the importance of secrecy and the guarded word, which has made many scholars believe that they did not develop written forms of the language. Winters has pointed to many characters carved on volcanic rock in the Sahara which are identical to the Manding syllabaries. He has deciphered an inscription at Oued Mertoutek in North Africa dated 3,000 B.C.using the Manding script. He has also used this to establish links between Africa and America in pre-Columbian times.

What emerges from all the above—the discovery of steel-making, astronomical observatories, mathematical systems, architectural constructions of great ingenuity and durability, agriculture and cattle-rearing of astonishing antiquity, navigation on inland waterways and the open sea, medicine and communication and writing systems—is that we know Africa only in vague outline. The lineaments of a lost science are now emerging and we can glimpse some of the once-buried reefs of this remarkable civilization. A lot more remains to be revealed. But enough has been found in the past few years to make it quite clear that the finest heart of the African world receded into the shadow while its broken bones were put on spectacular display. The image of the African, therefore, has been built up so far upon his lowest common denominator. In the new vision of the ancestor, African-Americans need to turn their eyes away from the periphery of the primitive to the more dynamic source of genius in the heartland of the African world.

AFRICAN OBSERVERS OF THE UNIVERSE:
THE SIRIUS QUESTION

Hunter Havelin Adams III

Summary: The complex knowledge of the Dogon of Mali about the Sirius star-system is sending shock-waves around the scientific world. These West African people have not only plotted the orbits of stars circling Sirius but have revealed the extraordinary nature of one of its companions—Sirius B—which they claim to be one of the densest and tiniest of stars in our galaxy. What is most astonishing about their revelations is that Sirius B is invisible to the unaided eye.

Eurocentric scientists have attributed this knowledge to the presence of space-men (Robert Tempels) Jesuit priests (Kenneth Brecher) and European travellers (Carl Sagan) among these Africans, who, according to Brecher, "have no business knowing this."

Hunter Adams III of the Argonne National Laboratory exposes the superficiality and racial arrogance of these claims. He points to the 700 year old antiquity of Sirius traditions among the Dogon, aspects of which are shared by other black peoples. Above all, he emphasizes the need for a revolution in scientific paradigms, a movement towards that synthesis of the intuitive and empirical modes which characterized early African science, making these discoveries possible.

Despite the huge success of movies like *Star Wars* and *Close Encounters of the Third Kind,* the renewed interest in astrology and in the search for life on Mars, we tend to take our celestial environment for granted. Only rarely do we focus our eyes on what is happening in the sky.

But to the ancients, space was of life-and-death importance. We know this because all over the earth stand their mysterious, megalithic monuments tuned to the rhythm of the stars, cycles they realized were the pulse of life. Through exacting long-term observation, our ancestors determined that seasonal cycles, vegetation growth cycles, and even animal migration and mating cycles correlated with the cyclic changing position of the moon and sun. That information provided them with a reliable and perpetual time frame—a calendar—to schedule their societal festivals and rituals and to know the optimum planting and harvest times. Their culture, along with their economy, was wedded to the sky.

In striving for greater calendrical accuracy, the astronomer priests of many African families, such as the Dogon of Mali in Africa, incorporated the rising and setting of certain stars or groups of stars into their various calendars. Such accuracy was necessary to make certain that the sacred holy days coincided precisely with the end or beginning of one of nature's basic cycles, thus maintaining their community's harmonious relationship with nature. Politics was also involved: priests derived their power and influence by keeping an accurate calendar.

One of the stars important to the ancients' calendrical systems was Sirius, the brightest star in the sky. In fact, many temples and even streets throughout Mexico and in Egypt are aligned to the rising of Sirius. But for the Dogon, the most sacred of their 700-year-old traditions revolve primarily around not Sirius, but its small and incredibly dense companion star, Sirius B[1], which to the unaided eye is invisible. Their extensive celestial knowledge, particularly that concerning this invisible star, is a mystery that has sent shock waves around the scientific world.

In a mountainous area of the Republic of Mali, approximately 200 miles south of the legendary city, Timbuktu, live several African families: the Dogon, the Bambara, the Bozo and the Minianka.

From 1931 to 1956 the Dogon were the focus of an intensive study conducted by two French anthropologists, Marcel Griaule and Germaine Dieterlen. Their great ambition to fully understand the Dogon, especially their religion, was realized in 1947 when elders of the double village of Ogol, along with the most important hogons (priests) of Sanga, held a conference and decided to reveal the more esoteric aspects of their religion. Four representatives from different communities were chosen to instruct the Frenchmen.

It must be understood that what was revealed about the Sirius system represents, as Griaule and Dieterlen point out, just "one phase of the revelations permitted to initiates who are top-ranking but not specifically responsible for the calculations to do with this part of the sky." Essentially initiates themselves, Griaule and Dieterlen had to go through the Dogon's system of education in order to learn the secrets of the universe from them—just as the many Greeks who went through the ancient Egyptians' mystery schools had to go through their system of education.

At first they received the "word at face value" (simple knowledge), then the "word on the side," then the "word from behind." Only in 1947—16 years later—had the elders decided that they were ready to receive the "clear word," the abstract and esoteric knowledge. Now they could learn the Dogon's most sacred knowledge—the realization of the nature of creation, from the creation of stars and spiraling galaxies to the creation of plants—and to know the purpose of human existence. Yet in the end, although privy to an extremely secret body of knowledge, Griaule and Dieterlen still had reached only the "slight acquaintance" level of the eight-level "clear word" phase of knowledge.

Here is a brief summary of the Dogon's cosmology as described in Griaule and Dieterlen's article "A Sudanese Sirius System" and in their book *The Pale Fox.*

Every 60 years, when the orbital periods of the planets Jupiter and Saturn come into synchronization, a ceremony called the "Sigui" is held and a new Hogon (priest) is chosen. Its purpose is the renovation of the world. This ceremony is related to the Sirius star system. Sirius, called "sigi tolo" by the Dogon (tolo means star), although it is important, is not seen as the basis of the system but as one of the foci of the elliptical orbit of its tiny invisible companion star called "po tolo" (Sirius B). Po is a cereal grain more commonly known throughout West Africa as "fonio" and known to botanists in Europe and America as "Digitaria exillis." Its seeds, being extremely small, explain why they named Sirius B after it.

The Dogon say the "po tolo" (Sirius B) though invisible, is the most important star in the sky. It is the egg of the world, the beginning and ending of all things seen and unseen. The period of its orbit around Sirius (the visible one) is counted twice, that is, 100 years, corresponding with their concept of twin-ness, principles of imperfection/perfection; singularity/duality; disorder/order; male/female and human/divine. These principles of twin-ness are very important, for through their antagonistic yet complementary character, which the entire philosophical, social, and territorial organization of the Dogon reflects, a systematic knowledge of the nature and purpose of human existence is revealed to the initiate. Over the period of one year Sirius B rotates on its own axis and this is honored during the *bado* celebration. This one-year rotation on its own axis is not yet known to modern astronomers. They have not yet ascertained it, although they have confirmed the 50-year orbit the Dogon have given for another star circling Sirius.

Sirius B is not only the smallest type of star in the sky, it is also the heaviest. It consists of a metal the Dogon call "sagala" which is a little brighter than iron and so heavy that all earthly beings combined cannot lift it (the Dogon know of 86 fundamental elements)! They say there is another star besides "po tolo" orbiting Sirius called "emme ya," which is larger than it but four times lighter and travels along a greater trajectory in the same direction and in a period of 50 years. This star

Among first photographs taken (1970) of Sirius B, which is the tiny dot to the lower right of the large star, Sirius (small multiple images of Sirius itself are seen here extending off to left and right). Adaptation by artist from a photo by Dr. Irving Lindenblad, U.S. Naval Observatory.   Adams - Fig. 1

Figure 2 — The heliacal rising of Sirius. Dogon drawing of Sirius and the sun joined together at this moment.

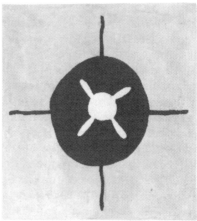

The heliacal rising of Sirius was so important to the ancient Egyptians (as indeed it is to the Dogon as well) that gigantic temples were constructed with their main aisles oriented precisely towards the spot on the horizon where Sirius would appear on the expected morning. The light of Sirius would be channelled along the corridor (due to the precise orientation) to flood the altar in the inner sanctum as if a pin-pointed spotlight had been switched on. This blast of light focused from a single star was possible because of the orientation being so incredibly precise and because the temple would be otherwise in total darkness within. In a huge, utterly dark temple, the light of one star focused solely on the altar must have made quite an impact on those present. In this way was the presence of the star made manifest within its temple.   Adams - Fig. 2

"emme ya" (sun of women) has a satellite called "nyan tolo" (star of women).

Griaule and Dieterlen learned much more. They were told that the moon is dry and dead, like dried blood, and turns like a conical spiral around the earth. Their chief instructor, Ongnonlou, drew in the sand a picture of the planet Saturn showing its rings and said they are permanent (distinguishing them from the rings occasionally seen around the moon). They were shown how, by the arrangement of large stones (megaliths) and altars over a wide geographical area, along with the location of mountain caves, the Dogon marked certain auspicious positions of the planet Venus which then determined their Venus calendar, which also is synchronized with their solar, lunar, and Sirius calendars; the rotation pattern of Jupiter's four largest moons were described to favor the growth patterns of the leaves of a plant called *sene.*

They were told that the earth is in the Milky Way and that the Milky Way has a spiral structure; that there are an infinite number of stars and spiralling worlds; and that the heavenly motions are likened to the circulation of the blood.

But why are these revelations so shocking? One answer might be that, as MIT physics professor, Kenneth Brecher, notes in the December 1977 issue of *Technology Review,* "Most myths conflict with scientific theory, a few do not. We are dealing here with the myth that is most nearly correct by our standards of truth."[2]

And what are these standards of truth? *Myths!* Here are some of Western science's tenets which in reality are just myths (the list is that of Morehouse College professor Carl Spight).

1. Science is fundamentally, culturally independent and universal.
2. The only reliable and completely objective language is scientific knowledge.
3. Science is dispassionate, unemotional, and anti-religious.
4. Logic is the fundamental tool of science.
5. The scientific method leads systematically and progressively toward the truth.[3]

These myths have now become maxims. Space will not permit an in-depth examination of them but several points concerning them must be made. We first must know the true meaning of science.

Science—all science—be it the physical sciences, the social sciences or the spiritual (and by the latter I mean music, art, philosophy/religion) is the search for unity or wholeness within or without *all* human experience. More explicitly, as theoretical psychologist Wade Nobles observes "science is the formal reconstruction or representation of a people's shared set of systematic and cumulative ideas, beliefs and knowledge (i.e., common sense) stemming from their culture."[4] Thus science cannot always spring from a universal or culturally independent base. It must be consistent with the essentials of its people's "common sense."

Because of the extensive influence the European has had on the world, *their* way of knowing, values, ideas, etc. (i.e., their reconstruction of reality) has become *the* model for the rest of the world and this has given the appearance of the overall superiority of their contributions to human history and the superiority of the present period to ancient and medieval periods of human history. "Thus the danger when one adopts *uncritically* the science and paradigms of another people's reality is that one adopts their consciousness and also limits the arena of one's own awareness."[5]

Therefore, we cannot take our thoughts for granted. We must critically examine them. We must constantly strive to become aware of what we are exposed to and decide ourselves whether or not we want to accept it. Especially in view of the fact, as physicist and nuclear policy planner Vince Taylor observes, in his article *Subjectivity and Science,* "pure objectivity does not exist since any observations, experiments, or analysis must be done by a *person,* who inescapably must have values, emotions, and feelings which influence his or her work."[6]

Today the model for all scientific desciplines is the experimental method. While it is quite obviously an effective tool for testing various hypotheses and thus discriminating between alternative explanations for *some* phenomena it is certainly not applicable to *all* phenomena. Nevertheless, "it has become, modified only by practical considerations, the only valid way to know something. Its alleged superiority lies in the fact that it assumes an obligation to impose reorder on every possible object, whether of immediate relevance or not...so that no mountain would be unscaled, no fact will remain unexplained."[7]

Since the Dogon apparently did not use either Western technology or its scientific methodology, we can understand the scientific community's amazement at their knowledge. As Brecher puts it, "The problem for us, therefore, is how the Dogon could have known a host of astronomical facts, all of which are invisible to the unaided eye." He adds, *"They have no business knowing any of this."*[8]

Trying to explain how the Dogon acquired their knowledge, Brecher maintains that "The most obvious possibility is the dreadful thought that it's all a fake. A second obvious possibility is that somebody (a Jesuit priest) told the Dogon all about Sirius before Griaule and Dieterlen ever arrived."[9] But another possible explanation, he adds, "is that the Dogon traded heavily with the Egyptians. There are in fact, many similarities in their cultures. It may then be that the Dogon got the information from the Egyptians at some time in the past. Of course, that would only push

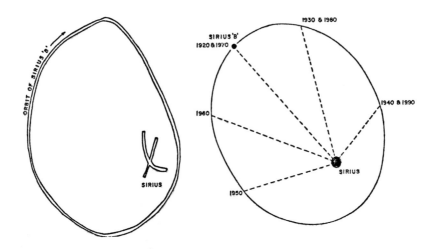

Figure 3 — On the left a Dogon sand drawing of the orbit of Sirius B (Po Tolo) around Sirius; on the right a modern astronomical drawing. Adams - Fig. 3

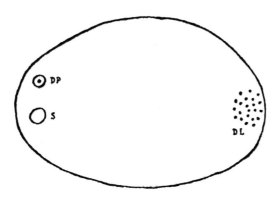

Figure 4 — A drawing showing the trajectory of the star 'Po Tolo' (Sirius B) around Sirius. The small circle on the left marked S is Sirius. Above it the circle with the dot in the center is 'Po Tolo' (DP) in its closest position. At the other end of the oval the small cluster of dots (DL) represents the star at its most distant position from Sirius. Adams - Fig. 4

the essential question backward in time: For how, then, did the Egyptians know that Sirius was a binary system that includes a white dwarf?"[10]

In his book *The Sirius Mystery*, Robert Temple presents a massive amount of evidence, based on eight years' research, which strongly suggests very close cultural and physical lineages between the Dogon, the ancient Egyptians, and the Sumerians. He convincingly demonstrates the striking similarities between many aspects of their mythologies. For example, Temple shows correspondence between the Bozo's mysteries and the highest level of Egyptian Mysteries—The Black Rite of AST (Isis) who was in hieroglyphic form symbolized by: ⌐

△ and identified with "spdt"—the Star Sirius. Ast as "spdt" in hieroglyphics was: △ ✶ △ ◠

"The goddess Ast was the companion of Asari (Osiris), 'The Lord of the Perfect Black' who was associated with the unseen, the 'underworld' and vegetation. One of Asari's hieroglyphic forms was: ◉ ⌐ ⌐

"The Bozo, cousins to the Dogon, describe Sirius B as the 'eye star,' and here we see the Egyptians designating Asari by an eye. The Bozo also describe Sirius A as 'seated,' and a seat (throne) was the first sign in the name Ast. In Egypt, Sirius was a star in the 'Bow and Arrow' constellation while the fifty great Gods of Sumer, the Anunnaki, are spoken of as being seated in the celestial regions of the Bow Star. One of these Gods was Asaru: in essence Asari of Egypt."

"In really early times the basic concepts of Egyptian astronomy and Sumerian astronomy were identical. Later many differences appeared; there were identical systems of dividing the calendar year into 12 months, composed of three weeks, which lasted ten days apiece." Space will not permit me to cite more comparisons, but as Temple maintains, "the connections between Egyptian and Sumerian words in sacred contexts become so multifold that it is impossible to ignore the continuities between the two cultures" (Temple, 1976).

One final comment about the Annunaki. The Annunaki of Sumer, as celestial entities, were known as Igigi. The Sumerians called themselves rather proudly "sag gigga" the black-headed people. "Gig" means black. In Tamil, a Dravidian language spoken in Southern India, "gig" also means black. Recent examinations of archaeological evidence, along with the grammatical and lexical structure of Sumerian languages, such as Ural and Elamite, has revealed striking correspondences with Dravidian languages suggesting that the Dravidians were among the founders of Sumerian civilization.

A calabash (gourd) found along the coast of Guinea with drawings on the bottom possibly representing a kind of zodiac—a star map. Adams - Fig. 5

A Babylonian design (maybe an interpretation of an earlier Sumerian one) carved onto an omphalos stone resembling some sort of zodiac.
Adams - Fig. 6

Remarking on all these similarities, at a symposium on Dravidian civilization in India, Andre F. Sjoberg observed, "it might be argued that Eastern Africa, the Near East, Iran, and parts of India formed a single cultural pool from the Neolithic period [28,000 years ago] onward almost to the beginning of the Christian era, a region wherein ideas and objects traveled back and forth."[11] Furthermore, Sjoberg states, "there is a good deal of archaeological evidence for maritime relations during the first three millenia B.C., and perhaps earlier, between the western coast of India and Iran, Mesopotamia, the Eastern Mediterranean, East Africa, Egypt, and parts of Arabia."[12]

President Leopold Senghor of Senegal, at a 1974 lecture delivered in India, pointed out that "geologists maintain that the Indian subcontinent was formerly attached to East Africa." Senghor also reminded his audience that "southern India is in the same latitude as Senegal, Mali, Niger, Chad, Sudan, Ethiopia, and Somalia."[13] He went on to draw comparisons between the African and Dravidian languages, noting that "as regards metallurgy, the following comparisons might be made: in Bambara (Dogon) *numu* is the word for forge, and in Telugu (Dravidian), *inumu,* iron; in Wolof and Telugu, *kamara* is the name given to the blacksmiths' caste."[14] Based on these and other similarities Senghor concludes: "It is indeed beyond question that the Dravidians share the same Black blood as their brothers in Africa and those of the diaspora."[15]

And yet, despite all of Temple's research comparing Black civilizations, he seems to believe that at all costs he must keep alive the Western myths. Thus in Eric von Daniken tradition, he believes unquestioningly that "civilization as we know it was an importation from another star [Sirius] in the first place." Here's an equally ludicrous observation: "The linked cultures of Egypt and Sumer in the Mediterranean area simply came out of nowhere. We know there were lots of people, but we found no traces of civilization."[16]

Temple also misinterprets what the Dogon told Griaule. For example, "Nommos" were represented by fish signs; the Dogon speak of Nommos as being "masters of the water," as the "Instructors," as "Monitors," as the "fathers of mankind" or as the *"guardians of the spiritual principles."* Temple interprets them as being amphibious creatures from a Sirian planet. At the "word at face value" stage of initiation this could be true because there are adventures of mythical beings, but not at the "clear word" stage.

Furthermore, in the Indus Valley Script there are also fish signs called "min," which also have several meanings: stars, or personal names of priests/instructors or "Nommos"![17] I might add that the God Siva is sometimes referred to as the "Great Fish" and represented by fish signs.

Also the Tamil word "min" conspicuously appears as the first syllable of the *Min*ianka, who share the Sirius cosmogony with the Dogon. Once we begin, as some Senegalese, Hindu, and other scholars have done, to systematically examine the languages of ancient Black people and their descendants with particular attention given to the sound of the spoken word, along with any associated astro-ontological symbolism, we will find a linguistic correspondence between them. Also, what the Dogon describe as "men with horns" and "men with wings," Temple interprets literally as horned and winged beings from other planets.[18] These "men with horns" were Dravidian dignitaries who had crowns made of animal horns, and the "men with wings" were Sumerian kings who sometimes were represented as men with eagle's wings.

According to astrophysicist Carl Sagan, "far more credible than an ancient extraterrestrial educational foray among the Dogon might be a comparatively recent contact with "scientifically" literate Europeans who conveyed to the Dogon the remarkable European 'myth of Sirius and its white dwarf companion, a myth that has all the superficial earmarks of a splendidly inventive tall story." He continues, "in my mind's eye I picture a Gallic (French) visitor to the Dogon people in the early part of this century. He may have been a diplomat, an explorer, an adventurer, or an early anthropologist [Brecher said a Jesuit priest]. The conversation turns to astronomical lore. Sirius is the brightest star in the sky. The Dogon regale the visitor with their Sirius mythology. Then, smiling politely, expectantly, they inquire of their visitor what *his* Sirius myths might be. Perhaps he refers, before answering, to a well-worn book in his baggage. The white dwarf companion of Sirius being a current astronomical sensation, the traveler exchanges a spectacular myth for a routine one. After he leaves, his account is remembered, retold and eventually incorporated into the corpus of Dogon mythology—or at least into a collateral branch (perhaps filed under 'Sirius myths, bleached peoples account'). When Griaule made mythological inquiries in the 1930's and 1940's he had his own European Sirius myth played back to him."

He concludes by saying, "is this not more likely than a visit by extraterrestrial spacefarers to ancient Egypt, with one cluster of hard scientific knowledge, in striking contradiction to common sense, preserved by oral tradition over the millenia, and only in West Africa?" (Sagan 1979)[19] With those comments, it is readily apparent he is full of contempt toward any non-European contributions to human progress.

Sagan goes on to cite three stories which purport to be examples of a full cycle return of a myth to its culture of origin. But there are serious deficiencies with them being all that he claims. Some of them Sagan himself points out: "All these stories underline the almost inevitable problems encountered in trying to extract from a 'primitive' people their ancient legends. Can you be sure that others (Europeans) have not come before you and destroyed the pristine state of the native myth? Can you be sure that the natives are not humoring you or pulling your leg?...Prescientific people are people. Individually they are as clever as (Europeans) are. Field interrogation of informants from a different culture is not always easy.'' (Sagan, 1979)[20]

In the course of his efforts for more than 25 years to learn the secrets of the Dogon, Marcel Griaule established a very close and cordial relationship with them. Wouldn't he have known if and when he was being humored? Not only was Griaule highly regarded by his peers but, when he passed, almost a quarter of a million of the Dogon people from the surrounding area gathered together to honor him, the *only* European ever so honored. With that degree of admiration, would they have lied to him? Sirius is no mystery to the Dogon: it has been part of their traditions for 700 years. It is important to look at the Dogon within this larger historical context (pre-European) in order to appreciate more fully the absurdity of the explanations advanced by Brecher, Temple and Sagan to deny credit to the Africans for their astronomical knowledge.

PART TWO

A wooden mask called the *Kanaga,* used by the Dogon to celebrate their Sirius-related Sigui ceremonies, is among the archaeological finds that indicate their preoccupation with this star for at least 700 years. The mask dates back to the thirteenth century, about the time of the first king of the Mali Empire, Sundiata. Mali was one of the three great empires of West Africa which succeeded Ghana and was in turn succeeded by Songhay. These empires were centers of trade and learning from 900 A.D. to 1594 A.D. Mali inherited the ancient knowledge of Ghana. "Ghana's known history goes back to beyond the 25th dynasty when the last Black pharoahs ruled Egypt" (Williams 1973).[21] Egypt and Ethiopia were Ghana's major trading partners.

Mali became well known as it rose to prominence in the medieval world, following upon Sundiata's conquest of Ghana, but its own history goes back much earlier. It has been traced back to paleolithic times through rock paintings, carvings and other archaeological finds. In its empire days it rewarded the man of learning as much as the man of commerce. Distinguished African and Arab scholars came to teach at the University of Sankore in Timbuktu. (The Moorish poet, architect and astronomer from Granada, Spain—Es-Saheli—who met the Mali Emperor, Mansa Musa, during his 1324 pilgrimage to Mecca, was one of these.)[22]

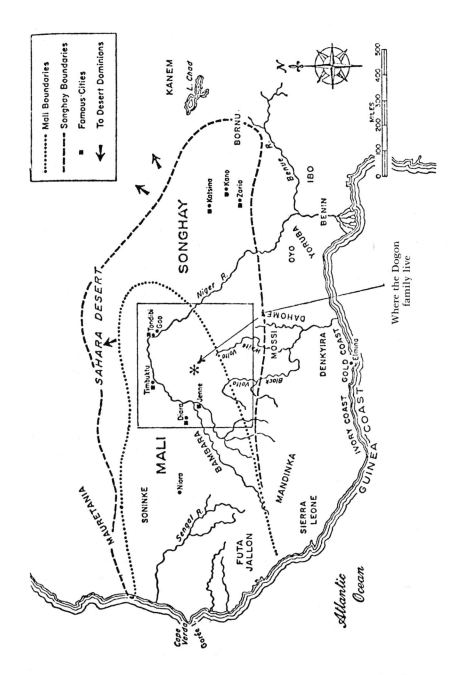

The West African Empires of Mali and Songhay: Ancient Centers of Trade and Learning   Adams - Fig. 7

During the Songhay empire under Askia Mohammed there were universities and learning centers established in the cities of Gao and Jenne also. "In these schools, colleges, and universities of the Songhay Empire, courses were given in astronomy, mathematics, ethnography, medicine, hygiene, philosophy, logic, diction, rhetoric and music."[23] At Jenne there was a medical school that trained physicians and surgeons of great skill. Among the difficult surgical operations performed successfully by doctors in Jenne was the removal of cataracts from the human eye.[24] The earliest traditions of the Songhay people go back to two groups known as "The Masters of the Soil" and "The Masters of the Water." The origin of these groups is not yet known. One theory has it that they came from the east near Lake Chad. The complex origin and history of these West African kingdoms make it clear that the Dogon had a wealth of knowledge from all over the African world to draw upon, apart from developments within their own traditions.

The attempt to dismiss the Dogon springs from a typically Euro-centric view of the world. Sagan and Brecher are taking issue with Temple's hypothesis of an extraterrestrial explanation for the Dogon's knowledge but their own hypotheses are equally absurd and arrogant. The real issue for them is not how the Dogon et. al. arrived at such an amazing amount of knowledge about the universe by themselves but who told them (Europeans or amphibious beings from a Sirian planet?) so nothing can be left unexplained! As Griaule and Dieterlen said themselves, "the *problem of knowing* how, *with no instruments* at their disposal, men could know the movements and certain characteristics of virtually invisible stars *has not been settled nor even posed!*"

Had not Sagan's, Brecher's and Temple's attitudes dominated their reasoning, they might have mentioned that in 1863, about a year after American astronomer, Alvin Clark, accidentally saw Sirius B with his new telescope, another astronomer, M. Goldschmidt, in an announce-ment to the Academy of Sciences at Paris, told of his discovery of not one, but *several companion stars* of Sirius—six in all! He said, "as long as Sirius was high enough above the horizon, I could see them; but afterwards I perceived only mere glimpses of light, without being able to distinguish the position of the stars." Very conspicuously the Dogon have a similar description; they say that "when Sirius B is close to Sirius, it is brighter, but when it is at its most distant point from Sirius it gives off a twinkling affect, suggesting several stars to the observer!"[25]

They would have mentioned that the calculated orbit of stars don't always agree with the observed orbit. Here's a case in point: In August of 1877 Camille Flammorion announced that the calculated orbit of Sirius B *did not agree* with the observed orbit (at that time), "suggesting the existence of one or more satellites of Sirius."[26]

Had not Brecher and Sagan been so bent on discrediting Temple, they would have given serious consideration to reports of other astronomers of the sighting of a third star of the Sirius System: Fox in 1920, 1926, 1928, and 1929; Van den Bos, Finsen, and others of the Ohio Observatory, although they mention that for several years when it *should have* been seen, it was not. Nevertheless, Zagar and Volet say it was there because there were wobbles that pointed to it.[27]

In Egypt, as well as Sumer and parts of Arabia, glass was used for glazing pottery. "Primitive" lenses made about 2000 B.C. have been found in Crete and throughout Arabia. In the British Museum there is a piece of ground glass probably used as a lens in the 8th century B.C. The Russians have recently discovered a crystal lens, perfectly spherical and of great precision, used in ancient Egypt.[28] It is a short and simple step to place one lens in front of another to make a basic telescope, and the chances are it could have happened and many times. Galileo himself noted that the 'ancients' were aware of telescopes. The question is just how good these telescopes were and how much knowledge the astronomer/priests of these early civilizations were able to obtain from them. Yet Brecher and Sagan give no consideration to this at all!

Their narrow vision cannot alter the facts, but their writings do cast light on the root of their problem: they are trying to deal with Dogon, Egyptian, Sumerian, and Dravidian knowledge as they would the Western scientists' way of knowing. To arrive at the truth, they feel, one must use the experimental method, so that—as political scientist Jacob Carruthers puts it—"no mountain will be unscaled, no fact will remain unexplained."

Nobody has a monopoly on truth. There is no one correct way of knowing; there are *ways* of knowing. And Western conceptual methodology cannot discover any more basic truths to explain the mysteries of creation than can a symbolic/intuitive methodology. Consider this: At least several thousand years ago the Dravidians knew that Mercury did not rotate on its axis with respect to the sun; this fact was only recently discovered, but with the help of modern instruments.

Albert Einstein understood the dilemma perfectly well when he said that "there is no inductive method which could lead to the fundamental concepts of physics. Failure to understand this constitutes the basic philosophical error of so many investigators of the 19th century."[29] Einstein also felt that "there is no logical path to these laws; only intuition, resting on a sympathetic understanding of experience, can reach them."[30] He, in fact, is said to have discovered his theory of relativity by actually seeing himself riding on a beam of light. Physicist Niels Bohr himself disclosed that in his dreams the structure of the atom was revealed.

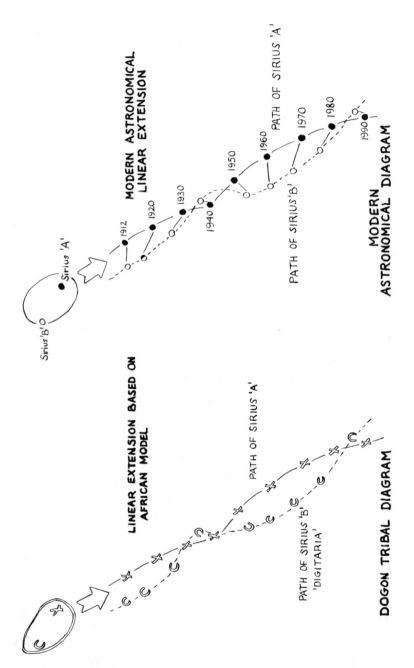

An extrapolated linear extension of the Dogon drawing of the orbit of Sirius B in comparison with a modern astronomical extension.   Adams - Fig. 8

In his book *Symbol and the Symbolic: Egypt, Science, and the Evolution of Consciousness*, R.A. Schwaller de Lubicz characterized Western science as "a research without illumination." He added, "This indecision colors everything: art as well as social organization, and even, in many cases, faith."[31]

Eastern societies, such as those of India and Africa, do not have this problem because there are no distinct separations between science and religion, philosophy and psychology, history and mythology. All of these are viewed as one reality and are closely interwoven into the fabric of daily life.

Astronomers, biologists, and physicists are gradually coming around to accepting that there is something transcendental behind the empirical. They are realizing that, despite the exponential increase in information about the universe and about life, they are no closer to the truth they so passionately seek than when the Greek philosopher, Democritus, speculated about the atom 2000 years ago. They are realizing that the precepts they are working so hard to master and apply are not immutable truths but *rules that are valid only in a certain range of conditions*, and that they presuppose limitations on one's description. As David Bohm points out, if you have a fixed criterion of what fits, you cannot create something new because you have to create something that fits your old idea...and that limits what we can think.[32]

We must realize that the high level of technical achievements humans have attained do not even touch the fringe of man's total possibilities. "We use but a fraction of our capacities, perhaps ten percent of our physical capacity, and five percent of our mental potential. What would happen if human beings generally could learn to use twelve percent, or fifteen? Surely we would have a very different situation—*a different human being, a different science*, different societies, and so on" (Houston 1975).[33]

Before there can be a different science in the West, there *first* must be a *transformation of values*: a *revolution in paradigms*. As Jean Houston, director of the Foundation for Mind Research, observes, "we may now be in the early stages of a qualitative and quantitative departure from the dominant scientific and social paradigms."[34] This change may bring science into a more creative dialogue with other ways of knowing, other intuitive models and methodologies which are synthesized with the empirical mode in the science of the early blacks.

This science was such a synthesis. It was a sacred science, whose fundamental paradigm was based on a spiritual principle: a principle which implicitly acknowledged the existence of One Supreme Consciousness or Force pervading the Universe, expressing itself in an infinite variety of transformations, from atoms to stars, from plants to men. This enabled them to "use not only logical yardsticks to measure scientific observation, but also emotional, intuitive and spiritual ones as well. By first feeling intuitively and then tempering that which he or she feels with logic, those black scientists became more sensitive or better able to make hidden unconscious ideas conscious."[35]

Sometimes the obvious blinds us. As de Lubicz observes, "One forgets that in sleeping to restore one's energy—the simple fact of eliminating cerebral consciousness—we are enabled to draw from the universal source of life, which might induce us to seek out (and find) its deeper cause.

"In order to know the true secrets of life it is necessary to learn how to examine that which, because we see it, we no longer observe."[36]

Every day, de Lubicz writes, "we apply secrets that if we only knew how to become conscious of them, would unveil for us all the powers and all the power that microcosmic man possesses."[37] Our ancestors were conscious of these "secrets" and their cosmologies, art, architecture, and social organization reflect their knowledge of them.

REFERENCES

1. The companion star to Sirius, Sirius B, is known as a white dwarf. A white dwarf has about the same mass as our sun. However, that same mass is so compressed that it is about 100 times smaller than the sun-planetary dimensions. The light from white dwarfs such as Sirius B (about 400 of these stars have been seen) is 10,000 times less than Sirius. Some white dwarfs display periodic light variations, known only within the last ten years by astronomers. However, the Dogon describe Sirius B as having periodic light variations in their 700 year old traditions.

2. Brecher, Kenneth, "Sirius Enigmas," *Technology Review*, p. 61, December, 1977.

3. Spight, Carl, "Towards Black Science and Technology," *Black Books Bulletin* Vol. 5, No. 3, p. 8-11, Fall 1974.

4. Nobles, Wade, "African Consciousness and Liberation Struggles: Implications for the Development and Construction of Scientific Paradigms" (1978) p. 21,22.

5. Idem.

6. Taylor, Vince, "Subjectivity and Science: A Correspondence about Belief," *Technology Review*, Feb. 1979, p. 54.

7. Carruthers, Jacob, "Science and Oppression," Northeastern Illinois University (1972) p. 4.

8. Brecher, Ibid, p. 59.

9. Idem.

10. Brecher, Ibid, p. 61.

11. Sjoberg, Andree, "Who Are the Dravidians?" *Symposium on Dravidian Civilization*, Editor, Jenkins Publishing Co., The Pemberton Press, Austin and New York, p. 13 (1971).

12. Sjoberg, Ibid, p. 13.

13. Senghor, Leopold, "Negritude and Dravidian Culture," *Journal of Tamil Studies*, No. 5, p. 2, September 1974.

14. Senghor, Ibid, p. 6.

15. Ibid, p. 4.

16. Temple, Robert, *The Sirius Mystery*, St. Martins Press, Inc., New York, p. 6, 1976. If, as Temple suggests, that life "civilization as *we* know it comes from another star" [Sirius]—that then would push the question at least one step back: for where did that life being/consciousness come from? The point is this: Black people and their descendants believe in the participatory nature of the universe; they have known that there are other levels of being [existence/consciousness] besides the one of the senses and the intellect of humans; that knowledge is different, and different on different levels of consciousness; that "the nature of all things in the universe was 'force,' or 'spirit' and that a natural feature of the universe was the multiplicity of forms (divine manifestations including man) and moments" of that same one spirit. See Wade Nobles, "African Consciousness and Liberation Struggles: Implications for the Development and Construction of Scientific Paradigms," (1978), p. 21,22.
   For these reasons "one cannot merely dismiss the divine manifestations and tales of beginnings as mythology—they are really dramatic presentations of truth-seeking and revelation of truth. And a truth to be fully comprehended must be perceived in as many dimensions as possible." Jacob Carruthers, "MAAT: The African Universe" Northeastern Illinois University, (1979), p. 1 and 4.

17. Mahadevan, Iravatham, "Dravidian Parallels in Proto-Indian Script," *Journal of Tamil Studies*, Vol. 2, No. 1, p. 180-181 and 199, May 1970.

18. Temple, Ibid, p. 209.

19. Sagan, Carl, *Broca's Brain—Reflections on the Romance of Science*, Random House, New York, p. 74-75, 1979.

20. Ibid, p. 79-80.

21. Williams, Chancellor, *The Destruction of Black Civilization*, Third World Press, Chicago, p. 210, 1973.

22. Ibid, p. 24.

23. Jackson, John G., *Introduction to African Civilization*, University Press, p. 217, 1970.

24. Ibid, p. 215.

25, Goldschmidt, M., "On the Companions of Sirius," *Monthly Notices of the Royal Astronomical Society*, Vol. 23, No. 5, p. 243, March 13, 1863.

26. Flammorion, Camille, "The Companion of Sirius," *The Astronomical Register*, No. 176, August 1877.

27. Temple, Ibid, p. 12.

28. Tompkins, Peter, *Secrets of the Great Pyramid*, Harper Colophon Edition, New York, p. 219, 1978.

29. Einstein, Albert, *Out of My Later Years*, Philosophy Library, p. 8, 1950.

30. Einstein, Albert, "Motiv des Forscens" in *Zu Max Plancks 60 Geburtstag*, Ansprachen in der Deutschen Physikalischen Gesellschaft, Karlsruhe, Muller

31. deLubicz, R.A. Schwaller, *Symbol and the Symbolic: Egypt, Science, and the Evolution of Consciousness*, translated by Lawlor, Robert and Deborah, Autumn Press, Brookline, Massachusetts, p. 87, 1978.

32. Bohm, David, *A Question of Physics: Conversations in Physics and Biology* (conducted by Paul Buckley and David Peat), University of Toronto Press, Toronto, Buffalo, p. 130, 1979.

33. Houston, Ibid, p. 254.

34. Idem.

35. King, Richard D., "Uraeus: From Mental Slavery to Mastership," *Uraeus, The Journal of Unconscious Life* Vol. 1, No. 3, p. 24, Summer Solstice Issue, 1978.

36. deLubicz, Ibid, p. 9.

37. Ibid, p. 88.

NEW LIGHT ON THE DOGON AND SIRIUS

Hunter Havelin Adams III

(With a note on Sirius B by Laurie Ryan)

The previous essay gave a very brief summary of the Dogon's celestial knowledge, and strongly suggested that the science of the Dogon and other Africans was paradigmatically different from what we know today as science. But despite that, the question remains: How did they know what they knew? With the evidence presented here—new archeological finds, the recent discovery of another star, apparently a part of the Sirius system, and some newly discovered insights into the perceptual range and capacity of "dark-adapted eyes"—we can now approach the threshold of an answer.

On page 132 of a Peruvian dictionary compiled by a Dominican monk, Domingo de San Tomas, published in 1560, there is a description of a *Quilpi*—an optical instrument for looking into the distance, i.e., a telescope. *Quilpi* is etymologically related to *quillaquiz*, meaning a planet or a star.[1] This is the first documented evidence to support Galileo's claim that the ancients had telescopes. How widespread they were and whether the Dogon had access to them we simply do not know.

Recently Xi Ze-Zong of China's Institute for the History of Natural Science Academia Sinica uncovered a record of one of China's earliest astronomers, Gan Dej. In it he reported *observing with the naked eye* one of the moons of Jupiter (known by the Chinese as Sui-Xing, the Year Star). This moon was probably Ganymede. This sighting occurred in the summer of 364 B.C., which is 2,000 years before Galileo's discovery of these moons. Theoretical calculations say it is in fact possible, if the conditions are just right, to see some of Jupiter's moons.[2]

Astronomer, Liu Jin-yi, of the same institute, along with six observers in a 1981 observation experiment, reported seeing Ganymede, Jupiter's largest moon. Three of them saw Europa as well.[3]

An American missionary, D.T. Stoddart, in an 1852 letter to astronomer John Hershel from Oroomisha, Persia, wrote, "at twilight Jupiter's satellites could be *seen with the naked eye* and the elongated shape of Saturn also."[4] In the Northern hemisphere, under the right conditions, a person can *see with the naked eye* two galaxies—M31 the Andromeda galaxy and M33 a spiral galaxy in the constellation Triangulum.[5]

These are extremely significant finds—they strongly support the Dogon's claim of observing four of Jupiter's moons, Saturn's rings, and spiral galaxies. Explaining some of the Dogon's observation techniques, film-maker/anthropologist Jean Rouch of the Musee de l'Homme in Paris, France, who worked closely with Marcel Griaule and Germaine Dieterlen, said, "the Dogon astronomer/ priests stay up all night and watch the sky. They watch from caves and from the roof-top terraces of their homes."[6] Their dark eyes would then be extremely dark-adapted i.e. very light sensitive.[7] They also make use of natural foresights and hindsights in their observations.

One of the most awe-inspiring and terrifying spectacles ever experienced by man are star flares—stars that explode at the end of their life-cycle (e.g., supernova) or stars that expand and contract in a rhythmic fashion, sometimes reaching a superluminosity (e.g., dwarf nova). Ancient records of star flares have been found by archeologists (e.g., the Crab Nebula supernovae of 1,054 C.E. was recorded by Chinese astronomers and depicted in rock art by Indians of the American southwest). The ancient Sumerians have a record of one that occurred in the constellation Vela about 6,000 years ago.[8]

Imagine an ancient Sumerian astronomer, with his dark-adapted eyes, watching the sky reverently every night when, "suddenly a dazzling ball of light blazed forth, hanging just above the watery southern horizon. Depending on the season, it was brillant as a second sun by day or brighter than the full moon by night, and its (shimmering) luminous reflection on the waters of the Persian Gulf stretched like a shiny ribbon from horizon to shore . . ."[9]

Recently another star flare has been found with the "Einstein" orbiting observatory. This one is a X-ray emiting dwarf nova 9' south of Sirius.[10] What is most significant is that the Dogon have a sand drawing which shows this star of the Sirius system in different states of emergence.[11]

Interestingly, the astrophysicists who made the discovery in March of 1979 found this same star in their cursory examination of about 70 photographic plates from 1894-1952 of the Harvard-Smithsonian Center for Astrophysics but it had gone unrecognized. That is a very important find because a host of scholars, such as Carl Sagan, have refused to accredit the Dogon's detailed astronomical knowledge to the Dogon themselves, always pointing out that *no* other star had ever been observed near Sirius except its white dwarf companion. Jean Rouch said that he and Griaule *never doubted* the authenticity of what they learned from the Dogon, even though they could not explain how they knew what they knew.

According to astrophysicist Michael Burns of NASA's Goddard Space Flight Center, "long term optical observations may reveal information concerning the star's orbit (if it is truly, as it appears, part of the Sirius system) and other characteristics of dwarf novae like supermaxima events."[12] At a supermaxima, the star's apparent magnitude could be 8-6. That could mean that the Dogon astronomer/priests could have seen it in the past (1,300 A.D.?) and recorded it. Perhaps that event was the catalyst that initiated the Dogon's new historical cycle.

Notes

1. Charroux, Robert, "The Mysterious Unknown," Neville Spearman, London 1972, pp. 39, 40.

2. Ze-Zong, Xi, "The Siting of Jupiter's Satellite by Gan Dej 2000 years before Galileo," *Chinese Journal of Astrophysics*, Vol. 5, 1981, pp. 242-243.

The brightness of any celestial body is known by its apparent magnitude. The four largest moons of Jupiter have an apparent magnitude of 6-5; Sirius A is 1.42 and Sirius B is 8.7 (the smaller the number the brighter the source.

3. Frazier, Ken, "Pre-Galileo Siting of Jovian Moon," *Science News*, 23 Jan. 1982, p. 59.

4. Banos, George, "Was the Star of Bethlehem the Planet Uranus?", *The Astronomy Quarterly*, Vol. 3, No. 12, 1979-1980, p. 168.

5. Hynek, Allen J., *Science Digest*, Dec. 1982, p. 38.

6. Rouch, Jean, interview at the Field Museum's of Chicago Anthropological Film Festival, Sept. 1980.

7. For blue- and green-eyed persons the apparent visual magnitude limit is 6.5 and is achieved only in very dark areas; however for dark-eyed, dark-skinned, and dark-haired persons under similar conditions the limit approaches 8.1

8. Michanowsky, George, "The Once and Future Star," Hawthorn, New York, 1977.

10. Its X-ray emission exhibits high and low states. Optical monitoring show outbursts occur at intervals of about 15 days. It has a visible magnitude of 10; it has a high magnetic field strength of 15-25 mega-gauss (10^7). Chlebowski, T., Halpern, J.P., Steiner, J.E., "Discovery of a New X-Ray Emitting Dwarf Nova 1E0643.0-1648," *Astrophysical Journal Letters*, Vol. 247, 1 July 1981, pp. L35-L38.

11. Griaule, M., Dieterlen, G., "Le Renard Pale" (Tome 1 Fasciule), Institute d' Etnologie, Musee de l'Homme, Paris, 1965, pp. 310 and 440.

12. Burns, Michael, personal communication, 1981.

A FURTHER NOTE ON SIRIUS B

By Laurie Ryan

Sirius A, the brightest star in the northern hemisphere has an apparent magnitude of -1.42. Sirius B has an apparent magnitude of 8.7. The apparent magnitude of a star is a measure of its brightness due to light from it reaching the earth. The lower the number, the brighter it will appear when seen from the earth. The limit that the naked eye can see is 6.5, although this is usually achieved in very dark areas. The limit is raised to 10 with a pair of binoculars and 13 with a small telescope. The position of Sirius in the sky from an observer in Mali is approximately 50-55 above the horizon within 700 years to the present. With an instrument only as powerful as binoculars Sirius B should be visible, except that it would be flooded by light from Sirius A. Perhaps they had a more powerful telescope, but even without one more powerful than binoculars, information on Sirius B could be obtained. In 1844, before Sirius B was discovered, Friedrich Bessel discovered a "wavy" motion of Sirius A, a sign that a companion star was disturbing its motion. He examined this sinusoidal motion to be 50 years, without ever seeing Sirius B. From continuous observations of the motion of Sirius A, the elliptical orbit and position of Sirius B can be inferred.

In examining their observations of the solar system, there is additional evidence that the Dogon may have been able to see Sirius B. The four largest moons of Jupiter have apparent magnitudes of 5-6 at their farthest position from Jupiter. Although this is within range of seeing with the naked eye, a flood of light from Jupiter may prevent this, but both the moons of Jupiter and the rings of Saturn can be seen with a small telescope. Galileo easily assembled his first telescope of three power magnification followed quickly by other instruments of up to 30 power magnification. The date of the principle of combining two lenses to magnify an object is not certain, and claims for discovery of this go back to Roger Bacon in the thirteenth century. Since all of the observations of the Dogon were within the range of the same small telescope, and it was possible for them to have such an instrument, their observations of the position and period of Sirius B must be valid.

NAMORATUNGA: THE FIRST ARCHAEOASTRONOMICAL EVIDENCE IN SUB-SAHARAN AFRICA

B.M. Lynch and L.H. Robbins

Summary: Namoratunga, a megalithic site in northwestern Kenya, has an alignment of 19 Basalt pillars that are nonrandomly oriented toward certain stars and constellations. The same stars and constellations are used by modern Cushitic peoples to calculate an accurate calendar. The fact that Namoratunga dates to about 300 B.C. suggests that a prehistoric calendar based on detailed astronomical knowledge was in use in eastern Africa.

This article is reprinted from **Science** Vol. 200, pp. 766-768, 19 May, 1978 with the kind permission of the authors and the American Association for the Advancement of Science.

NAMORATUNGA: THE FIRST ARCHEOASTRONOMICAL EVIDENCE IN SUB-SAHARAN AFRICA

In recent years there has been a growing interest among archeologists and astronomers in the possible relationships between megaliths erected by prehistoric peoples and the positions of constellations and other solar phenomena (1). Much of this work has centered on European sites such as Stonehenge. In Africa, especially in Ethiopia, megaliths are known that are believed to have been associated with Cushitic speakers (2); but, as far as we are aware, none of them have been related to astronomical evidence.

Our recent research in northwestern Kenya has resulted in the discovery of evidence warranting archeoastronomical investigation which probably dates from about 300 B.C. Lynch was excavating the site of Namoratunga I (2°0'5"N, 36°6'50"E) located along the Kerio River valley, southwest of Lake Turkana (Fig. 1.) This is a large cemetery and rock art site where the graves are surrounded by massive standing stones which have been engraved with cattle brand symbols (3). The burial practices at Namoratunga I closely parallel customs practiced recently by the Konso of southern Ethiopia, a Cushitic-speaking group (4). Namoratunga I has recently been radio-carbon-dated to 2285±165 years before present (B.P.) (5). The name Namoratunga means "stone people" in the language of the local Turkana tribe: the Turkana believe that a malevolent spirit had the power to turn people who mocked the spirit to stone. Namoratunga I was so striking in its isolation from similar sites with massive upright stones that we thought that any other similiar sites would surely be known by the people, who are nomadic and possess a great knowledge of the area they inhabit. Local elders informed us of another site with the same name located 210 km to the north near the Ferguson's Gulf area of Lake Turkana (3°24'N, 35°50'E) (Fig. 1). Namoratunga II is located on the eastern edge (3) of the Losidok range overlooking the Lake Turkana basin with an unobstructed view of the entire horizon. Central Island, in the middle of the Lake, is due east and can be clearly seen from the site.

We investigated this site and found that it was definitely related to the Namoratunga I site. There was at least one grave marked by upright slabs, and other upright basalt columns were faintly engraved with the same brand symbols. Although Namoratunga II has not been dated, it is clearly part of the same cultural complex and probably dates to the same general period (300 B.C.) as Namoratunga I. Yet Namoratunga II contrasted significantly with Namoratunga I because the large stone columns were in an unusual alignment (Fig. 2). At Namoratunga I, standing stones were only found circling graves. In addition to the standing stones circling the one grave at Namoratunga II, 19 large stone columns were arranged in rows that were not part of any grave. Because the distribution of these stones appeared to be markedly nonrandom (6), we decided to examine the possibility that their arrangement was correlated with certain astronomical events, especially since present-day Eastern Cushites have a sophisticated calendar which uses the rising of seven stars or constellations in conjunction with various phases of the moon to calculate a 12-month, 354-day year. The seven stars or constellations include Triangulum, Pleiades, Aldebaran, Bellatrix, Central Orion, Saiph (Kappa Orionis), and Sirius (7). For half of the year they identify months by the rising of each of the seven stars or constellations in relation to the new moon. Each star or constellation appears successively in conjunction with the new moon in the order Triangulum, Pleiades, Aldebaran, Bellatrix, Central Orion, Saiph, and Sirius. Only Triangulum is utilized for the second half of the year beginning when Triangulum rises in conjunction with a full moon. Each successive month is identified by Triangulum's relation to progressively declining phases of the waning moon. Such months are approximately 29.5 days long (7). Since the site was Cushitic in origin, we checked the rising of these seven stars or constellations against the possible stone alignments at Namoratunga II (8).

Because of gradual changes in the earth's axis of rotation, called precession, it was necessary to determine the azimuths of these constellations for the year 300 B.C. (9). In some cases these stars exhibited a difference of as much as 12° in their present azimuths as compared with those of 300 B.C. (Table 1).

Table 1. Present azimuths and azimuths in 300 B.C. of seven stars used in conjunction with the stone pillars at Namoratunga II to calculate a calendar.

Star or constellation	Present azimuths	Azimuths in 300 B.C.	Namoratunga	
			Stone alignment	Error
Triangulum (Beta)	35° N of E	23° N of E	1-7	0°
Pleiades	24° N of E	14° N of E	1-8-12	0°
Aldebaran	17° N of E	9° N of E	1-2-9	0°
			5-13	0°
Bellatrix	6° N of E	1° N of E	1-3-4	1°+
			17-18	0°
Central Orion	2° S of E	10° S of E	5-10	1°
			16-18	1°
Saiph (Kappa Orionis)	10° S of E	13° S of E	5-6-7	0°
			14-18	0°
Sirius	17° S of E	17° S of E	5-6-9	0°
			15-18	0°

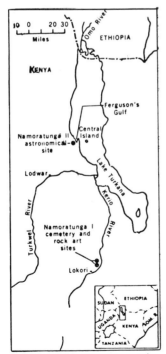

Fig. 1. Location of Namoratunga sites.

We first assumed that if the stone "pillars" at Namoratunga II did indeed align with the stars, the stones in the far west of the site would be the most obvious stones to initially sight from since the rising of the stars was the phenomenon of calendric importance. This would allow the observer maximum use of all the stone pillars. Despite the fact that many of the stones were placed in the ground at angles, we considered only the tops of the stones when checking for possible alignments. The angling of the stones was apparently intentional since present-day Eastern Cushites also place both wooden and stone pillars into the ground at angles. The first position that we examined was stone 18 (see Fig. 3 for all alignments). From this vantage point it was possible to align other stones with the rising of four stars: Bellatrix with stone 17, Orion with stone 16, Saiph with stone 14, and Sirius with stone 15. Only the alignment with stone 16 yielded a 1° error.

Fig. 2. Pattern of stones at Namoratunga II

From stone 1 alignments were found with Triangulum (1-7), Pleiades (1-8-12), Aldebaran (1-2-9), and Bellatrix (1-3-4). Only the alignment with Bellatrix displayed any error, slightly more than 1°. Three of the four alignments from stone 1 consisted of a row of three stones. In view of the close proximity of these stones, a three-stone alignment would allow for more accurate sightings. This was not necessary for the alignments taken of stone 18 since the stones the particular constellations would rise over were as much as 12 m away.

Alignments were also noted for stone 5. From here, alignments could be formed with Aldebaran (5-13), Orion (5-10), Saiph (5-6-7), and Sirius (5-6-9). The Orion alignment was off by approximately 1°. Like three of the four alignments from stone 1, the Saiph alignment and possibly the Sirius alignment were formed by a row of three stones. Stones 1 and 5 were oriented exactly true north.

Each of the three sighting points (1,5,18) produced four alignments. Five and possibly six of these alignments were formed by three stones (six if the 5-11-10 alignment is included). In no case were any of these alignments off by more than 1°. In addition, with one exception all of the 19 stones at the site were used in forming the alignments. Stone 11, which had fallen down, would most likely have fallen on the 5-10 Orion alignment. Only stone 19 was not used, but this stone was the smallest at the site, only 15 cm above the surface, and as such would have been of questionable value as a line of sight. Since Central Island, the only geographical feature readily visible from the site, is due east of Namoratunga II, it seems likely that some of the alignments may have used Central Island as an additional distant line of sight.

We followed the same procedure to check for alignments, using the present azimuths of these seven stars. Only four of them matched the stone alignments at Namoratunga II. In the case of Sirius, for example, there was no difference between the present azimuth and that of 300 B.C. This information adds further support to the idea that the Namoratunga II alignments are nonrandom and gives weight to the idea that the stones were used in calendric reckoning in 300 B.C.

The archeoastronomical information described for Namoratunga II adds significantly to the growing body of evidence attesting to the complexity of prehistoric cultural developments in sub-Saharan Africa. It strongly suggests that an accurate and complex calendar system based on astronomical reckoning was developed by the first millennium B.C. in eastern Africa. Furthermore, it raises the possibility that other megalithic sites will be found that will have astronomical implications.

REFERENCES AND NOTES

[1] G. S. Hawkins, *Stonehenge Decoded* (Dell, New York, 1955).

[2] G. W. B. Huntingford, *East. Anthropol.* **3**, 119 (1950).

[3] M. Lynch and L. H. Robbins, *Curr. Anthropol.* **18** (No. 3), 538 (1977); M. Lynch, *Azania*, in press.

[4] A. E. Jensen, *Im Lande des Gada: Wanderungen Zwischen Volkstrummern Sudabessiniens* (Strecker and Schroder, Stuttgart, 1936); C. R. Hallpike, *The Konso of Ethiopia: A Study of the Values of a Cushitic People* (Oxford Univ. Press, London, 1972).

[5] Human bone sample GX-5042A.

[6] The mean height of the portion of the stones visible above the ground was 55 cm. The stones are estimated to weigh between 45 and 270 kg. each.

[7] A. Legesse, *Gada: Three Approaches to the Study of African Society* (Free Press, New York, 1973).

[8] The elaborate grave construction, evidence of clan burial areas, and other information clearly relate Namoratunga I to Cushitic prehistory (M. Lynch and L. H. Robbins, in preparation).

[9] All alignments at the site were determined with the aid of a transit and as such are accurate to within 1°.

[10] Fieldwork was generously supported by the National Science Foundation. We are grateful to the Government of Kenya for permission to do this research. We thank R. E. F. Leakey and J. C. Onyango-Abuje of the National Museums of Kenya and N. Chittick and D. W. Phillipson of the British Institute of Eastern Africa for facilitating our research. We are grateful to S. E. Telengoi for leading us to the site. We thank P. Uland for her excellent drawings. We are especially grateful to R. Victor of the Michigan State University Planetarium and Department of Astrophysics for his advice and calculation of the azimuths of the stars used in the analysis.

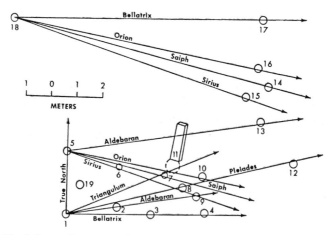

Fig. 3. Stone alignments relative to the seven stars at Namoratunga II.

AN ANCIENT HARVEST ON THE NILE

Fred Wendorf, Romuald Schild, and Angela E. Close

The most profound revolution in human history, anthropologists have long felt, was the switch from hunting and gathering to farming. It was only after this transition thousands of years ago that wandering hunter-gatherers could settle down into villages and begin to develop true civilization.

Until recently most anthropologists thought they had a good idea of when and how this transition happened. But new discoveries by our research team—representing Southern Methodist University, the Geological Survey of Egypt, and the Polish Academy of Sciences—digging in the arid sands of Egypt's Nile Valley, now appear to challenge many major assumptions about the origin of agriculture.

People used to think farming began about 10,000 years ago, just after the last ice age, somewhere in southwestern Asia—probably in the region where wild strains of wheat and barley grow today. People used to think it happened because human population in the region outstripped the supply of foods gathered from the wild, forcing deliberate cultivation of wild food plants. People used to think that once the abundance of agriculture was available, populations grew even larger, forcing still greater reliance on more intensive farming. Burgeoning populations, it was held, led to the creation of villages, increasingly complex governments, and all the resulting accoutrements of civilization.

Our excavations at Wadi Kubbaniya, a desolate region in Egypt's Western Desert, throw all this into doubt. We have found that, between 17,000 and 18,500 years ago—while ice still covered much of Europe—African peoples were already raising crops of wheat, barley, lentils, chick-peas, capers, and dates. They were doing it in the floodplains of the Nile, much as people would continue to do for another 13,000 years until the classical Egyptian civilization arose, and on into modern times.

Moreover, there is every indication that the rise of this diversified agriculture did not lead directly to the beginning of village life. Probably people continued their wandering ways as hunters and gatherers for thousands of years more.

Fred Wendorf is an anthropologist and Angela Close is a research associate at Southern Methodist University. Romuald Schild is associate director of the Institute for the History of Material Culture, Polish Academy of Sciences.

Reprinted by kind permission of the American Association for the Advancement of Science from *Science*, November 1982.

Farming was just one more resource in a broad-based way of life. These conclusions raise anew the question of why civilization emerged.

In the days of the ancient farmers, Wadi Kubbaniya probably looked much as it does today—undulating sand dunes crossed by small riverbeds that are dry most of the time. It rains only about once every 15 years. But the level of the Nile was higher then. River water flooded the lower part of the wadi, or gulch, creating an embayment. Each year then, as it did until the Aswan dam was built, the Nile would overflow its banks, flooding the surrounding areas and depositing a layer of rich silt.

Lower Wadi Kubbaniya must have been an unusually attractive environment for people of the late Paleolithic: fish in the river, ducks and geese in the marshlands, various bushes, trees, and grasses fringing the water. Antelope and wild cattle roamed the vegetated area. Beyond the narrow band watered by the Nile, there was then, as now, desert, We have found the remains of ancient camps in several distinct places—high up on the dunes next to the floodplain, lower down on the ridges between the swales, or depressions, in the embayment, and still farther down at the mouth of the wadi where it empties into the Nile channel.

Although we do not know what the ancient people of Wadi Kubbaniya looked like, we do know in significant detail how they went about their lives. In fact, by piecing together evidence dug up from their campsites, we have reconstructed the annual cycle these ancients lived as they moved from place to place with the seasons.

In addition to the remains of various crops—mainly seeds—we found stones used to grind grain to flour, including large milling stones and smaller mortars and pestles. We also found other stone tools such as cutting blades, engraving burins, and hide scrapers.

The high dune areas appear to have been used during two different periods of the year. First, the ancient people camped here during late August and September, during or immediately after the late summer flooding of the Nile. They hunted hartebeest and wild cattle, but mainly they fished. As the flood waters receded, isolated ponds were left to dot the lower depressions, and catfish were stranded in the ponds. Almost all the fish bones we have found in the nearby campsites are from the heads of catfish. The rest of the fish must have been carried away to be eaten elsewhere later in the year. We found a lot of ash and charcoal in the campsites, so it is possible the fish were preserved by smoking.

When the water in the highest ponds dried up and the fish were depleted, the still-damp pond beds, covered with rich river silt, made an ideal spot for crops. Probably at this time the people of Wadi Kubbaniya planted the cereals, barley and wheat, and the legumes, lentils and chick-peas.

As the river continued to fall and the floor of the wadi dried out, groups of people apparently moved from the high dunes down to the ridges between the swales on the lower floodplain. It looks as if the people simply moved to these

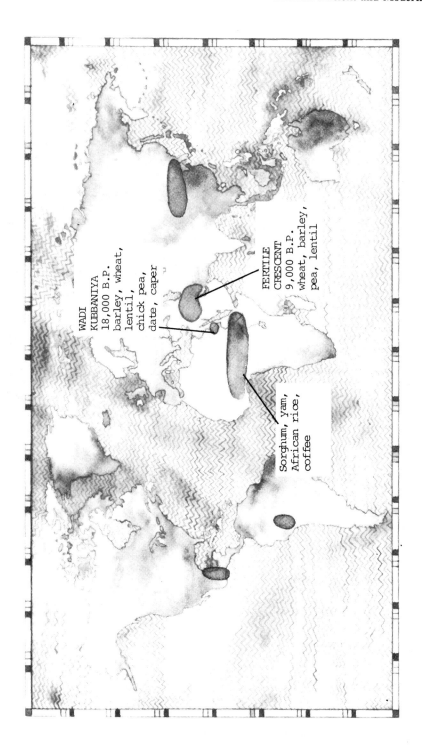

WADI
KUBBANIYA
18,000 B.P.
barley, wheat,
lentil,
chick pea,
date, caper

FERTILE
CRESCENT
9,000 B.P.
wheat, barley,
pea, lentil

Sorghum, yam,
African rice,
coffee

areas, leaving their newly planted crops behind and resuming hunting and fishing until the lowest ponds dried.

Although it seems they might have planted these areas, too, we found not evidence of it. For example, while we found grinding stones in the high dunes areas, indicating that ground the grain there, there were none in the floodplains. This is a mystery, for the season when the lower ponds dried up would still have been right for planting. We believe the explanation lies in the lack of a suitable method of preparing the ground. Up in the soft, sandy dunes, a simple digging stick would have been enough. But the floodplains are made of heavy clay. A hoe would have been needed, preferably a plow. It seems these implements were unknown in the late Paleolithic.

When all the fish in the swales had been collected, the Kubbaniya people may have left the wadi and gone elsewhere in the Nile Valley until December or January, when the crops in the dunes would be ready for harvest. It is a common practice today for primitive farmers to leave an area once the fields are planted and to return only at harvest time. We know that the Kubbaniya people spent at least a part of the year near Esna, some 90 miles to the north (stone tools showing the same idiosyncrasies of technique were found in both Wadi Kubbaniya and Esna), but we cannot be sure it was during the late autumn-early winter period.

In December or January—the harvest season—the people returned to Wadi Kubbaniya and again camped on the high dunes. The cereals and perhaps also the chick-peas were ground to flour. Lentils were probably left whole or perhaps pounded to a paste in the stone mortars we found. Animal bones in the campsite dumps indicate the people were also hunting local game, including the ducks and geese that wintered in southern Egypt.

We cannot be certain that after the harvest the people stayed in Wadi Kubbaniya through the early spring, although it is quite possible. In any case, they were there in late spring or early summer when they camped on the floodplain at the mouth of the wadi. By this time the crops were all in and the winter birds had flown north for the summer. The river was at its lowest and this was the very driest time of year. Gazelles, which normally lived along the fringes of the desert, were drawn closer in to the river by their need for water, and they became a more important source of meat for the Kubbaniya people. Judging by the bones, however, most hunting was still for larger animals—the wild cattle, hartebeest, and an occasional hippo.

As the summer wore on, however, the floodplain sites had to be abandoned when the river rose and began to spill over. We are not sure where the people went during the flood. But when the water began to fall in late August or September, the cycle began all over again as the people returned to the high dune ponds to catch the stranded catfish.

One of the chief questions we had to answer to interpret our evidence was whether wheat and barley grew wild in southern Egypt 18,000 years ago. Were the ancients simply gathering wild grain or were they planting it deliberately?

From what we know of the growing conditions, it seems possible that wild plants might have been present in the area of Wadi Kubbaniya, but if so, their existence would have been marginal at best.

But since the ancient people relied heavily on these grains, marginal wild stands alone are not likely to have been sufficient. The evidence points to the use of the pond beds as fields—sites where the grains could not have survived naturally because of the unreliability of the annual flooding.

There is another way to distinguish wild grain from domesticated strains. They look different under the microscope. Wild cereals, to reseed, must drop their grain from the parent plant when ripe. When people gather grain, however, they collect not the fallen grain but the stalk with the head of grains attached. Threshing later separates the wheat from the chaff. This form of harvest automatically selects the grains more firmly attached to the stalk and eliminates the looser grains. If the next crop is planted from seed harvested this way, it will be more likely to retain any genetic tendency to have firmly attached grain.

Domesticated grains have a rough fracture zone at one end of the kernel where the grain has been torn, in threshing, from the stalk. By contrast, wild grains of the same species are smooth. Microscopic study of the only fracture zone found at Wadi Kubbaniya shows that it is rough. This evidence is not conclusive, since a single specimen could have been wild but harvested while unripe. There is another indication that the cereals are domestic. Many of the grains have the twisted form which is peculiar to six-row barley, and all six-row barley is domestic. This suggests that the people who harvested the grain deliberately planted it. Moreover, since it could have taken many generations under domestication for the rough spot and the twists to be established as normal features of the grain, the earliest stages of wheat and barley domestication may have occurred still further back in time.

Other lines of evidence indicate that the dates were clearly domesticated and that the chick-peas may have been as well. The domestication question cannot be answered so clearly for the lentils and capers. In any event, we are tempted to pose the heretical question of whether genetically defined "domestication" is really so important or so conducive to cultural advances as the older theories would have us believe. Domestication may not be something that human beings deliberately *do* to other species but, rather, the result of an unconscious interaction between people and the species they eat.

If the use of these early domesticated plants by the Wadi Kubbaniya people is viewed in the wider context of more general animal-plant relationships, then it can be seen to fall into a pattern. Other animals make use of plants, and when this use is consistent and sustained, then the plants will adapt to it and will frequently take advantage of it to further their own population. The simplest examples of this are the development by some plants of sweet scents or of brightly colored flowers to encourage pollination by insects, or the change of fruits to bright and attractive colors when the seeds inside them are ripe and ready for dispersal.

Other, more complex cases constitute true symbiosis between the animals and plants involved. For instance, some types of acacia trees are "infested" with ants that feed on a specially produced nectar and on a leaf tip that is especially rich in proteins. In return, however, the ants destroy any other insect that attacks the plant and will even attack and drive away large leaf-eating animals. The symbiosis in this case is so highly developed that the acacia trees will die from the unaccustomed attacks of other insects and herbivores when their own ants are removed.

Many plants seem to use the animals they support to spread their seeds to areas they could not otherwise reach. Squirrels not only harvest and store acorns, they also sow them; at least, it must seem so from the oak tree's point of view. And man himself has been used with great success by the plants with which he maintains a continuous interaction. This is readily seen by comparing the very limited distributions of wild wheat and barley with the global distributions of domesticated wheat and barley. We have done as much for them as they have for us.

Domestication, or genetic adaptation by a plant to use by and of an animal—as in the case of ants and acacias—seems to be very common phenomenon with nature, and we strongly suspect that it is also a common phenomenon within the history of our own species. Unfortunately, plant remains are rarely both preserved and recovered in early prehistoric sites, so we lack the evidence to detect consistent use of any particular type of plant. Nevertheless, there is every reason to believe that early peoples were not haphazard feeders but were making regular and systematic use of plant foods.

Because plant remains are rarely preserved, we have only a tantalizingly small body of evidence attesting to consistent use of any one plant food in prehistoric times. In Europe, for instance, our ancestors were eating grapes 400,000 years ago and were collecting hackberry seeds shortly after that. In southern Africa, there are grinding stones at least twice as old as those of Wadi Kubbaniya, although we can only speculate as to their use. Given the ease with which it seems to occur in nature, there is no reason why genetic domestication should not have occurred frequently in the past.

The findings at Wadi Kubbaniya conflict with orthodox views on the beginnings of agriculture. However, they do fall into a pattern with other discoveries in the Nile Valley, and this pattern suggests the need to rethink the causes and consequences of food production. During the international campaign to save the archeological remains threatened by the New High Dam at Aswan, excavations disclosed numerous grinding stones in sites dated to about 14,500 years ago. There were also bits of flaked stone with polished edges, the sort of tool that we know from other discoveries were set like sawteeth into a wooden stick to serve as a sickle. No cereal remains were found, but the sediments did yield wheat rust spores and several pollen grains from an unidentified grass that might have been a cereal. Another site has yielded barley pollens from several levels. Interestingly, the concentration of pollens increases suddenly in the level correlated with human occupation of the area. The stone tools differ from one site to another, suggesting that people of several different cultural traditions are represented. Only in the most recent site, dated to 12,000 years ago, is there any evidence of an increase in population size and density beyond that of small bands.

These Nile sites indicate not that Wadi Kubbaniya was an isolated occurrence but rather that the use of cereals was widespread, occurring among diverse cultural groups and persisting as an important economic activity for at least 6,000 years after the time of Wadi Kubbaniya. These findings suggest that previous beliefs connecting intensive use of cereals to growth in population density and to a changing social structure are wrong.

The Wadi Kubbaniya data also seriously challenge the idea of food production as a consequence of environmental stress or population pressure. Although the sites were occupied during extreme dry periods, the rising Nile greatly expanded the habitable life belt along the river and provided new opportunities for the harvest of fish from the dune swales along the edge of the floodplain.

There does not, in fact, seem to be any single "cause" for the beginning of agriculture. It may well have begun as a natural interaction between early peoples and the plant species they came to exploit regularly. It probably happened many times in the past, whenever Paleolithic peoples made extensive and sustained use of plant resource. it is important in this instance because the plants used were cereals, and these cereals provided the economic base for the development of our civilization. The rise of agriculture, however, did not lead rapidly or inevitably to identifiable social or economic change. It simply provided another resource in a broadly based hunting, fishing, and gathering economy.

AFRICAN CATTLE BONES STIR SCIENTIFIC DEBATE

Bayard Webster

A University of Massachusetts anthropologist has found that the earliest known domestic cattle lived in East Africa some 15,000 years ago. The finding questions the long-held theory that the "cradle of civilization" lies in the Middle East, where domesticated cattle, a hallmark of civilization, were known to exist some 8,000 years ago.

Dr. Charles M. Nelson reported in Boston yesterday that he and his assistants had uncovered the teeth and bones of cattle at three separate sites in the Lukenya Hill District in the Kenya Highlands, approximately 25 miles from Nairobi. With the help of anthropologists in Nairobi, he identified the cattle from which the bones and fragments came and, with radiocarbon dating techniques, determined their age.

His findings led him to conclude that nonindigenous cattle figured in the economy of the region's pre-Iron Age people, indicating that a relatively sophisticated society existed at the time. Such a society, he reasoned, could have spread its mores, living modes and philosophy, eventually reaching the fertile crescent of the Euphrates River Valley, where the present-day regions of Iraq, Syria, Lebanon, Jordan and Israel are often referred to as the cradle of civilization.

New Evidence Raises Doubts

"From our earliest school days we are taught that civiliztion first developed in the Middle East and then spread to India, Central Asia, Europe and North Africa," Dr. Nelson said in an interview. But he noted that the evidence his team had unearthed in Africa and recent discoveries by other scientists of 18,000-year-old domesticated grain crops in Africa raised doubts about that position.

He said that such findings suggest that many of the elements necessary for the development of civilization — agriculture and animal husbandry and their accompanying technologies — may have originated in surrounding areas and were exported to the Middle East through trade and cultural diffuison of information and ideas.

"We know that in areas where complex societies first developed, they had domesticated plants and animals — barley, other grains, sheep, goats, pigs and cattle — and this led to changes in the structure of their society," Dr. Nelson said.

No Wild Cattle in Area

The researchers determined that the cattle were domestic by analyses and archeological examinations that showed there had never been any wild cattle in the area. "If there were any, we would have found their remains widely distributed over the area. But we found cattle bones and teeth in the ancient middens," Dr. Nelson said.

Further studies have shown that tsetse flies, the principal cause of cattle deaths in Africa, would have wiped out any wild cattle. But domesticated cattle herds, kept penned-up in the fly-free highlands and not permitted to wander off to water holes where tsetse flies abound, could survive without trouble.

"What we are finding in East Africa," Dr. Nelson said, "are the elements of a food-producing economy. And that in a big geographical system like a continent, many different aspects of civilization are found in different places. And then these things come together in a kind of coalescence of knowledge. Instead of looking for simple, quickie types of explanations, we're going to have to go to big regional projects in which scientists cooperate with one another."

The researchers noted that 15,000 years ago was unexpectedly early for domestic animals to be incorporated into a hunting and gathering economy. The discovery may lead to a way to gauge the evolution of domestic cattle and to reassess evidence from other areas to determine how and when domestication occurred there, he said.

The anthropologist, who specializes in ancient pastoral nomadic societies, has spent more than a decade excavating sites in Africa, with Drs. Richard Leakey and John Kimengich among his collaborators.

THE PYRAMIDS:
ANCIENT SHOWCASE OF AFRICAN
SCIENCE AND TECHNOLOGY

Beatrice Lumpkin

Summary: The pyramids and other great stone monuments of Egypt and the Sudan are the product of a long development of African science and technology. Development took the course from mud bricks to huge stone monoliths, from tally marks for numbers to hieratic ciperization of numbers and complicated formulas, from earliest prehistoric agriculture to highly organized, irrigated farming, from early picture writing to largely phonetic script, and from tribal organization to central government.

This development which proceeded from African beginnings, on African soil, by African peoples, eliminates any need to fabricate an external, foreign source for pyramid building or the ancient Egyptian civilization as a whole.

The development of pyramids and other great monuments is traced from the mud brick beginnings to the great pyramids and temples. Planning of the monuments is described; examples are given of written plans, and the level of mathematics and technology required for pyramid building are discussed. Possible methods of construction of the pyramids are considered.

Much has been said about the artistic grandeur and the religious conviction involved in the colossal construction projects of ancient Egypt. This article, instead, will be concerned with what these stone structures tell us about the level of science, technology and administration required for their construction. I have used as my sources the works of leading Egyptologists although my conclusions are different. In evaluating ancient Egypt, the pervasive role of racial prejudice in the United States and Western Europe introduces a fog of confusions. As W.E.B. DuBois cautioned in his *The World and Africa* "Reisner was born in sight of Negro slavery in America and never forgot it."[1]

George Sarton, a respected historian of science, has written an excellent introduction to this subject:

"Pyramids? Did I mention pyramids? Do not these gigantic witnesses of the Egyptian genius speak loudly enough? The great pyramid of Gizeh dates from the beginning of the thirtieth century B.C. In our age of mechanical wonders, its mass is still as imposing as when it was built almost five thousand years ago; it seems as permanent as the hills and in all probability will outlast most of the skyskrapers of which we are so proud. However startling our first vision of it, our admiration increases as we analyze the achievement and measure the amount of mathematical and engineering skill, of experience and discipline, which were needed to bring it to a successful conclusion."[2]

Sarton preceeds his discussion of the pyramids with remarks about the mathematical papyrus copied by the scribe Ahmes.

"Here we have a mathematical treatise which was written more than thirteen centuries before the time of Euclid!...it contains already such elaborate results that we must consider it, not as a beginning, but rather as a climax, *the climax of a very long evolution.*"[3] (my emphasis)

We do not know all the steps in the evolution of the Ahmes papyrus although Ahmes himself said it was a copy of a much earlier papyrus. We know that the first calendar had already been developed in Egypt thousands of years before Ahmes. As for the development of Egyptian numbers, the last issue of this Journal[4] showed the Ishango bone from Central Africa, over 8,000 years old, which uses tally marks to represent numbers. Clearly, there are many links missing between these simple tally marks in central Africa and the highly developed number symbols of dynastic Egypt. Perhaps we never shall recover all of these links. Still I agree with Carl Boyer that "...continuity in the history of mathematics is the rule rather than the exception. Where a discontinuity seems to arise, we should first consider the possibility that the apparent "hiatus" may be explained by the loss of intervening documents."[5]

EARLIEST AGRICULTURE IN EGYPT

Recent evidence pushes back to an extremely early date the beginnings of agriculture in Egypt. There is now evidence that agriculture began in Southern Egypt 10,000 years earlier than previously believed. Near Aswan, an international team of Egyptian, Polish and U.S. scientists found remnants of barley with a radiocarbon date of 17,000 to 18,300 years ago. During the Nubian salvage campaign, numerous agricultural tools dated 14,500 + 490 years were uncovered, giving further proof of an African site for the earliest known origin of cereal cultivation.[6]

This early evidence of agriculture, the discovery by Wertime of the use of tin in Egypt hundreds of years earlier than previously believed*.

*SCIENCE, 4 January 1980, V. 207, No. 4426, pp 50,51, book review by Vincet C. Pigott of "The Search for Ancient Tin", Theodore A. Wertime and Nubian salvage evidence of pharaonic (Horus falcon) kings in Nubia twelve generations before Menes, should end, once and for all, the hypothesis of a "sudden" emergence of Egyptian civilization, full-blown and without roots in African soil. Such theories of a non-African source of Egyptian writing and civilization are rooted in racial prejudice rather than scientific evidence. Still the prejudice persists and is too often repeated by people who should know better.

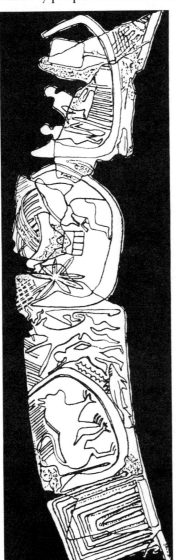

Images carved on a stone incense burner used about 3,300 B.C. by the Nubians. Near the middle is a seated figure wearing a crown known from later Egyptian times. Above royal figure is falcon god, Horus. Concentric rectangles, at left are palace symbol (see Editorial). (Adaptation of drawing in Oriental Institute, University of Chicago, by kind permission—Artist Sylvia Bakos)

Lumpkin — Fig. 1

The source of much of our information is the fragile Egyptian book roll made of papyrus paper. The rolls did not survive in large number, no matter how dry the climate. In contrast, the clay tablets used in Mesopotamia were preserved in abundance. From one Babylonian locality alone, that of ancient Nippur, 50,000 tablets have been taken.[7] The very factors of lightweight portability which gave the papyrus the advantage in ancient times has resulted in a disadvantage to the modern historian because only a few scientific papyri are extant. Many papyri and clay tablets, robbed from Egypt and Mesopotamia by greedy "explorers" in the days before independence, were allowed to crumble to dust in some Western collections.

Neugebauer gives a poignant example from his own experience, with an astronomical papyrus:

"One of its subjects is the description of the travel of the "decans" over the body of the sky goddess, who was depicted on the ceilings of tombs and temples as a representation of the vault of heavens under which we live. Our papyrus was first seen in the possession of an antiquities dealer in Cairo. At the time, the text still contained at the beginning the picture of the sky goddess with all the constellations and their dates of rising and setting. When the text reached Copenhagen the picture was gone. No doubt it was sold to some private collector and is probably lost forever. Thus a vital part of the understanding of the text vanished almost at the same moment its importance was recognized.[8]

The possible importance of this missing document is indicated by the "Moscow Mathematical Papyrus" which, although in poor condition, is the only source of complicated pyramid problems and measurement of curved surfaces. Without this fragment, our concept of Egyptian mathematics would be that of a mathematics far less advanced than the Moscow papyrus indicates.

THE PYRAMIDS TODAY

Fortunately the pyramids remain, at least some of them. In their haste to examine the interior of three pyramids and find the treasure they contained, European treasure hunters of the last century tore down three Meroitic pyramids, stone by stone.[9]

The remains of eighty pyramids are still recognizable, some in the Sudan but most built in the desert, west of the Nile, near Memphis. Tradition had it that Memphis was built on ground just reclaimed from the water by diverting the Nile to a new channel east of its original course.[10] Memphis was built by Menes, the first king to unite all Egypt. His undisputably African features underscore the black origins of the world's first great government.[11]

The Great Pyramid at Giza, first of the seven wonders of the world, was built as a tomb for Khufu, a black king whose statue in the Cairo museum shows classic black African features.[12] The size and precision of the Great Pyramid boggle the mind. The square base originally measured 755.43 ft., 755.88 ft. and 755.77 ft. on its north, south, east and west sides respectively. The height was 481.4 ft. and the base covered an area of 13.1 acres.[13] The right angles, at each corner of the base, line the walls up almost perfectly with the four cardinal points. These angles were accurate within 0.07°, a degree of precision which has raised many questions about possible use of the pyramid for astronomical purposes. It is a fact that half the perimeter of the base divided by the height is 3.1408392; compared to the modern value of pi of 3.1415927 the difference is only 0.0007535. This is dismissed as mere coincidence by the official Egyptologists who point out that the Egyptian value for pi was, $4 \times (8/9)^2 = 3.1604938$, a difference of 0.0189012 from the modern value. Either way it is taken, it is clear that the Egyptian value for pi was more accurate than any other approximation of ancient time. I would suggest that we have too few mathematical documents at this time to reject, out of hand, the possibility that the ratio of the Great Pyramid semiperimeter to its heights was significant.

Large enough to hold the English Westminster Abbey and St. Paul's Cathedral plus the cathedrals of Florence, Milan and St. Peter's in Rome, the Great Pyramid is so massive that if broken up into 1-foot cubes it would stretch 2/3 of the way around the equator.[14] The interior of the pyramid has been excavated by its builders to form a grand gallery of great beauty. Gleaming in polished limestone, it extends 153 feet in length and rises to a corbelled ceiling 28 feet high. The passageway is so designed that seven courses of stone begin above the 7½ ft. walls, each course projecting 3 inches inward until the top courses on each side are just 3½ ft. apart. The huge ceiling slabs which top off the vault are "set each at a steeper slope than the passage in order that "the lower edge of each stone should hitch like a pawl into a ratchet cut in the top of the walls; hence no stone can press on the one below it, so as to cause a cumulative pressure all down the roof; and each stone is separately upheld by the sidewalls across which it lies."[15]

The grand gallery leads to a passage which opens to the famous "King's Chamber," which is roofed and paved with finely dressed and polished red granite...The northern and southern walls each have an air channel. Ahmed Fakhry, an Egyptian Egyptologist who has spent much time at the pyramids, reports that one of the air channels "still functions and serves to keep the air of the chamber wonderfully fresh."[16]

Each of the roof slabs of granite is estimated to weigh 50 tons. However, relief chambers were built in above the "King's Chamber" to relieve the pressure on its roof.[17]

Section of relieving chambers above the King's Chamber in the Great Pyramid. (After Perrot & Chipiez, *Histoire de l' Art dans l' Antiquite, pge 227.)*

Lumpkin — Fig. 2

DEVELOPMENT OF THE TRUE PYRAMID

How was the great pyramid designed and built? Did those who designed it and organized the construction come suddenly on the Egyptian scene and perform a series of miracles?

Although not all the answers to the questions about pyramid building are known at this time, enough is known to be sure that the science and technology of pyramid building developed over the centuries. A whole succession of structures show the development of this science. The miracle, if there was a miracle, lies in the genius of the Egyptian people.

Pyramid building "developed directly from crude brick construction," according to Lauer.[18] Thus the basic technology for pyramid building came from the genius of the common people, the unknown inventors who progressed from mud-daubed reed huts to shaping the Nile mud into bricks to bake in the sun for more comfortable, durable housing.

The first pyramid ever built was designed by the great Imhotep for King Zoser at Saqqâra. Imhotep made the important innovation of using stone instead of bricks, but the stones were relatively small and arranged like bricks with frequent alternation of headers and stretchers. Decorative details frequently imitate the rush matting and reeds that were used in humble dwellings and palaces alike. Even wood doors were shown, engraved in the stone, either in open or closed position.[19]

Imhotep's decision to build in stone could not have been taken lightly. It depended on an extension of the stonecutters' technology and the skill accumulated by the people who had learned how to shape delicate stone vessels over the centuries. The important role of experiment, the "cut and try" of the modern engineer, is evident from the five separate stages in which the first pyramid was designed and built.

The first step was to build a large stone mastaba, resembling the huge mud brick tombs of earlier kings, but built in lasting stone. Mastaba is the modern Arabic word for the benches built outside of peasant homes which have the same shape as these tombs. Then the base was enlarged. Taking advantage of the strength of the stone blocks, Imhotep made a further innovation. He added, on top of the mastaba, a series of three other mastaba, each smaller than the one beneath. The base was enlarged again and additional layers added to make a total of 6 steps, all made of stone from nearby quarries. The step pyramid which resulted was then encased with fine limestone quarried from the Tura and Masura hills across the river and ferried to the west bank.

Almost as impressive as the pyramid itself was the stone wall which enclosed the pyramid, 30 ft. high and 909 ft by 1,785 ft. in its length and width, with 14 imitation gates cut into the stone.[20] The burial chamber itself, for such was the purpose of the pyramid, was in a chamber cut out of the rock beneath the pyramid and reached by a passageway outside of the pyramid. Although relatively small stones were used in the basic construction, a 3-ton granite plug sealed the hole in the ceiling of the burial chamber.

The use of inclined courses of stone was an important innovation in this first step-pyramid, imparting the stability to the structure that would make possible further development of the pyramid design.

Several of the pyramids which followed Zoser's show the steps in transition to true pyramids with smoothly sloping sides. Among the changes was the use of larger, massive blocks which had the advantage of greater stability and required less cutting labor. Evidently these advantages outweighed the greater difficulty of transporting larger stones.

At Meidum, a 7-step pyramid was built. Then the steps were filled in until the sides sloped like a true pyramid. A final casing of good limestone finished the first true pyramid. The angle of inclination was similar to that of Zoser's, 75°. But this angle proved too steep for a pyramid at Dashur, one of the first designed originally as a true pyramid.

The famous Bent Pyramid of Dashur was started with an incline of 54°31'. Supporting timbers, still in place, indicate that structural weaknesses developed. The angle of incline was abruptly decreased to

43°21' and the reduced pyramid was finished in haste.21 This experience possibly led to excessive caution in building the nearby Northern Stone Pyramid of Dashur, the earliest tomb completed as a pyramid. Its angle of inclination is only 43°40' instead of the 52° used in subsequent pyramids, resulting in a lower pyramid.22

This record of experimentation in pyramid-building provides the background for appreciating some of the Egyptian mathematics which has come down to us. Very likely we know only a fragment of the mathematics of these ancient Africans, but it is a very interesting fragment.

The Ahmes paprus (bought by a Scot named Rhind) has several problems in pyramid mathematics. In their study of pyramids, the

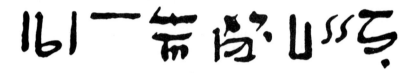

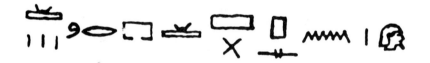

Problem in pyramid mathematics from the Ahmed papyrus (bought by Rhind)
Top, Hieratic script
Bottom, same in Hieroglyphs   Lumpkin — Fig. 3

Egyptians used the property of similar triangles which is the basis of trigonometry. To assure smooth (straight) sides of the pyramid and to assure that the four sides would terminate in a point, the ratio of "run" to "rise" would have to be kept constant. We call this ratio the contangent of the angle of inclination. They called it the *seked* of the pyramid. The property of similar triangles used is, of course, the proportionality of corresponding sides. Problems 56 - 60 of Ahmes (Rhind Mathematical Papyrus) use this proportion to calculate the altitude of a pyramid given the seked and the length of one side of the square base, a very practical problem for pyramid builders.23

But the greatest puzzle to modern mathematicians is to try to reconstruct the method used by the Egyptians to discover their formula for the volume of a truncated pyramid, as given in problem 14 of the Moscow Mathematical Papyrus.24 This formula for a pyramid of square base with sides a, cut off at a height h, with a square top of side b is:

$$V = \left(\frac{h}{3}\right)(a^2 + ab + b^2)$$

Here is a formula which clearly does not fit into the standard evaluation of Egyptian mathematics as "primitive." Indeed it is a challenge to modern historians of mathematics to reconstruct the Egyptian method. Many dissection models have been proposed. Of those I've seen, I prefer that of Gillings because it is done in the spirit of the scribes, proceeding from a number of specific cases to derive a general method. However, I would not reject out of hand the method proposed by Lancelot Hogben who broke up the volume of the pyramid into many very small steps, like a step pyramid whose steps were so small that they approximated a true pyramid.[25] Although summation of infinite series could not be expected in ancient mathematics, the great facility of the Egyptians with finite series, arithmetic and geometric, has been explicitly shown in the Ahmes papyrus.[26] Also, as we have already seen, pyramid building began with step-pyramids showing, for all to see, the relationship between the volume of step pyramids and true pyramids.

HOW THE PYRAMIDS WERE BUILT

Some of the most fascinating discussions which shed light on the science and technology of the ancient Egyptians, are the modern attemps to figure out how the pyramids were built or how the obelisks were installed. The full answer to these questions must wait for more complete scientific study of these monuments. Significantly, it was only after independence, in the years of the Nasser government, that the Egyptian government was able to begin to finance this type of study of the pyramids. Only in this part of the 20th century have there been Egyptian Egyptologists directing such work. Since excavations at pyramid sites are very expensive and yield relatively little in treasure, there has been little subsidy of such work by Western organizations.

The same sort of talents that brought together a centralized government in ancient Egypt, that constructed the vast network of irrigation canals, that developed the first phonetic writing and imbedded an alphabet into the beautiful picture writing, that wrote the first medical treatises, composed a body of literature and phenomenal art that we still admire today, that invented the first ciphers to represent numbers, these were the talents that underlay the ability to create the awe-inspiring pyramids, obelisks and temples.

The authors of *Ancient Egyptian Masonry,* a classic study in this field, said these ancients were "perhaps the best organizers of human labor the world has ever seen...Their powers of transport by water were astonishing; whether thousands of blocks were required for a temple or whether a single block weighing 1000 tons had to be brought, their boat-building powers were fully equal to the demand made upon them."[27]

This seems to be the place to put to rest the unbased slanderous assumptions that the pyramids were built with slave labor cruelly driven by the overseer's lash. These great construction projects provide evidence, instead, of the tremendous productivity of Egyptian agriculture and the efficiency of the central administration which made possible the feeding of many thousands of people while they worked on construction. Most were farmers, working in the off season when the fields were flooded, who made extra income on public works, perhaps an early form of work relief. Many were skilled craftsmen.

King Menthuhotep IV of the XIth dynasty sent 10,000 men to the Hammamat quarry for a large sarcophagus. To move the lid, from the quarry to the river, 3000 sailors were used. It was claimed that "not a man perished, not a trooper was missing, not an ass died and not a workman was enfeebled."[28] Not so lucky was an expedition for Rameses IV who sent 9,262 persons to the same quarry of whom 900 perished. Of the 8,362 survivors, 2,000 were slaves and 5,000 classified as "infantry" and the remainder in special categories, indicating that the bulk of the work was done by free Egyptians.[29] Most of the slaves were prisoners taken in foreign wars and there was no racial element involved. Slaves were permitted to marry into Egyptian families.

An Egyptian Egyptologist, Ahmed Fakhry, defends Khufu, the pharaoh of the Great Pyramid:

"Some of the classical authors wrote that Khufu was a great tyrant and was hated by his subjects because he enslaved the whole nation to build his great tomb; unfortunately such ideas are still repeated. But ancient Egyptian history provides no evidence at all to support these stories. Khufu was apparently an able and energetic ruler, during whose reign the land flourished and art reached perfection."[30]

WRITTEN PLANS

Some written plans have survived, showing scale drawings; front and side views are known and even an example of sectional representation of a house has been found.[31] Next to a curved, saddleback solid was found a sketch for its construction. Although little known, this sketch is of the greatest importance because it is an example of the use of rectangular coordinate to draw a curve, a prerunner of coordinate geometry.[32]

Vertical lines, equally spaced, are used in the sketch in a manner reminiscent of our common graph paper. The height of the vertical lines gives the desired height at the horizontal location indicated by the

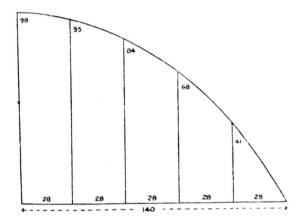

Fig. 4A. Scale-drawing of the curve whose particulars are indicated on the ancient diagram shown in Fig. 4B.
                                                          Lumpkin — Fig. 4A.

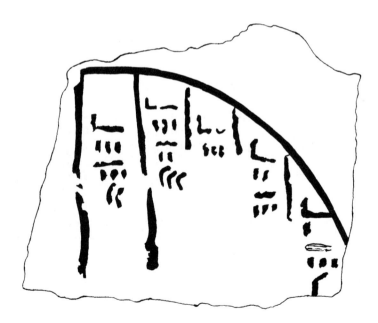

An architect's diagram, defining a curve by co-ordinates. Probably III rd dynosty. Saqqara.
                                                          Lumpkin — Fig. 4B

spacing between vertical lines.

A better known example of rectangular coordinate grids is that used for star maps shown on the ceilings of some famous Egyptian tombs. But the usage in this sketch, for constructing a curved surface, is even more advanced in concept. A grid of squares was also used as a convenient method of scaling up plans for actual construction.[33] Such grids are seen on some of the plans, also on unfinished artwork.

We know something about the pyramid builder's plan although only a few fragments remain of the thousands of plans that were probably used. Reference to earlier plans appeared in Egyptian literature when a king made repairs to an old monument. We know only a little about their methods of measurement and further study is needed of their cubit, remen and double remen measuring units as an example of Pythagorean triples.[34] But the question still remains of how the pyramid builders mined, hauled and put into place immense slabs of rock without modern tools. Mere numbers of workers alone is not the answer. The tools, we believe, were simple but the process of organizing the labor force was complex.

FROM QUARRY TO PYRAMID

Engelbach and Clarke have given what appear to me to be explanations consistent with the evidence found in the huge quarries. Especially valuable evidence is supplied by the partly mined obelisk at Aswan, left at the quarry after it was found to be flawed.[35] Other convincing evidence comes from the unfinished pyramid of Sekhemkhet which is practically covered with embankments built as ramps to move the stones to the required height.[36] In the quarries "Boulders from which blocks have been detached by means of wedges can be seen by the thousand, and all over the area great embankments, which facilitated the transport of the blocks to the Nile can be traced leading from the quarries."[37] The following explanation is after Engelbach and Clarke.

A trench was started around the desired block by pounding in copper chisels. The surface of the boulder was probably prepared by heating with fire; then water was used on the hot stone to crumble the granite.

Once the trench was begun, balls of dolorite (very hard rock found at the sites) were used to pound out the trench and even-out the surfaces of the desired block. For undercoating the rock, wedges were often used. Many generations of stonecutting skill went into selecting a proper site, stones that were desirable and accessible, both for cutting and transport to the river.

Quarrymen's wedge-slots. Preparing the stone for cutting. Lumpkin — Fig. 5

Handling such huge blocks could have presented even more of a challenge than the quarrying. There is no question that the Egyptians used levers; the ancient shadduf which is still used to haul water up from the low Nile to the high fields is a lever. Many blocks still retain grooves for the attachment of ropes. A combination of levers, ropes and well-organized work crews could have moved the massive stones out of the quarry.

Only one drawing has come down to us showing the transport of a huge statue overland. The statue is tied to a sled being pulled by 172 men as other men pour a lubricating liquid in front of the sled. Three other men are shown carrying logs in the rear, perhaps to place them in front of the sled.[38] A modern news article should dispel any doubt about the practicality of this means of transport:

"...when contractors recently needed to drag an immense nuclear reactor across the sands into place at the Bailly Nuclear Power Plant near Gary, they put in a call...Could they supply six wooden skids that could bear 550 tons of reactor without being ground into match sticks?"[39]

It seems that the Egyptians anticipated this method of moving a very

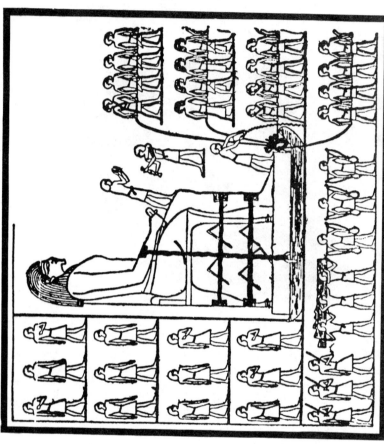

Lumpkin — Fig. 6

Transport of a huge statue overland.
The statue is tied to a sled being pulled by 172 men as other men pour a lubricating liquid in front of the sled. 3 other men are shown carrying logs in the rear, perhaps to place them in front of the sled...In 1978 at Gary, a U.S. nuclear reactor was dragged across the sands, using the same Egyptian method which proved to be the most practical in these conditions.

heavy load over sand by some thousands of years. There is little evidence of use of wheels during the pyramid building age, except for one painting in the tomb of Kaemhesit at Saqqâra.[40] (see Fig. 7) But it was no lack of wheels in the year 1978 at Gary that led to the dragging of a heavy reactor across the sand. It may well be that in sand this was the most practical method.

Lumpkin— Fig. 7

Scaling ladder, fitted with wheels and kept from slipping by a handspike, from the Vth dynasty tomb of Kaemhesit at Saqqâra. This is the only representation of a wheel known in the Old Kingdom.

Loading and unloading the ships presented another problem. The shipbuilding art was clearly up to the task of carrying the megaliths[41] because the murals at the tomb of Hatshepsut, woman Pharaoh of the New Kingdom, show one barge, carrying a 600-ton load of two obelisks, being towed by a fleet of 30 ships. But how to get the obelisk on and off board?

Some think the obelisk may have been rolled into place in the ship which had been previously buried in the sand. Then the sand could have been removed and a channel dug to the Nile to bring water in to float the ship onto the Nile. This is not the type of operation that would leave evidence behind for thousands of years. For the time being it remains an interesting hypothesis.

In summary, this brief treatment of some outstanding architectural achievements of the African people of Egypt has discussed the skill of the craftsmen, the mathematical ability of the architects and engineers and the administrative ability of the planners. These skills had their beginning in the development of agriculture in Africa, the evolution of brick structures for the people's housing, early shipbuilding and tribal administration which merged, first into regional, then into one central government.

It is appropriate to end with a brief comment about the Egyptian language and its written forms. It was a very rich language and well suited to expression of abstract ideas. African in origin, with some Semitic elements, its written form began with pictographs showing African plants, animals, subjects.[42] With the beginning of the first dynasty, under Menes, written history began. By this time, the prehistoric development of the hieroglyphs and faster hieratic script had reached a very advanced level. Phonetic elements, including 24 alphabetic symbols, were used to spell out the words, sometimes after the pictograph, sometimes alone, with a determinative character at the end of the word to guarantee against misinterpretation. The language and its written form proved an important factor in building the advanced civilization of the Egyptian people. The forthcoming translation of Diop's work,[43] which shows the close relationship between the old Egyptian language and his own African language of Wolof, will further strengthen our understanding of the African basis of the ancient Egyptian civilization.

NOTES AND REFERENCES

1. W.E.B. DuBois, *The World and Africa*, Viking, N.Y., p. 118.
2. George Sarton, *The Life of Science*, Books for Libraries Press, Freeport, N.Y., 1948, 1971 p. 138.
3. ibid, pg. 137.
4. *Journal of African Civilizations* Vol. I, No 2, Claudia Zaslavsky, pp. 22-23.
5. Carl Boyer, *History of Mathematics*, Wiley & Sons, N.Y., 1968, p. 257.
6. *SCIENCE*, 28 Sept. 79 V. 205 No. 4413 pp 1341, "Use of Barley in the Egyptian Late Paleolithic", Wendorf, Schild, El Hadidi, Close, Kobusiewicz, Wieckowska, Issawi, Haas.
7. Boyer, op. cit., p. 27.
8. Otto Neugebauer, *The Exact Sciences in Antiquity*, Dover, N.Y., 1957,1969, p. 58.
9. Ahmed Fakhry, *The Pyramids*, University of Chicago, 1967, pp 246-8.
10. I.E.S. Edwards, *The Pyramids of Egypt*, Penguin, Middlesex Eng., 1947,79 p. 20.
11. Cheikh Anta Diop, *The African Origins of Civilization*, Lawrence Hill, Wesport,N.Y., translated by Mercer Cook, 1974, Fig. 5.
12. Diop, op. cit Fig. 7
13. I.E.S. Edwards, op. cit. p. 117-118.
14. ibid
15. W.M. Flinders Petrie, *The Pyramids and Temples of Gizeh*, Field & Tuer, London 1885, p. 25.
16. Fakhry, op. cit. p. 120.
17. Somers Clarke and R. Engelbach, *Ancient Egyptian Masonry*, Oxford, London, p. 189 (Fig. 228).
18. Jean-Phillipe Lauer, *Saqqâra*, Charles Scribners, N.Y., 1976, p. 12.
19. ibid
20. Zakaria Gonheim, *The Lost Pyramid*, Rinehart, N.Y., 1956, pp. 13-47.
21. I.E.S. Edwards, op. cit., p. 97
22. Fakhry, op. cit., p. 95.
23. A.B. Chase, L. Bull, H.P. Manning, and R.C. Archibald, The Rhind Mathematical Papyrus, Mathematical Association of America, Oberlin, Ohio, V. I, 1927, V. 2, 1929.
24. Richard J. Gillings, *Mathematics in the Time of the Pharaohs*, M.I.T., Cambridge, 1972, pp. 187-193.
25. Lancelot Hogben, *Mathematics in the Making*, Doubleday, N.Y., 1960, pp. 70-1.
26. Gillings, op. cit., pp. 166-180.
27. Somers Clarke and Engelbach, op. cit. p.3.
28. Clarke and Engelbach, op. cit. pp. 32-33.
29. James H. Breasted, *Ancient Records*, 1-447,448,453 U. of Chicago, 1906.
30. Fakhry, op. cit. p. 103.
31. Somers Clarke & Engelbach Fig. 53, pp. 52,53.
32. ibid Fig. 48.
33. ibid, p. 47.
34. Gillings, op, cit., pp. 207-9
35. I.E.S. Edwards, op. cit, Fig. 32B.
36. Fakhry, op. cit., p. 44.
37. Somers Clark and Engelbach, op. cit., p. 23
38. Newberry, *El-Bersheh*, PL XV, statue of Dhuthotpe (Somers, Clarke & Engelbach, p. 85).
39. *Chicago Sun Times*, Feb. 26, 1978, p. 48.
40. Somers Clarke and Engelbach, op. cit. p. 86, Fig. 83.
41. Bjorn Landstrom, *Ships of the Pharaohs*, Doubleday, N.Y., 1970, pp. 60-2.*Also see pp. 12-22* for evidence of African origin of sailing ships.
42. E.A. Wallis Budge, *The Dwellers On the Nile*, Dover, N.Y., 1977, orig. 1926, p. 172.
43. Diop, Cheikh Anta, *Parents-Genetique de l'Egyptian Pharaonique et des Langues Nègres Africaines*, IFAN, Dakar, 1977.

GREAT ZIMBABWE:
AN ANCIENT AFRICAN CITY-STATE

Molefi and Kariamu Asante

Great Zimbabwe is a massive stone complex seventeen miles south of the Zimbabwean city of Nyanda, formerly Fort Victoria. With the exception of the extensive pyramids of Egypt and Sudan and the Bigo Ruins of Uganda, Great Zimbabwe is the most immense ancient construction site found in Africa (Caton-Thompson, 1971). A substantial, though not altogether informed, interest has been shown by European writers about the origin of the site. Only now, since independence, have African scholars ventured to the site itself for serious study.

During 1981-82 we visited the Great Zimbabwe with the intention of studying the physical layout to ascertain how an ancient people may have developed a communication network and organized areas for dance and theater rituals. We had imagined that the internal construction of the site and the type of occupations required within such a huge complex might provide us with clues to the uses of ritual and communication. Inasmuch as no human society exists without communication, and since dance is ubiquitous in African societies, it seemed clear enough, and easy enough to arrive at plausible conclusions regarding the communication and movement systems operative within Great Zimbabwe.

We were surprised, however, by the extent of the physcial complex. Nothing we had read had given us the proper perspective with which to approach a study of the ancient complex, and yet numerous works relating to Great Zimbabwe have been published (Bent, 1896; Caton-Thompson, 1931; Garlake, 1970). It occurred to us after considerable deliberation, that a more interesting thesis, particularly as it related to the African historiography, could be developed around the question of the place of Zimbabwe in African history as a locus of civilization. Subsequently, we traversed the length and breadth of the ancient walls and concourses with our modern calculators and 35mm camera hoping to gather data and assess them in terms of the locus of civilization theme. Since we had accepted Diop's position that Nubia and Egypt represented one locus of civilization in Africa we believed that Great Zimbabwe, while much later, had to represent another key area of African civilization.

Description of Site

The ancient plan of Great Zimbabwe is in two parts: the hill complex and the valley complexes. The hill complex is now commonly called the Royal Enclosure; the valley complexes comprise nine separate stone sites including the *Imba Huru*, Great Enclosure. The hill complex was Eurocentrically called the "Acropolis" by Rhodesians. It is traditionally referred to as "Dzimbabwe". Although the name came to be associated with all former royal residences it is appropriate for us to refer to the hill complex where the king kept many of his treasures as "Dzimbabwe." Although he lived in the Great Enclosure in the valley, he spent considerable ritual time on the hill.

An ancient cliff ascent with narrow passageways and stone steps approach the Royal Enclosure from the South. Huge boulders and sharp turns indicate that this ascent was a secret entrance to the Royal Enclosure. At the top of the hill, one can normally survey the surrounding valley for thirty miles. The Great Enclosure and the eight other valley complexes are clearly visible from the Royal Enclosure. This allowed the king to observe the comings and goings of traders and warriors from his hilltop home. Rising nearly 90 meters above the valley, the Royal Enclosure shows a bare southern cliff.

Several important enclosures exist within the hill complex. The principal ones are the ritual enclosure, the smelting enclosure and the iron-keeping enclosure. The king apparently kept the iron-smiths and copper craftsmen in the Royal Enclosure, as there is also a small cave, made by a huge granite rock which housed the copper and iron. Since the major royal treasure, as far as can be discerned, was located in the valley complexes, then the secret cave in the Royal Enclosure must have been only one site where the king kept his wealth and magical secrets.

The valley complexes are dominated by the *Imba Huru*, Great Enclosure. The wall is 250 meters long and it utilizes 15,000 tons of granite blocks. We estimated that within a section one meter long, from top to bottom, two meters thick, there were approximately 4500 stone blocks. The height of the main wall of the *Imba Huru* is about ten meters. It is this great impressive structure that has become so symbolic of Zimbabwe. To build any of these complexes took skill, will and industry. Yet, the *Imba Huru* demonstrates administrative and social achievement by bringing workers together on such an elephant scale to erect the complex. Peter Garlake (1982) estimates that over 10,000 people lived in Great Zimbabwe making it one of the largest cities of its day. Most of these people lived in the area of the valley complexes. Houses, *imbas*, were erected inside the wall enclosures.

Historical Note

The first European to see the Great Zimbabwe was the German, Karl Mauch, who had initially entered the territory under a limited permit granted by the aging King of the Matabele, Mzilikazi, in he 19th century. Mauch had requested permission to hunt in the land of the Matabele but soon revealed his real interest to be the search for gold. In numerous trips into the territory systematically covering the land in large sections, he discovered ancient mine works and rare miner-

PLAN OF DZIMBABWE

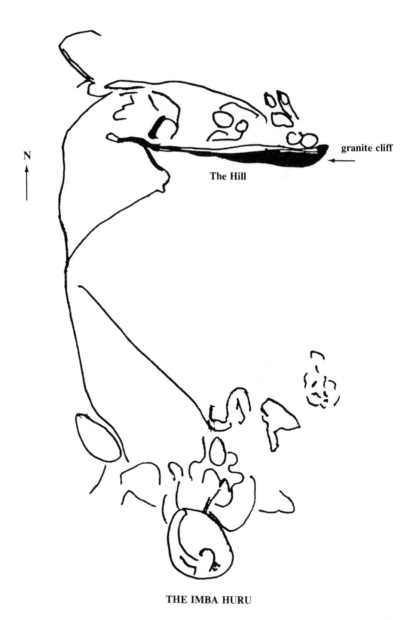

Figure 1. From South to North the entire area is approximately 3000 feet or more than half a mile in length.

als (Burke, 1969). Mauch, led by his African guides, entered the perimeters of the valley complexes. Since that time there have been numerous theories and conjectures, some preposterous, such as the one that claims Great Zimbabwe was built by the Persians for the worship of Ashtar, regarding the province of Great Zimbabwe.

The majority of these conjectures have been made in ignorance of Southern African history and archeology. There exists more than two hundred (200) Mazimbabwes, the name given to the stone village sites, scattered over Zimbabwe and Mozambique. Great Zimbabwe attracts much more attention than the sites at Dhlo Dhlo, Khami, Mtoko, and Chisvingo, because of the enormous scale of the site. One claim puts the figure for the number of sites at 500. This figure usually includes stone sites that are so small they may have been district posts for tribute collectors rather than actual villages. Nevertheless the prominence of the same type of structural concept over such a wide area indicates that the builders were indigenous people.

The question of the origin of the Great Zimbabwe would probably never have occurred if the structure had been found on a continent other than Africa. Few writers have ascribed the building of Teotihuaucan to people other than the Aztecs or Chichen Itza to other than the Mayans or Macchu Picchu to other than the Incas. However, in Africa the pyramids have been questioned in long treatises attempting to prove that the pre-Arab black inhabitants did not build them. And in many books written by ethnocentric European writers, the claim has been made that the Great Zimbabwe, five-hundred miles inland, was built by Persians, Phoenicians, Portuguese, Arabs, and Chinese. But it is clear from serious study that "all objects found in the ruins prove it was built by the local Shona-speaking people" (Garlake, 1982). Unfortunately the colonizers of Africa had no interest in the possibility of African genius creating Great Zimbabwe. Rather than taking the obvious, they began by trying to show the ridiculous.

Trade and Commerce

Much of the intellectual wizardy utilized by some white writers to cast doubt on the ability of the Africans to erect Great Zimbabwe stems from the city-state's highly developed trade sector. Around the perimeter of the Great Enclosure, it is still possible for one to discover relics from the ancient society. Authorities have wisely curbed all but the most serious research examinations of the site. Nevertheless, enough evidence exists to demonstrate that the Zimbabweans controlled the internal trade for a large part of Southern Africa.

Six ancient coins have been found in the various places throughout Zimbabwe, evidence of widespread commercial activity (Huffman, 1972). The earliest coins to be found in the nation of Zimbabwe are a third century copper coin of the Kushan dynasty in India (Anon, 1939:5-6) and a third century copper "Antoni-

Figure 2. This is the conical tower in the Zimbabwe Great Enclosure. The tower now reaches thirty-four feet skyward. The walls nearby are up to twenty feet thick, built of expertly cut and fitted granite blocks held together for centuries, through the care and skill of the original craftsmen, without mortar. These are the largest of more than three hundred stone ruins in Zimbabwe and nearby countries.

Figure 3. At this point the wall of the "Temple" of Great Zimbabwe is thirty-one feet tall. The masonry compares with the finest work to be found anywhere. The double chevron pattern at the top of the wall is found in many ruins in the area of the Monomotapa empire, and signifies the residence of the king.

nians'' of Claudius II Gothicus (Spicer, 1930:45-46). The one coin found and reported so far inside Great Zimbabwe is an Islamic coin dating from the 14th century and bearing the name of Sultan al-Hasan bin Sulaiman, who was Sultan from 1320 to 1333, thus during the time of Ibn Battuta's visit to the East Coast, where a large Islamized African community existed, the remnants of which can be seen in seaports such as Mombasa, Sofala, and Beira.

A flourishing trade existed between the African interior and the coast. Traders from Great Zimbabwe journeyed to the coast to trade ivory and gold for ceramics, beads, faience, glass and celadon. Early European explorers found thousands of glass beads and large quantities of other imported goods as well as gold, copper, and bronze bracelets and rings in the ruins (Huffman, 1972, p. 4). Much of the wealth which remained at Zimbabwe through the centuries was removed by pillagers. In fact, several soapstone sculptures called *hongwes*, sacred birds, which dominated each enclosure were taken by a succession of white 'explorers'. Willi Posselt came to the Great Zimbabwe in 1889 and found the stone sculptures intact. According to his diary:

> I examined the best specimen of the four 'bird' stones and decided to dig it out; but while doing so, Andizibi and his followers became very excited and rushing around with their guns and assegais. I fully expected them to attack us ... I was able to tell Andizibi that I had no intention of removing the stone ... but that I was quite prepared to buy it. (Posselt, 1924)

Posselt dug up the stone sculptures, and collected soapstone divination bowls and dishes, ritual phalli and buried them in the hill complex, intending to retrieve them at a more auspicious time. He said that they were too heavy to haul down the hill (Posselt, 1924). Two years later Theodore Bent began excavating in the region of the Great Zimbabwe. He found Posselt's booty and additional relics and hauled them away. In time the South African Museum, the Paul Tishman collection of New York, the British Museum and the Museum Fur Volkerkunde of Berlin held valuable relics of this ancient African city-state.

The site has withstood successive raids by European treasure hunters, souvenir seekers and plunderers. In 1892 the Imba Huru and other buildings were ransacked by the English Royal Horse Guards. Sixty men gutted the insides of the great building taking everything that was light enough to be removed. When they left the scene the Imba Huru was nothing more than a shell of stone. But even so in its bewildering emptiness it remained an impressive example of African workmanship. They also vandalized the smaller buildings surrounding the Imba Huru. It is necessary to understand the incredible attraction Great Zimbabwe had for European visitors. They could not believe that Africans built the city. In 1871 a German prospector had carted away stone posts and a beautiful platter which he later sold to Cecil Rhodes. In 1889 another European hunter-prospector removed carved stone birds. Many of these relics are in European and South African museums although some stone birds have been returned recently.

A Perspective

Great Zimbabwe rose in significance from the twelfth century and flourished as the capital of the Munhu Mutapa empire for three hundred years. Despite the impression given by the massiveness of the structure the buildings were not designed as fortifications as were the ancient walls of Kano in Nigeria, for example. Great Zimbabwe was the residence of the paramount ruler of the southeastern interior of Africa, surrounded by the houses of his family, tributary rulers, officials of his court and servants. There were also a few dwellings erected in the thirteenth century for traders.

According to Garlake (1982) the walls of Great Zimbabwe were built to display the power of the state. We observed no battlements, bastions or ramparts capable of being used for warfare. Furthermore, the prominent conical tower which rises from the Imba Huru has no access to the top; it is built of solid stone throughout. Cliff tops which would be inaccessible are beautifully walled, while more accessible routes are left unwalled. Thus, the enormity of the structure symbolizes the power, permanence and authority of the Munhu Mutapa, paramount ruler.

Our thesis which follows that of Garlake is that Great Zimbabwe was more a political statement than a place for shelter or protection. Everything in the Great Zimbabwe expressed the traditional religious values of the Shona people. However, since Shona religion is a personal and family affair, there were no major temples or shrines. Inasmuch as the religion expressed relationships between the living and dead it did not demand public display. The collective recognition of community was expressed in the visual sight of the Great Zimbabwe itself. The private shrines of the King were rarely seen by the ordinary people.

It is conceivable that the *mbira* dance which utilizes the popular mbira instrument often referred to as a thumb piano developed in the small enclaves of the Royal Enclosure. As a dance of the ancestors it could have served as a source of remembering the *Mutupos* or totems of the people.

Numerous objects of value were found in the Dzimbabwe, suggesting trade with countries as far away as India and China. African traders may have gone to the coast to trade gold for glazed stoneware, glass beads from India and Chinese celadon dishes in hues of blue and green. In 1902 European treasure hunters unearthed over fifty pounds of iron hoes, an iron gong, such as might be used in calling the city to attention for the paramount king, two massive spearheads of iron used as gong strikers, ten pounds of iron already twisted into bangles, a huge bounty of copper and bronze bracelets, stone molds for copper ingots, numerous ingots themselves and other valuable relics.

The hoard also included wrought iron lampstands, a large iron spoon, tiny bronze hawkbells, a copper-sheathed jewelry box, a spiralled copper finger ring, a copper necklace, a large chain of coral, small sheets of beaten gold pierced so that it might have served as backing for a chair or chest and great stores of ivory. We observed these objects in the museum established to preserve some of the relics. However, we were certain that the vast majority of the treasures of Great Zimbabwe have long disappeared so thorough had been the plunder.

Finally, the evidence demonstrates that a city-state with so many diverse objects of ritual and decoration had a well developed system of administration. Since there are numerous ancient sites similar to Great Zimbabwe and scattered throughout Zimbabwe and Mozambique, it seems remarkable that African and African American anthropologists and archaelogists have not taken a more definite investigative attitude toward these sites; of course, part of the problem has been political; Zimbabwe received its independence in 1980. Quite possibly, with the freedom to travel and study throughout the nation, others will begin to study the relationship between the past and the present, knowing well that roots are necessary for the branches to grow.

References

Anon (1939). Ancient coin found in Inyanga District. *Bulletin of the Stanley Society, volume 3, pp. 5, 6. Cyclostyled Report on file, Zimbabwe Historical Monuments Commission.*

Bent, J.T. (1893). *"On finds at the Great Zimbabwe Ruins (with a view to elucidating the race that built them)." Journal of Anthropological Institute,* volume 22, 1893.

Bent, J.T. (1895). *The Ruined Cities of Mashonaland.* Bulawayo: Books of Rhodesia, 1969, fascimile of the 3rd edition.

Burke, E.E. (1969), Ed. *Journals of Carl Mauch.* Salisbury: National Archives.

Caton-Thompson, G. *The Zimbabwe Culture.* London: Cass, 1971 (first published by Clarendon Press, Oxford, 1931).

Garlake, P. (1982). *Life at Great Zimbabwe.* Salisbury: Mambo Press.

Garlake, P. (1970). "Rodesian Ruins: A Preliminary Assessment of Their Styles and Chronology." *Journal of African History,* volume 11, no. 4.

Huffman, T. (1972). "An Arab Coin From Zimbabwe," Arnoldia 32, no. 5, July.

Posselt, F.W. I. (1924). "The early Days of Mashonaland and a Visit to the Zimbabwe Ruins." *NADA,* volume 2.

AFRICAN EXPERIMENTAL AERONAUTICS: A 2,000-YEAR-OLD MODEL GLIDER

Dr. Khalil Messiha, Guirguis Messiha,
Dr. Gamal Mokhtar, and Michael Frenchman

Summary: Khalil Messiha's discovery indicates that the Egyptians were experimenting with flying machines as early as the 4th or 3rd century B.C. This article is based on several related pieces, collected and presented to the Editor by an official at NASA. The Journal gives credit to those mentioned above for authorship of these materials, which have been edited and arranged for publication in this issue.

AN ANCIENT EGYPTIAN AEROPLANE MODEL

Khalil Messiha and Guirguis Messiha

This extraordinary scientific model was placed among the models of birds in room No. 22, bearing No. 6347, in the Egyptian Museum. It dates back to hundreds of years B.C. (Late period Egypt) The model attracted my attention as it was very much like the aeroplane models I used to make some 20 years ago. It was discovered in Sakkara in 1898 and is made of sycamore wood. It is the model of a *Monoplane* and weighs 39.120 gms. (See Photos and Fig. 1).

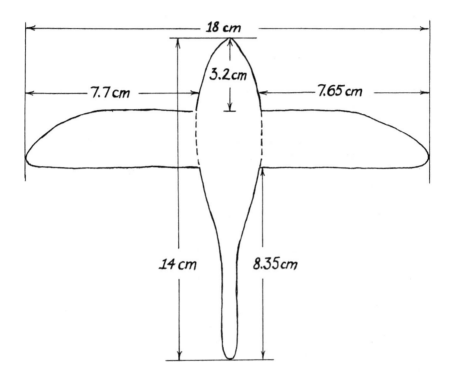

Plan of the model (ventral view)

The Wing:

The wing is made of one piece of wood, and its span is exactly 18 cms. The part over the body is the thickest — 8 millimeters. Then it tapers in thickness towards the tips. One can note also that there is a *Dihedral angle* which is slightly unequal on both sides due to slight distortion of the wood, caused by passage of time (see Fig. 2). In Fig. 2 which is an actual tracing scale 1:1 looking from the tail, one can see clearly the Dihedral angle.

The Body (See Fig. 2 & 3)

The body is made of the same wood as the wing and has an *aerofoil shape* beautifully carved and smooth. Its nose is pyramidal in shape with one eye painted on its right surface. It increases in thickness as it moves towards the tail, and the thickest part is that holding the wing. It has a heart shape section, then the body gets slimmer assuming a compressed (fish body) shape and has an elliptical section in its two thirds. The last third is the tail which is an integral part of the body. There is a rectangular grooved part to hold the wing which is 3 cms in length. The upper surface of the wing is flush with the body. The part of the body joining the tail is 1.8 cms high, and the entire body measures 14 cms from nose to tail. The tail is nearly rectangular in shape. It is 3 cms high and about 4 millims thick and has an upright position. The lower part of the tail is broken which I think may be an evidence that the tail was attached there.

It should be noted, however, that there is no trace of any decoration of "feathers" painted on the body with the exception of the eye, and two faint reddish lines surrounding the belly under the grooves. There are also *no legs* or marks to suggest any such fittings as on the other bird models of Ancient Egypt.

1(b). Flight Engineer Guirguis Messiha presented the following comment:

"The negative dihedral angle of this model has the same effect of a positive dihedral angle giving good effect on the flight of the model. The wing section shows that the wing surface is part of an ellipse, which gives stability in flight. Generally the body is an aerofoil shape which lessens the drag, a fact that has been discovered after years of experimental work in aeronautics".

I have already made a similar balsa wood model, and added the tailplane (which I suppose was lost) and was not astonished to find that it could sail in the air for a few yards when thrown by hand.

A 2,000-YEAR-OLD MODEL GLIDER

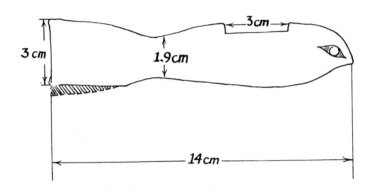

Side view (right side)

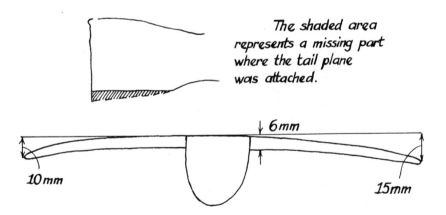

The shaded area represents a missing part where the tail plane was attached.

This diagram shows the tapering wings and the dihedral angles

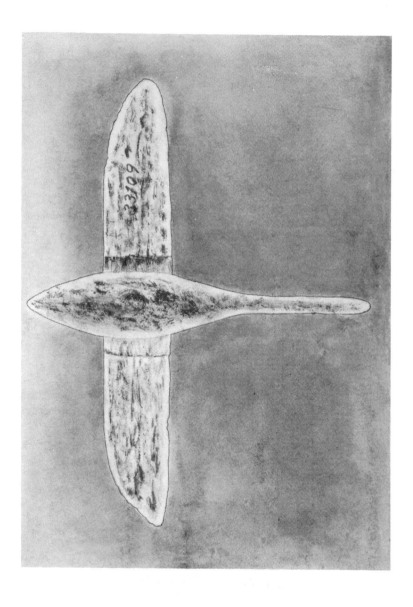

1. The maker of this model made several models before he could reach the "fine finishing" apparent in our model.
2. This ancient aeroplane model represents a diminutive of an original monoplane still present in Sakkara.
3. The name of the inventor of this model is "Pa-di-Imen" which means the "Gift of Amon".*

Editor's Footnote Amon is an African deity with origins in southern Egypt.

OFFICIAL STATEMENT ON THE MESSIHA DISCOVERY

Gamal Mokhtar

Few days ago, members of the International Aerospace Education Committee, who met in Cairo for the first time, were surprised when they visited the Egyptian Museum.

This was not the normal surprise of visitors coming to the Museum for the first time, but also a surprise to see the model of an aeroplane 2300 years old.

The model was found in Sakkara in the 19th century and brought to the Museum where it was officially registered in 1898.

No one here had then known anything about aeroplanes, and the model was kept as a bird.

For many years it was kept in a glass box with other birds, until a young Egyptian physician and artist noticed that it was different from birds. The difference was clear in his eyes, because birds' tails are horizontal, while aeroplanes have vertical tails.

The piece has a vertical tail. It also has wings completely different from birds' wings, but exactly like aircraft wings.

Being a model aircraft amateur, the Egyptian physician and artist was able to distinguish the model plane from the models of birds surrounding it.

There is no doubt that this piece of wood, though quite small, only 18 by 14 centimeters, has a very great meaning. Archeologists and scientists over the world are invited to study this fantastic piece which will no doubt change the history of aviation.

A 2,000-YEAR-OLD MODEL GLIDER

Michael Frenchman

Dr. Khalil Messiha rediscovered a model glider or sailplane dating from the fourth or third century BC. The glider, which is made of sycamore wood, looks remarkably futuristic and bears a close resemblance to the American Hercules transport aircraft which has a distinctive reverse dihedral wing.

Dr. Messiha, who has made a study of bird figures, came across the glider model in 1969 when he was looking through a box of bird models in one of the Cairo Museum's storerooms.

"I was looking for odd things when I found this particular model. It was very like some of the scale model planes which I used to make 20 years ago", he said. Most bird figures that have been found are often half human, half bird. But this one was very different.

It was in a box of relics found at Saqqara in 1898. The model is of a high-wing monoplane and weighs 39 gms. The aerofoil-shaped wing is in one piece with a span of 18cm and a greatest thickness of 8mm over the fuselage. Seen from the front the wing tips droop slightly. The fuselage is heart shaped in section and assumes a compressed elipse towards the tail.

"It is the tail that is really the most interesting thing which distinguishes this model from all others that have been discovered", Dr. Messiha said. At the end of the fuselage is a vertical fin. According to Dr. Messiha there is no known bird that sports a fin "rudder", certainly not in Egypt. No bird can produce such a contortion at the rear of its body, to assume anything that looks like the model. Furthermore there is a groove under the fin for a tailplane which is missing.

All other bird models have usually been expensively decorated and have fittings for legs, or marks to suggest that such attachments once existed. This model has no legs and only very slight traces of a painted eye on one side of the nose and two faint reddish lines under the wing and around the fuselage. Dr. Messiha says that a lot of work and skill went into the production of the model to produce the very fine aerofoil shape in the wing. Many attempts must have been made before perfection was achieved.

He is convinced that the find is a scale model of a full-sized flying machine of some kind. He has spent many hours making a replica of the model, which when fitted with a tailplane of the correct proportions will actually fly or glide when thrown into the air.

His brother, Mr. Guirguis Messiha, who is a flight engineer, commented that the aerofoil-shape of the body would lessen the drag effect, a fact that has been discovered only comparatively recently after many years of aeronautical engineering research.

Although the model seems at first sight something of an anti-climax because of its size, there is no doubt that it does bear a striking resemblance to a man-made machine of some kind. Dr. Messiha points out that the ancient Egyptian engineers always made models of contemporary things, from their funeral boats to war chariots. All these existed, and the full-scale versions have been found, so why not a scale model of some kind of glider?

The Cairo Museum is at least taking the whole thing seriously enough to stage a special "aeroplane" exhibition. The diminutive model is shown perched on a pinnacle of velvet in a rather unbecoming lead-sealed glass case. Displays of the more conventional bird models surround it.

Dr. Messiha, who won a prize some years ago for constructing model aircraft, is convinced that other "glider" models exist and that somewhere there should be the remains of a full-scale version. He hopes to carry out excavations at Saqqara, where he believes other models will be found. He is also going to examine other items discovered previously and stored in the museum.

"This is no toy model", he says. "It is too scientifcally designed and it took a lot of skill to make it. The man who did this studied bird flight very carefully. The bird that this model most resembles is the kite, which has a horizontal tail which can be twisted to a near vertical position in flight."

The doctor, who is 48, studied fine art for five years before taking up medicine, and is also an illustrator and engraver. He is at present engaged on research into ancient Egyptian sciences and engineering. He believes they were very advanced in certain areas of knowledge, including elementary aeronautics.

AFRICA IN THE MAINSTREAM OF
MATHEMATICS HISTORY

Beatrice Lumpkin

SUMMARY: For thousands of years, Africa was in the mainstream of mathematics history. This history began with the first written numerals of ancient Egypt, a culture whose African origin has been reaffirmed by the most recent discoveries of archaeology. With a longer period of scientific work than any other area of the world, progress in mathematics continued on the African continent through three great periods, ancient Egyptian, Hellenistic and Muslim. The language changed from Egyptian to Greek to Arabic. But the tradition of African science continued, despite change of language. The Renaissance in Europe was triggered by the science and mathematics brought to Spain and Italy by the Moors of North Africa. Although all peoples and continents have played a role in the history of mathematics, the contributions of Africa are still unacknowledged by western historians.

One of the earliest examples of writing were the hieroglyphs on Narmer's pallette, named for the first king of upper and lower Egypt, who was also known as Menes. The numerals used cited thousands of heads of cattle and thousands of prisoners, indicating the numerals and hieroglyphs already had a long history in Egypt. [1] It has recently been learned from the findings of the International Nubian Rescue Mission which salvaged ancient artifacts and monuments before the Aswan Dam flooded the Sudanese area that pharaonic kings and hieroglyphic writing were known south of the first cataract 20 generations before Menes.

These findings have reaffirmed the African origin of the great ancient civilization. From this region, in the interior of Africa, has come evidence of the earliest known cultivation of grain.[2] With this new evidence, the date of the Egyptian calendar must also be reconsidered. Originally thought to date back to 4241 b.c. when first analyzed by European scholars, its apparent date was arbitrarily changed to 2773 b.c. It was claimed that "Such precise mathematical and astronomical work cannot be seriously ascribed to a people slowly emerging from neolithic conditions."[3] The internal evidence is consistent with either date, based on the Sothic cycle of 1468.[4]

Struik, himself, has kept an open mind on light that could be shed by new discoveries. In correspondence with this author, he wrote: "As to mathematics, the Stonehenge discussions have made it necessary to rethink our ideas of what neolithic people knew. Gillings has shown that the ancient Egyptians could work with their fractions in a most sophisticated way."[5]

The early beginnings of algebra and geometry in ancient Egypt are briefly covered in many history books. But the full scope and depth of ancient Egyptian mathematics have been largely overlooked because the first judgement of the European translators of the papyri dismissed this mathematics as "primitive."[6] It is only in the last ten years that a full-length study of this mathematics was published. It is often not realized that African contributions did not end with the ancient Egyptians but continued through the Hellenistic and Muslim empires. Indeed, Africa continued in the mainstream of mathematics for thousands of years, right up to the European Renaissance.

Any unprejudiced view of world history must acknowledge that many different peoples and races on every continent have made great mathematical discoveries. The Mayans[7] of Central America used a zero hundreds of years before 876 A.D.,[8] its earliest known use in India. And the ancient Chinese, almost 2,000 years ago, solved systems of equations with a method similar to the modern elementary transformations of matrices.[9]

But it was through Africa that the science, mathematics and knowledge of the entire Eastern world reached Europe. This was true in the time of the classical Greeks and continued through the middle ages when Muslim scholars dominated the intellectual life of Europe, Africa and the western and central parts of Asia.

Very different from the above is the theory of history now taught at most North American universities and accepted as "fact" by thousands of practicing mathematicians and teachers. They teach the purely European origin of mathematics. According to this version of history, mathematics began in Greece in the 5th century b.c. With the decline of the Greek empire, no further progress was made until Europe, the true home of mathematics, was ready to advance again during the Renaissance.[10]

To those, such as Kline, who dismiss all mathematics before the Greeks as less than "true" mathematics, George Sarton, the encyclopedist of science, replies: "It is childish to assume that science began in Greece. The 'Greek miracle' was prepared by millenia of work in Egypt, Mesopotamia and possibly other regions. Greek science was less an invention than a revival."[11]

Three great periods of African mathematics will be briefly considered in this article. They are: The ancient Egyptian mathematics of the pyramids, obelisks and great temples,[12] the African participation in classical mathematics of the Hellenistic period and the African participation in Muslim mathematics. Other periods and locales of mathematics on the African continent are not described although future research may well show that these played an important role in the history of mathematics. This vast subject, not covered here, includes the mathematical games so widespread in Africa,[13] the systems of measurement used in the African forest kingdoms, and the mathematics used in building the great stone complex of Zimbabwe. Perhaps now that Zimbabwe has its own government, more information will become available and new chapters in the history of mathematics will be written.

The great accuracy of the dimensions of the pyramids[14] still gives rise to wonder. Geometry, literally the measurement of the land, required a high technology in addition to theoretical mathematics. The famous "rope stretchers" to whom Democritus compared himself, used special ropes, twisted of many fine strands to assure high stability and constant length. The accuracy of the Egyptian value for pi (the constant ratio of circumference to diameter of any circle) was probably a result of theoretical analysis of "squaring a circle"[15] and confirmation of experiment and accurate measurement. The Egyptian value of pi was 3.16, much closer to the modern 3.14 than the Biblical value, 3.0.

Contrary to the reports that the ancient Egyptians did not derive any general principles and limited themselves to specific examples, many of the problems in the mathematical papyri ended with general statements. For example, in the papyrus written by the scribe Ahmes (Rhind Mathematical Papyrus 61B) the solution was followed by: Behold! Does one according to the like for every uneven fraction which may occur. Gillings lists over 10 such statements in this papyrus.[16]

In his book, *Mathematics in the Time of the Pharaohs,* Gillings tries to discover methods that may have been used by the ancient Egyptian scribes to derive their often amazing results. By approaching the subject without prejudice, with the keeness of a mathematical detective, Gillings investigated the terse clues left by the scribes and has revealed some unsuspected achievements. These include formulas for the summation of arithmetic and geometric series and the measurement of the area of a curved surface.

An efficient irrigation technology, efficient central administration, and the skill of the farmers of ancient Egypt made possible a large food surplus, enough to support the mathematicians, teachers and other intellectuals. In turn, these ancient African mathematicians contributed to production by developing methods of measuring the land through formulas for the areas of rectangles, triangles, circles and even the area of a curved dome. Properties of similar triangles were known and some trigonometry, the equivalent of our contangent, helped assure a constant slope for the faces of pyramids.

Their very system of measurement shows knowledge of some

Pythagorean triads. An area measured in cubits was doubled if remens were used while the shape remained similar.[17] Alone of the ancients, the Egyptian's knew the correct formula for the volume of a truncated pyramid, thus stumping the modern experts who wonder "How did they do it?"

First and second degree equations were solved by the method of false position, a method that continued in use up to this century. But perhaps it was in their use of arithmetic and geometric series that the Egyptians' work has almost a modern ring. Indeed the formula used for the sum of n terms of an arithmetic series is the equivalent of one we use today, $s = n/2 (2a + (n-1) d)$.

Sometimes these ancient problems seemed pure mathematical fun. For what practical significance could there have been in problem '79 of the Ahmes papyrus which seems to anticipate this Mother Goose rhyme by 3,500 years,

"As I was going to St. Tues,
I met a man with seven wives.
Each wife had seven cats..."

Compare with:
>Houses 7
>Cats 49
>Mice 343
>Spelt 2,401

(ears of grain)
>Hekat 16,807

(measures of grain)[18]

Egyptian fractions were, perhaps, the most important application of mathematics in those times because they were used for the extensive bookkeeping needed for large public works such as pyramid construction. These were unitary fractions using 1 as the numerator. For example, instead of 2/5 they wrote the equivalent 1/3 + 1/15. These fractions remained in use in Europe until fairly recent times when they were replaced by the decimal fractions which the Moors had introduced. With their fractions, the Egyptians could add, multiply, divide and take square roots.

ALEXANDRIAN MATHEMATICS

Egyptian contributions to science and mathematics did not end with the conquest by the Macedonian, Alexander the Great. Attracted by the great wealth and learning of Egypt, Alexander, in 332 B.C., ordered the construction of Alexandria, a city which became the intellectual center of the Greek speaking world. In Alexandria the products and ideas of the city states of North Africa, Asia Minor, Greece, India and China mingled and took firm root on African soil. A great museum and library attracted the best scholars and educated many generations of Egyptian students.

It was in the fourth century before our era[19] that Greek mathematicians developed the deductive, axiomatic method, establishing the logical foundation on which mathematics so proudly rests today. As Struik wrote, "This again may be connected with the fact that mathematics had become a hobby of a leisure class which was based on slavery, indifferent to invention, and interested in contemplation."[20]

Of course, no modern scholar has tried to belittle this great Greek accomplishment because it rested on an economic base of slavery. Contrast this with the case of Egypt, where slavery played a much lesser role. Yet Hollywood movies and popular texts claim that the greatness of the pyramid period is lessened because slave labor was used.

Up to the fourth century b.c. according to Neugebauer, Greek mathematics was similar to, and no doubt an outgrowth of Egyptian and Babylonian. He cautions that "if modern scholars had devoted as much attention to Galen or Ptolemy as they did to Plato and his followers, they would have come to quite different results and they would not have invented the myth about the remarkable quality of the so-called Greek mind to develop scientific theories without resorting to experiments or empirical tests."[21]

It was in Egypt that Hellenistic mathematics reached its peak. Struik attributes this flowering of mathematics to the central position that Egypt occupied during the Ptolemaic period as the intellectual and economic center of the Mediterranean world.[22]

Who were the people of Alexandria? They were the African people of Egypt with a few immigrants from Greece, Western Asia and neighboring African countries. Sarton reminds us that "Greek emigrants were too few in pre-Christian times and too little interested in science and scholarship to affect and change Eastern minds."[23] The ruling class, itself, was mixed from the first days of Alexandria because Alexander, the Macedonian, ordered his officers to marry and mix with the local population.

Nonetheless, although no pictures have come down to us of any of the great men and women of Alexandria, false portraits have been published which portray them as fair Greeks, not even sunburned by the Egyptian sun. This misleading practice is decried by George Sarton, in an article on "Iconographic Honesty" in which this dean of science history declares "I do not believe there is a single ancient scientist of whose lineaments we have any definite knowledge; thus to publish "portraits' of Hippocrates, Aristotle or Euclid is, until further notice, stupid and wicked."24

In the case of Euclid, best known of the Alexandrian mathematicians, there is not a shred of evidence to suggest that he was anything other than Egyptian. Euclid's fame is based on his 13 major texts, *The Elements*, a strictly logical deduction of theorems from accepted definitions and axioms. For over 2,000 years these books dominated the teaching of mathematics to the delight of mathematicians and the discomfiture of students. In a similar manner, *The Almagest*, written by another Egyptian, Claudius Ptolemy, c. 150 a.d., dominated astronomy until finally replaced by Copernicus' theory of a sun-centered planetary system, c. 1543.

The Almagest (the greatest in Arabic) contains in its 13 books the foundations of spherical trigonometry, a catalogue of 1028 stars and the epicycle system of an earth-centered astronomy. By some peculiar racial reasoning, Ptolemy is often described as Egyptian only because his work was of a practical, applied nature, differing in this respect from the strictly theoretical work of Euclid. The fact is that both were Alexandrians and therefore it is highly probable that they were Africans. In Ptolemy's time, Alexandria was already 400 years old and very much a part of Egypt.

Of Heron, another Alexandrian who wrote *Metrica* on geometric measurement and *Pneumatica,* a book about machines, Howard Eves says "There are reasons to suppose he was an Egyptian with Greek training."25 Another great mathematician of that time, Diophantus, of the Alexandria of the 3rd century, continued the tradition of Egyptian algebra. His *Arithmetica* on number theory marks the author as a genius in his field26 and introduced brief symbols to simplify algebraic expressions (syncopation) in place of the long, wordy forumlations then in use (rhetorical algebra.)

All of these Alexandrian mathematicians wrote their books in Greek. Their use of Greek makes them no more European than the use of English by Nigerians today changes that nationality.

To this very incomplete list of Egyptian mathematicians who worked in Alexandria must be added Theon and his daughter Hypatia, whose memory still inspires women to become mathematicians.

AFRICAN MATHEMATICS DURING THE MUSLIM EMPIRE

In the lengthy period between the decline of the Greek and Roman empires to the eve of the Renaissance, a period of almost 1,000 years,

Europe disappears from the mainstream of the history of mathematics. That is, with the exception of Moorish mathematicians in Spain and Italy who came from North Africa and brought with them 4,000 years of African-Asian mathematics.

In Moorish Spain, "Cordoba, in the tenth century, was a great centre of learning, where one could walk for several miles in a straight line by the light of the public lamps."[27] A whole series of new inventions became available during this period — steel, silk, porcelain and paper. African papyrus paper was still used and appreciated for its fine qualities but pulp paper from China was coming into wider use.[28]

Struik, who has read the Muslim mathematicians in the Russian translations (unfortunately much of this work is still not available in English) stresses ther continuity of culture under Arabic rule. "The ancient native civilizations had even a better chance to survive under this rule than under the alien rule of the Greeks."[29]

In North Africa, the Arabs, as the Greeks before them, intermarried with the African people of these countries and quickly absorbed the culture and learning of Egypt. The rapid physical expansion of the Islamic empire had its intellectual parallel in the exchange of knowledge among Egypt, Persia, India, and China.

From the 8th century until the 15th, Arabic was the language of mathematics and science. About 773 Al-Fazari translated the Indian Siddhanta to Arabic, popularizing the Hindu decimal system — the zero is believed to have come into use later. Thabit ibn Qurra and his school produced excellent Arabic translations of Euclid, Appolonius, Archimedes, Ptolemy and Theodosius and made important additions of their own (826-901). To this day, most of these classics are known to us only through the Arabic translations, the original Greek versions having been lost.

But one book, more than any other, was the vehicle for introducing Europe to Muslim algebra and the Hindu-Arabic numerals and arithmetic, l-Khowarizmi's "Al-jabr wa'l muqabalah. From the author's name we get the common mathematical term, "algorithm." From the title, al-jabr, we get the modern term, "algebra."

Some of the greatest scholars of this time came to Egypt to work, where they could enjoy support for the full scope of their research. Among them was the outstanding mathematician-physicist Alhazen (Al-Haitham). Although born in Basra, his productive life was spent in Egypt, pioneering in optics and geometry.[30] Alhazen is the first of three Muslim mathematicians who opened the door to non-Euclidean geometry. Through his work and that of his successors, Omar Khayyam and Nasir Eddin, European mathematicians hundreds of years later were inspired to create new geometries.

MUSLIM MATHEMATICS REACHES EUROPE

The main routes of transmission of Muslim learning were from North Africa to Spain, also to Sicily and Southern Italy, where Moorish rule lasted for many generations. The Europeans who appear in the mathematical history of the time had studied with the Muslims. Constantine the African (d.1087), a merchant from Carthage, brought a precious cargo of manuscripts to Salerno where a school was founded to translate and study the Arabic works. Adelard of Bath (1116-1142) made a long voyage to Arab countries and translated Arab classics into Latin. Fibonacci (Leonardo Pisano) (1170-1240) got his start in mathematics during his long residence in the North African coastal city where his father was a merchant.[31]

In short, as summarized by Haskins, "The full recovery of this ancient learning, supplemented by what the Arabs had gained from the Orient and from their own observation, constitutes the scientific renaissance of the Middle Ages."[32]

INTERRUPTED PROGRESS

The period which follows the European Renaissance and brings us down to the modern era saw the pillaging of Africa, Asia and the Americas by European colonialism. Slavery depopulated Africa and drastically interrupted African progress. But it is no mere academic exercise to reconstruct without prejudice the thousands of years of history during which Africa contributed to the mainstream of mathematics. World science will become much richer when the former colonial peoples take their place, once more, in the mainstream of mathematics and science.

REFERENCES

1. Sir Alan Gardiner, *Egyptian Grammar*, Griffith Institute, Oxford, 1927, 1978 p.5.

2. *Science*, 28 Sept. 79 V. 205 No. 4413 pp. 1341-7, "Use of Barley in the Egyptian Late Paleolithic," Wendorf, Schild, El Hadidi, Close, Kobusiewicz, Wieckowska, Issawi, Haas.

3. Dirk J. Struik, *A Concise History of Mathematics*, Dover, N.Y. 1967, pp. 24-5.

5. Letter dated April 4, 1978. Gillings is the author of *Mathematics in the Time of the Pharaohs, cited in 14, below.*

6. Morris Kline, *Mathematics, A Cultural Approach*, Addison Wesley, Reading, Mass., p. 14.

7. J. Eric S. Thompson, *The Rise and Fall of Maya Civilization*, U. of Oklahoma Press, Norman, 1954, p. 158. For possible African influence in Olmec and Maya civilizations, see; Ivan Van Sertima, *They Came Before Columbus*, Random House, N.Y., 1976.

8. Boyer, op. cit., p. 235.

9. Boyer, ibid, p. 219.

10. Morris Kline, *Mathematics in Western Culture*, Oxford Press, N.Y. 1953, p. 23.

11. George Sarton, *A History of Science*, Harvard U., Cambridge, 1959, p. IX.

12. Beatrice Lumpkin, *The Pyramids, Ancient Showcase of African Science and Technology*.

13. Claudia Zaslavsky, *Africa Counts*, Prindle, Weber & Schmidt, N.Y., 1973 Section 4.

14. I.E.S. Edwards, *The Pyramids of Egypt*, Penguin, Middlesex Eng., 1947, 9 p. 118.

15. Richard J. Gillings, *Mathematics in the Time of the Pharaohs*, M.I.T., Cambridge, 1975, pp. 141-5.

16. Gillings, ibid, p. 233.

17. Gillings, ibid, p. 208.

18. Chace, Bullard and Manning, *The Rhind Mathematical Papyrus*, Mathematics Association of America, Oberlin Ohio, 1927, V. 1, Photographs XXV-XXVI, Problem 79.

19. Otto Neugebauer, *The Exact Sciences in Antiquity*, Dover, N.Y. 1957, 1969 p. 148.

20. Struik, op. cit., pp. 48, 49.

21. Neugebauer, op. cit., p. 152.

22. Struik, op. cit., pp 49, 50.

23. Sarton, op. cit., p. 4.

24. George Sarton, "Iconographic Honesty," *Isis* 30 (1939) p. 226.

25. Howard Eves. *An Introduction to the History of Mathematics*, Holt, Rinehart and Winston, N.Y. 1964, 1969, p. 159.

26. Eves, ibid, p. 159.

27. H.J.J. Winter, *Eastern Science*, John Murray, London, 1952, p. 62.

28. J.D. Bernal, *Science in History*, Cameron, N.Y., 1954, p. 195.

29. Struik, op. cit., p. 69.

30. Aldo Mieli, *La Science Arabe*, E.J. Brill, Leiden, 1938, p. 105.

31. Mieli, op. cit., p. 243.

32. Charles Homer Haskins, *Studies in the History of Medieval Science*, Harvard U., Cambridge, 1927, p. 3.

THE YORUBA NUMBER SYSTEM

Claudia Zaslavsky

Summary: *This excerpt is taken from a pioneer work in African mathematics—AFRICA COUNTS: Number and Pattern in African Culture and is reprinted by kind permission of the author and her publisher, Prindle, Weber & Schmidt. At the present time, no other extensive study exists of mathematical methods that are distinctly African and sub-Saharan. In this article Professor Zaslavsky sketches in the historical background to African mathematics and then focuses on the amazingly intricate system of numeration based on twenty developed by the Yoruba of Southwest Nigeria.*

Historical Background to Early African Mathematics

Man apparently first emerged on the African continent. The scientific world was astounded when Drs. Mary and Louis Leakey announced the discovery in 1959 of the remains of *Homo habilis,* a tool-making hominid estimated by the potassium-argon dating technique to be 1,750,000 years old. The scene of the discovery, Olduvai Gorge in northern Tanzania, has since yielded much information about the development of man.

Later, two human skulls and stone tools were excavated in Kenya, east of Lake Rudolph; their age is estimated to be 2.6 million years. In February, 1971 came the announcement that a human type of jawbone from the same area was five and a half million years old! No part of the world has proved as fertile a field for the discovery of skeletal remains and stone tools. The most impressive to date is the finding at Fort Ternan, Kenya, of a man-like creature and animals estimated to be fourteen million years of age.

A spectacular discovery, reported early in 1970, was that of an ancient mine in an iron-ore mountain in Swaziland, in southeast Africa. Stone age mining tools were found, and samples of charcoal remaining from old fires were tested by the radio-carbon dating technique. The mine turned out to be 43,000 years old! The ancients appeared to have been seeking specularite, a valuable pigment and cosmetic.

Rock paintings, executed ten thousand years ago, point to an era when the Sahara was green and lush, inhabited by cattle and horses, and by human beings who hunted, rode in chariots, danced, worshipped, and loved. Other such paintings, some dating back thirty thousand years, have been found in South and East Africa, giving us clues to the lives of the people who lived in ancient times.

During the later stone age, hunting and fishing societies developed in the Nile Valley, in West Africa, and in East Africa. From the mathematical point of view the most interesting find is a carved bone discovered at the fishing site of Ishango on Lake Edward, in Zaire (Democratic Republic of the Congo). It is a bone tool handle having notches arranged in definite patterns and a bit of quartz fixed in a narrow cavity in its head. It dates back to the period between 9000 B.C. and 6500 B.C. The discoverer of the artifact, Dr. Jean de Heinzelin, suggests that it may have been used for engraving or writing.

He is particularly intrigued by the markings on the bone. There are three separate columns, each consisting of sets of notches arranged in distinct patterns. One column has four groups composed of eleven, thirteen, seventeen and nineteen notches; these are the prime numbers between ten and twenty. In another column the groups consist of eleven, twenty-one, nineteen and nine notches, in that order. The pattern here may be $10 + 1$, $20 + 1$, $20 - 1$, and $10 - 1$. The third column has the notches arranged in eight groups, in the following order: 3, 6, 4, 8, 10, 5, 5, 7. The 3 and the 6 are close together, followed by a space, then the 4 and the 8, also close together, then another space, followed by 10 and two 5's. This arrangement seems to be related to the operation of doubling. De Heinzelin concludes that the bone may have been the artifact of a people who used a number system based on ten, and who were also familiar with prime numbers and the operation of duplication.

There is a difference of opinion about the markings on the bone. Alexander Marshack, who has examined the markings on the artifact by microscope, says:

> It represents a *notational* and *counting* system, serving to accumulate groups of marks made by different points and apparently engraved at different times. Analysis of the microscopic data shows no indication of a counting by fives and tens but that the groups of marks vary irregularly in amount. That this is an early system of notational counting is clear; however, this does not necessarily imply a modern arithmetic *numerical* system. I have tracked the origins of such early notational systems back to the Upper Paleolithic cultures of about 30,000 B.C.

In *The Roots of Civilization* Mr. Marshack gives his conclusions:

> When I examined this tiny petrified bone at the Musee de'Histoire Naturelle in Brussels, I found that the engraving, as nearly as microscopic examination could differentiate the deteriorated markings, was made by

thirty-nine different points and was notational. It seemed, more clearly than before, to be lunar.

He plotted the engraved marks on the Ishango bone against a lunar model, and noted a "close tally between the groups of marks and the astonomical lunar periods. A number of other readings in the long series of tests that were conducted gave even closer lunar approximations." Here, then, is possible evidence of one of man's earliest intellectual activities, sequential notation on the basis of a lunar calendar, comprising a period of almost six months.

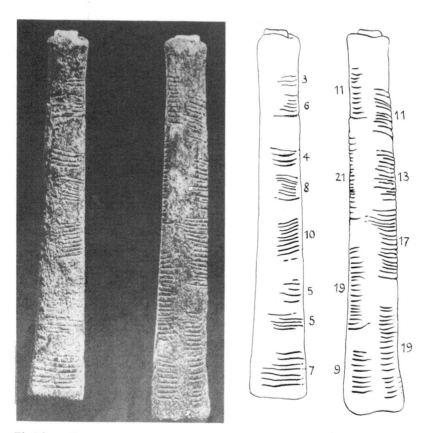

The Ishango bone, over eight thousand years old. This carved bone, discovered at Ishango, on the shore of Lake Edward in Zaire (Congo), indicates that a calendrical or numeration system was known to the fishing and hunting folk of the area. The schematic drawing of the bone shows the arrangement of notches visible to the naked eye. They suggest a knowledge of multiplication by two and of prime numbers. Microscopic examination revealed further detail.   Zaslavsky - Fig. I

It is hardly likely that this artifact was unique in the culture of the Ishango area. The newly evolved techniques of microscopic analysis may reveal other such examples. It is also possible that tallies of this sort were made in a more perishable form—on wood, on animal skins, or by an accumulation of pebbles or seeds; if this was so, the evidence would have been lost in the course of time.

When did man first have occasion to keep mathematical records? Was it to note the passage of time, to predict the season for planting the seed, the flooding of the rivers, the coming of the rains? The first calendars, notches on a bone, were probably lunar, following the phases of the moon. But an agricultural economy required the development of a solar calendar and the reconciliation of solar and lunar time-keeping methods. We believe that tallies of the solar year began several thousand years ago in Egypt, and somewhat earlier in Mesopotamia. From the development of the calendar arose the science of astronomy.

The man who herded the cattle and the farmer who cultivated the fields had to observe the passage of the days and the seasons. But it was a separate class of priests who abstracted the practical knowledge into both a scientific study and a religion. Their observations over a period of many centuries enabled them to foretell the behavior of the seasons and the appearance of the heavenly bodies. This knowledge they kept secret. They were agents through whom the people propitiated their gods to ensure the coming of the rains, the appearance of the new moon—the survival and prosperity of the society. Through religious observances the priests exerted their influence over the populace. Knowledge of natural events enabled the priests to predict and claim credit for their occurrence. Frequently they also held the power to divide the land, to demand tribute from the people, to organize public works, and to build vast monuments to the glory of the gods and the kings. Only a stable society, one that had passed the bare subsistence level, could afford to maintain such a superstructure of unproductive rulers and priests.

Mathematics in Ancient Egypt

In ancient Egypt the flooding of the Nile River necessitated annual redivision of the land. Private ownership of land and the ability to produce a surplus of commodities enabled the owners to exchange their products for their private gain or to store them for future use. Thus arose the need for a system of weights and measures. Mathematical operations of addition, subtraction, multiplication, division, and the use of fractions are recorded in Egyptian papyri in connection with the practical problems of the society.

Their methods of doubling and halving, called "duplication and mediation," were still considered separate operations in medieval Europe. This is how the method is used for multiplication. Let us find the product of 27 and 11. The process consists of successively doubling one factor and halving the other:

11*	27
5*	54
2	108
1*	216

Now we find the sum of those multiples of 27 which correspond to odd numbers (starred) in the first column: 27 + 54 + 216 = 297, the desired product.

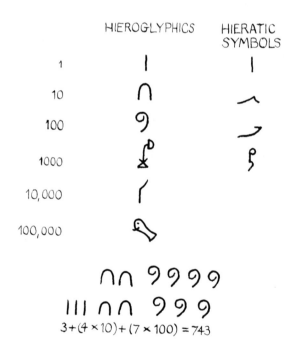

$3 + (4 \times 10) + (7 \times 100) = 743$

Egyptian numerals. Hieroglyphic symbols appeared as early as 3400 B.C., chiefly in inscriptions on stone. The priests used hieratic symbols when writing on papyrus.   Zaslavsky - Fig. 2

The feats of Egyptian engineering are astounding to present-day architects. They were able to construct their pyramids and temples with most minute accuracy. The Egyptian value of π, the ratio of the circumference of a circle to its diameter, was 3.16, much closer to the correct value (3.14159...) than was the Babylonian and Biblical approximation of three. They worked out the correct formula for the volume of the frustum of a pyramid (a cut-off pyramid). An early example of rectangular coordinate geometry was discovered in the tombs of the Pharoahs in the form of astronomical texts showing how to consult the position of the stars to determine the time during the darkness of night. This "star clock" indicated the appropriate times for the nightly services in the temples.

Western culture owes a great debt to Egypt and Mesopotamia. The ancient Greeks have been regarded as the fathers of Western civilization. But many centuries before their time the Egyptian priests had developed a complete curriculum for the training of their members. This included philosophy, writing, astronomy, geometry, engineering, and architecture. Indeed, the upper-class Greeks completed their education by studying with Mesopotamian or Egyptian teachers. The Hellenic astronomers adopted the Egyptian civil calendar, the first of its kind in human history. The year consisted of twelve months of thirty days each plus five additional days. (The Egyptians also used the lunar calendar to set their religious observances. This is still done today in computing the dates of the Christian Easter and the Jewish Passover.) The extensive Egyptian libraries were available to visitors. No doubt a great deal of the learning of centuries was written down by the Greeks. Thus they have been credited with discoveries that they merely transmitted from Egypt and the East.

What has happened to the enormous accumulation of literature, science, and technical achievements? Much has been lost; on the other hand, archaeology is revealing to us how much has been assimilated and taken over by later societies. The Bible contains selections which we now realize were taken almost word for word from the Egyptian Mysteries of the Dead. Hellenic science arose on the foundations of several thousand years of accumulated knowledge, and its influence was to be dominant from India to Western Europe until the European Renaissance.

Thus far there has been very little effort to investigate the two-way influence between Egypt and the lands to the south and west in Africa. Until recently students of Egyptian history and archaeology have refused to include Egypt and the Nile Valley as an integral part of the African continent. Indeed, the ancient Egyptians were classified as a "Hamitic" branch of the "white race," in spite of ample evidence that blacks played a prominent role in their society. Fortunately the racist "Hamitic" myth has been exploded . . .

Sixteenth century states of the Nigerian region. From Claudia Zaslavsky's Africa Counts.

Zaslavsky - Fig. 3

Editor's Note: Professor Zaslavsky goes on to deal with several mathematical systems used by African peoples below the Sahara and shows the way in which social organization has influenced the development of mathematical knowledge. The Yoruba and their system of numbers is but one of the many peoples and systems she examines but we have chosen to highlight her chapter on the Yoruba since they have engaged in intensive trading for more than a thousand years before the coming of the Europeans.

The Yoruba and the Kingdom of Benin

We are just beginning to discover the history of southern Nigeria, the most densely populated region of the whole continent of Africa. Since the peoples of this area apparently left no written records, the key to their history must lie in archaeological excavations, works of art, oral traditions, language analysis, and reports of foreign visitors.

The recently developed technique of radiocarbon dating has brought infinitely greater accuracy to the field of archaeological research. By early 1967 thirty-one dates were known for all of Nigeria. It is estimated that five thousand dates are needed for the period 500 B.C.—A.D. 1500 to enable archaeologists to make an adequate reconstruction of the history of the country.

In the Nok area of northern Nigeria have been found stone implements whose age is estimated at more than 39,000 years. The iron-based Nok culture is believed to have existed in approximately 400 B.C.—A.D. 200; the terracotta art figures of this period are thought to have directly influenced the later art of the Yoruba people and of the adjoining city-state of Benin.

Concentrated efforts are being made to gather the oral traditions, but the difficulties are great. On the site of the former Oyo Empire of the Yoruba one now finds ruined settlements, some deserted during the Nupe invasion of the fifteenth and sixteenth centuries, some sacked by the Alafins (kings of Oyo) in the seventeenth and eighteenth centuries and many emptied by the nineteenth-century invasion of the Islamic Fulani from the north, as well as the Dahomean slave raids from the west. Lions occasionally greet the present visitors to these sites.

Essential to every African royal household was the professional historian, whose duty it was to memorize and recite the dynastic lists of the kingdom. His function was similar to that of the rhapsodists of the Homeric age. No doubt the facts were colored somewhat to please the current rulers; nevertheless, these lists constitute a fairly reliable record.

Toward the end of the nineteenth century the Rev. Samuel Johnson (Anla Ogun), a Yoruba Anglican minister, undertook to write down these oral traditions, so that the history of his fatherland might not be lost. Although educated Yoruba, schooled in the Western tradition, were familiar with the history of Greece and Rome, the were taught nothing during colonization about their own land. Johnson spent over twenty years collecting his material and recorded it in *The History of the Yorubas*, which comprises the myths, history, and customs of his people.

Many traditions indicate that the Yoruba people came originally from the east. There are many similarities to the ancient Egyptian culture in religious observances, works of art, burial customs, and the institution of divine kingship; however, these cultural traits are shared by other African peoples. The ancient town of Ife, called Ile-Ife, was the spiritual center and cradle of the Yoruba people, and it was from Ife that the people of the neighboring state of Benin got their long line of kings. At this site have been found remarkable bronze, stone, iron, and terracotta works of art, dating back almost a thousand years.

One version of the creation legend begins with the Flood. Olorun, the supreme god, let his son Oduduwa down on a chain, carrying a handful of earth, a cockerel, and a palm nut. Oduduwa scattered the earth over the water, and the cockerel scratched it so that it became the land on which the palm tree grew, spreading its sixteen branches. The sacred number sixteen is believed to represent the sixteen crowned heads of Yorubaland.

According to another version of the creation myth, the Oba of Benin and the heads of the six Yoruba kingdoms were all descended from a common ancestor, Oduduwa. Oranyan, the youngest king, is supposed to have been the founder of the Oyo state.

By the year A.D. 1300, the Yoruba people had built numerous walled cities surrounded by farms. Trade was carried on with the peoples of the north; they exchanged cloth and kola nuts for products they needed. In turn the Yoruba states were exposed to the intellectual stimulation of the northern neighbors and the University in Timbuktu.

During the following centuries, the state of Oyo expanded until its dominion extended over a vast area, including even Dahomey to the west. Meanwhile the kingdom of Benin, to the southeast, had become independent of the Yoruba, and had grown into a mighty empire. When the Portuguese, the first Europeans to visit this part of Africa, entered Benin City in the late fifteenth century, they were truly astounded by the level of culture they encountered. Later European travelers described the thirty main streets of the metropolis, all straight and wide, laid out at right angles to one another, the longest extending four miles. "The people are as clean as the Dutch. Their houses shine like a looking glass," reported a Dutch visitor. The Oba's palace alone was reputed to be as large as a Dutch town. Brass-casting by the lost-wax method had been introduced from Ife, making possible the marvelous plaques on the walls of the palace, a history of Benin in art form.

With the Europeans came missionaries, gin, firearms, and the intensification of the slave trade. Slave raiding and wars with neighboring peoples alternated with periods of stability and peaceful trade—until the dissolution of the empires and the conquest by the British at the end of the nineteenth century. In 1897 a British delegation insisted upon seeing the Oba of Benin at a time when his religion forbade him to meet with strangers. Several of the British were killed in this incident. In retaliation the British sent a punitive expedition to burn the entire city. They removed 2500 beautiful Benin bronzes; these are now on exhibit in the museums of Europe and the United States.

The Yoruba city of Ibadan is the largest black city in Africa, a metropolis of more than 1,400,000 people, and the seat of the famous University of Ibadan. Although axes dating back to the Stone Age have been found in the area, Ibadan was only a small village built around a central market prior to the nineteenth century. During the time of the internal wars, it became a settlement for the army, a town free of the fear of invasion, a refuge from strife. Today three-quarters of the inhabitants are farmers who live in the city and work on the farms which surround it in a ring twenty miles wide. Actually, it is a city-village; farmers, craftsmen and traders live in large compounds in the town center.

Although Benin and the Yoruba states now form part of the republic of Nigeria, their language and culture remain very much alive. The Oba of Benin still reigns today. Modern Yoruba artists have adapted traditional Yoruba art forms to new subjects, producing works of great vigor and originality. As separate states within the Federal Republic, these enduring civilizations continue to flourish.

The Yoruba System of Numbers

"One of the most peculiar number scales in existence," wrote Conant of the Yoruba system of numeration. Indeed, one must be a mathematician to learn this complex system.

The Yoruba expresses forty-five, for example, as "five from ten from three twenties." In symbolic notation:

$$45 = (20 \times 3) - 10 - 5$$
$$106 = (20 \times 6) - 10 - 4$$
$$300 = 20 \times (20 - 5)$$
$$525 = (200 \times 3) - (20 \times 4) + 5$$

Quite a feat of arithmetic, involving addition, subtraction, and multiplication to express one number.

It is a vigesimal system, one based on twenty, of which we find many examples in western Africa. The unusual feature of the Yoruba system is that it relies upon subtraction to a very high degree. But to the Yoruba it seems perfectly natural, and he uses it with the ease with which we write IX (ten minus one) for nine in Roman numerals, or read the time as "twenty (minutes) to three."

A summary of the system is given by the Rev. Samuel Johnson in the introduction to his book, *The History of the Yorubas* (Preface, pages liv-lv).

> From one to ten, different terms are used, then for 20, 30, 200 and 400; the rest are multiples and compounds. Thus 11, 12, 13 and 14 are reckoned as ten plus one, plus two, plus three, and plus four; 15 to 20 are reckoned as 20 less five, less four, less three, less two, less one, and then 20.
>
> In the same way we continue 20 and one, to 20 and four, and then 30 less five (25), less four, and so on to 30, and so for all figures reckoned by tens.
>
> There is no doubt that the digits form the basis of enumeration to a large extent, if not entirely so. Five, ten, twenty, i.e., the digits of one hand, of two, and

the toes included, and their multiples form the different stages of enumeration.

Beginning from the first multiple of 20 we have *Ogoji*, a contraction of *ogun meji*, i.e., two twenties (40), *Ogota*, three twenties (60), *Ogorin*, four twenties (80), *Ogorun*, five twenties (100), and so on to ten twenties (200), when the new word *Igba* is used.

The intermediate numbers (30 having a distinct terminology), 50, 70, 90, 110, 130 to 190 are reckoned as: 60 less ten (50), 80 less ten (70), a hundred less ten (90), and so on up to 200.

The figures from 200 to 2000 are reckoned as multiples of 200 (400, however, which is 20×20, the square of all the digits, has a distinct terminology, *Irinwo* or *Erinwo*, i.e., the elephant of figures—meaning the highest coined word in calculation, the rest being multiples)....

By a system of contraction, elision, and euphonic assimilation, for which the Yoruba language is characteristic, the long term *Orundin-ni (Egbeta* or *Egberin* and so on) is contracted to *Ede* or*Ode*, e.g. *Edegbeta* (500)...and so on....

Summary. Thus we see that with numbers that go by tens, five is used as the intermediate figure—five less than the next higher stage. In those by 20, ten is used as the intermediate. In those by 200, 100 is used, and in those of 2000, 1000 is used.

Cardinal	Counting	Adjectival	Ordinal
1. okan	ookan = eni	kan	ekin:ni = ikin:ni = akoko
2. eji	eeji	meji	ekeji = ikeji
3. eta	eeta	meta	eketa = iketa
4. erin	eerin	merin	ekerin = ikerin
5. arun	aarun	marun	ekarun = ikarun
6. efa	eefa	mefa	ekefa = ikefa
7. eje	eeje	meje	ekeje = ikeje
8. ejo	eejo	mejo	ekejo = ikejo
9. esan	eesan	mesan	ekesan = ikesan
10. ewa	eewaa	mewaa	ekewaa = ikewaa

Table 1 - Yoruba Numerals from One to Ten.

The figure that is made use of for calculating indefinite numbers is 20,000 (*Egbawa*), and in money calculation especially it is termed *Oke kan*, i.e., one bag (of cowries). Large numbers to an indefinite amount are so many "bags" or rather "bags" in so many places.

I have relied heavily for the analysis of Yoruba numerals upon Robert G. Armstrong's study, *Yoruba Numerals*. Armstrong states: "It is testimony to the Yoruba capacity for abstract reasoning that they could have developed and learned such a system."

Table 1 shows the words for the first ten numbers in the four principal applications. The double vowel with which each of the counting numbers begins is actually a contracted form of the word *owo*, meaning "cowrie" or "money." The original system, whose age is unknown, was expanded for the purpose of counting cowries.

The names of the numbers for the counting series, as well as their derivations, are given in Table 2. After 200 the system becomes quite irregular, and these irregularities are maintained on the higher levels.

The construction of the numerals from 35 through 54 is represented in Table 3. Of the twenty numerals, only five do not involve subtraction at all, and five numerals involve subtraction in two columns!

The idea of infinity is expressed in the Yoruba proverb: "There is nothing as numerous as the locusts; they are found at home and in the farm." Although some farms were as much as twenty miles from the towns in which the farmers lived, the locusts covered every bit of foliage on the route.

Dr. Akinpelu, of the University of Ife, gave me the following constructions for unit fractions, for doubling, and for powers of a base:

ebu = fraction
Idaji = one-half (divide into two)
Idameta = one-third (divide into three)
Idamerin = one-fourth
Idamarun = one-fifth
etc.

Ilopomeji = two times, or doubling
Erin lona meji = 4^2 (4 in 2 places)
Erin lona meta = 4^3
Erin lona merin = 4^4
etc.

Table 2 - Yoruba Counting Series

1	ookan	11	ookan laa (*laa* from *le ewa* = in addition to ten)	18	eeji din logun (20 — 2)
2	eeji				
3	eeta	12	eeji laa	19	ookan din logun (20 — 1)
4	eerin	13	eeta laa		
5	aarun	14	eerin laa	20	ogun
6	eefa	15	eedogun (from *arun din ogun* = five reduces twenty)	21	ookan le logun ("one on twenty" = 20 + 1)
7	eeje				
8	eejo	16	eerin din logun (20 — 4)	25	eedoogbon (30 — 5)
9	eesan	17	eeta din logun (20 — 3)		
10	eewaa			30	ogbon

35 aarun din logoji
    [five less than two
    twenties = (20 × 2) - 5]

40 ogoji
    ("twenty twos")

50 aadota
    [(20 × 3) - 10]

60 ogota
    (3 × 20, or more literally,
    "twenty in three ways")

100 ogorun = orun
    (20 × 5)

105 aarun din laadofa
    [(20 × 6) - 10 - 5]

200 igba

300 oodunrun = oodun
     [20 × (20 - 5)]

315 orin din nirinwo odin
     marun
     [400 - (20 × 4) - 5]

400 irinwo

2000 egbewa (200 × 10)

4000 egbaaji (2 × 2000)

20,000 egbaawaa (2000 × 10)

40,000 egbaawaa lonan meji
       (ten 2000s in two ways)

1,000,000 egbeegberun
          (idiomatically
          1000 × 1000)

Table 3 - Analysis of Yoruba Numerals 35—54.

	twenty	ten	unit
35	2	0	-5
36	2	0	-4
37	2	0	-3
38	2	0	-2
39	2	0	-1
40	2	0	0
41	2	0	1
42	2	0	2
43	2	0	3
44	2	0	4
45	3	-1	-5

46	3	-1	-4
47	3	-1	-3
48	3	-1	-2
49	3	-1	-1
50	3	-1	0
51	3	-1	1
52	3	-1	2
53	3	-1	3
54	3	-1	4

Origin of the Subtractive System

Early investigators concluded that the evolution of this complex system for large numbers could be attributed to cowrie counting, the earliest occasion that required the Yoruba to count in such large denominations. In 1887 Mann described to a meeting of British anthropologists the procedure for cowrie-counting among the Yoruba. First the bag of 20,000 shells is emptied on the floor. The cowrie-counter kneels or sits beside the heap and rapidly draws four groups of five to make a small pile of twenty. Five twenties are combined into a pile of one hundred, and then two hundreds are swept together to form the important unit of two hundred. He attributes the subtractive principle in the numeration system to the practice of counting cowries by fives. Marianne Schmidl writes (page 94): "It is particularly evident in the case of the Yoruba that reckoning with cowrie shells was basic in the construction of the number system. With the single exception of the first decade, all numbers from five on are formed by subtraction from the next multiple of ten, which demonstrates that they were counted in fives and collected in stacks of ten and twenty units."

Although this method of cowrie-counting was widely used, few peoples besides the Yoruba and their immediate neighbors formalized the procedure in this unique subtractive system of reckoning.

Armstrong ventures the opinion that the pattern originated so that one could count the ten numbers with the fingers of one hand. If the multiples of ten are understood, and not shown by finger gestures, then one finger at a time can be extended to denote 21, 22, 23, and 24, respectively. When the fifth finger is extended, it is subtracted from 30; and when it is retracted, the remaining four fingers are deducted from 30 to give 26, etc.

Yoruba Record-Keeping and Computation

Thus far I have not been able to determine what computational methods were used in past centuries by Yoruba merchants in commercial transactions involving many thousands of cowrie shells. Nor have I yet found whether they kept written records of debts, or whether trade was strictly on a cash basis.

Dr. Ajayi, of the University of Ibadan, writes that computations are usually performed mentally. Records of numerical transactions are "sometimes marks on walls, beans or sticks in a jar, etc. to represent large units of what is being counted; e.g., a hundred or a thousand cowries or heads of cattle, etc. owed, or years of a monarch's reign. In some kingdoms, censuses of the number of families in each village or district are kept in the same manner."

Yoruba Children Learn Their Numbers

Chief Ayorinde, the authority on Yoruba folklore, commented upon the teaching of numerical concepts:

> The knowledge of numerals among the Yoruba People is as old as life itself. It is usually taught or imparted in different forms from childhood or as soon as a child can recognize an object. Pebbles, beans or stones are sometimes used in the teaching of numbers through demonstration. This teaching is also continued through traditional games as in Ayo, otherwise known as the "Warri Game," and it often sharpens one's mental capacity for calculations.
>
> Children also learn the art of buying and selling while in company of their mothers to the market. Apart from helping with the supervised sales of the parent's articles, the children are sometimes given a few wares of their own so as to give them confidence and as a test of their understanding of money values. The teaching of mathematics could also be formal and informal, indoors and outdoors, and takes many forms.

Today in this country, commercially produced materials are designed by educators to give the American child concrete experience with numbers—the kinds of experiences that are a normal aspect of Yoruba upbringing.

Updating the Yoruba Numeration System

During the colonial period, the languages of the dominating European powers were used in African schools, except possibly in the primary grades. Since they gained independence, however, the African peoples have been eager to revive interest in their own languages and culture; hence there is a new desire to expand the native vocabulary to include concepts hitherto unexpressed. Although English is still used today in Nigerian institutions of higher learning as a common means of communication for students of varied linguistic backgrounds, the Yoruba language is being expanded to accommodate new ideas.

Dr. Armstrong, the Director of the Institute of African Studies at the University of Ibadan, has developed a decimal number system which used Yoruba words throughout and eliminates all the irregularities of the traditional system. Thus modern arithmetic would become readily accessible to average people and to youngsters in the elementary grades, without requiring that they learn a language other than their own. Dr. Armstrong's reforms include terms for all the arithmetic operations, as well as fractions, decimal fractions, and percents. Dr. Armstrong has confidence that these reforms will encourage people to take a great interest in mathematics, as they realize they are citizens of an increasingly mathematical world. He concludes: "...a nation that could develop and transmit the complexities of their [numeration] system has obviously a great deal of mathematical talent and interest."

The Numeration System of Benin

The construction of the number words in the Edo language, spoken by the people of Benin, is similar to that of Yoruba, with the exception that in Edo the words for numbers having five in the units place are formed by addition, rather than subtraction. Take, for example, the words for 45 and 46.

$$45 = (60 - 10) - 5 \quad \text{in Yoruba}$$
$$45 = 40 + 5 \quad \text{in Edo}$$
$$46 = (60 - 10) - 4 \quad \text{in both Yoruba and Edo}$$

In Edo the first five numbers following a multiple of ten are formed by addition to that multiple of ten, while the next four are based on subtraction from the next higher multiple of ten.

In his paper, "How the Binis Count and Measure," Peter Idehen gives this interesting interpretation of the word for fifteen: "*Ekesugie* means either 'mid-way between *Igbe* (10) and *Ugie* (20)' or 'five out of twenty.'" For twenty-five he gives two forms:

25   *Isen-yan Obgen* (5 and 20) or *Ekesogban* (midway between 20 and 30)

I have at hand four sources for the Edo number words, all differing from one another. Since the most recent is that of David A. Munro (1967), I am using this book as the basis for the numeration table, with some modifications suggested by Mr. Idehen's paper (Table 4).

On the subject of counting beyond one hundred, Idehen writes that in the past most people either had no occasion to use such large numbers, or else they resorted to English. He urges that people learn to count in Bini up to the millions, so that they can translate into their own familiar language, for instance, a radio broadcast stating that the government plans to spend two million pounds on a project.

For the higher numbers he gives:

1000	*aria isen*	(5 × 200)
2000	*aria isen eva*	(2 × 1000)
10,000	*aria isen igbe*	(10 × 1000)
1,000,000	*aria isen aria isen*	(1000 × 1000)
1,000,000,000	*aria isen aria isen aria isen*	(1000 × 1000 × 1000)

Table 4 - Edo Number Words

1	owo or okpa	16	ener-ovb-ugie (4 out of 20)
2	eva	17	eha iro vb-ugie (3 out of 20)
3	eha	18	eva iro vb-ugie (2 out of 20)
4	ene	19	okpa iro vb-ugie (1 out of 20)
5	ise	20	ugie
6	eha	30	ogba
7	ihiro	40	iy-eva (20 × 2)
8	erere	50	(e)k-igbe s-iy-eha [(20 × 3) - 10]
9	ihiri	60	iy-eha
10	igbe	70	(e)k-igbe s-iy-ena [(20 × 4) - 10]
11	oworo	100	iy-ise (20 × 5)
12	iweva (10 + 2)	190	igbe iro vb-uri (10 out of 200)
13	iwera	200	uri *or* aria okpa
14	iwene	300	uri okpa vb-iy-ise *or* iyisen yan uri
15	ekesugie		(100 + 200)
		400	uri eva *or* aria eva (200 in 2 places)

BLACK CONTRIBUTIONS TO THE EARLY
HISTORY OF WESTERN MEDICINE

Frederick Newsome

Summary: During several millenia, blacks in ancient Egypt made numerous contributions to medicine and were acknowledged as the inventors of the art of medicine. They produced the earliest physicians, medical knowledge, and medical literature. They contributed to the development of medicine in ancient Greece. Ancient writers, including Herodotus, Isocrates, and Diodorus, affirm this. Modern presentations of ancient medicine, however, deprive blacks of the knowledge of their early contributions to medicine by ignoring or subtly misrepresenting the black identity of the ancient Egyptians. Blacks are currently underrepresented in US medical schools. It is proposed that the recognition of the contributions of blacks to the early history of Western medicine would inspire black students to study medicine.

(This article is reprinted from the *Journal of the National Medical Association*, Vol. 71, No. 2, 1979, p. 189-193 with their kind permission)

Concern has been expressed about the need to increase black representation in the medical profession.[1-3]

It is evident that the correction of this black under-representation will require affirmative action programs developed for high school students as opposed to college and medical school students.[2] For a reason to be considered here, many young American blacks lack confidence in their mathematical and scientific ability and display disinterest in scientific, premedical subjects.[4] It is probable that the interest in medicine among young blacks would increase if the contributions of blacks to the history of medicine were more widely known and included in general education. Knowledge of the successes of other blacks in medicine would serve as an inspiration to young blacks to qualify themselves to enter the profession. However, if the young black student in search of such inspiration were to review existing books and periodicals on the history of medicine, he or she would gain the impression that blacks have had little success in medicine and had contributed nothing to its long and exciting history. This impression, which most of the literature of the history of medicine creates, is historically false. Blacks entered, or more accurately, began the drama of Western medicine where one would suspect—in Africa.

The early African people known today as the ancient Egyptians lived along the Nile and called their nation Kmt. In ancient Egyptian script, called hieroglyphs, the word Kmt means black village, black city, or, in modern parlance, black community.[5] It is written with four signs: the sign for black which has the phonetic value of "k" (a crocodile skin), the sign for "m" the sign for "t," and the sign for city, village or community (two intersecting roads). Thus, this discussion will consider three major contributions made to the early history of Western medicine by the ancient people of Kmt or, literally, of the black community. (1) They produced the world's first physicians who for millenia enjoyed the reputation of being the most skilled in the world. (2) They produced the world's first medical knowledge and literature. (3) They influenced and contributed to Hippocrates, the Hippocratic tradition, and the development of medicine in ancient Greece. It is proposed that knowledge of these African accomplishments by the young people of African origin in the United States would increase their interest in medicine as well as their confidence in their ability to study medicine.

The first king of Egypt was Menes (3200 BC). According to Manetho (300 BC), Menes had a son, Athothis, who also became king, ruled for 27 years, practiced medicine, and wrote books on anatomy.[6] Unfortunately, these books have never been found. It is uncertain who was the first physician in history. However, if Manetho is to be believed, one of the earliest physicians, if not the first, known to history by name was the versatile author, anatomist, and African king, Athothis.

Even if the anatomy books allegedly written by Athothis are never found, a little knowledge of hieroglyphs is convincing evidence that the Egyptians at a very early date knew considerable gross human and animal anatomy. Many of the signs which represent consonants, vowels, things, and concepts are well-reproduced animals and parts of anatomy. Graphical reproduction of anatomical parts requires knowledge of anatomy. This is also true of sculpture and embalming which, as is well known, they also practiced. Anatomical parts for which there were signs include: the pupil of the eye, the cornea, the heart, the trachea, the lungs, the vertebral column, the long bones, the brain, the meninges, the spinal cord, the ribs, the intestines, the spleen, the male and female genitals, the uterus, and, possibly, the kidney.[5]

Notwithstanding Athothis, mentioned by Manetho, the African multigenius Imhotep is usually regarded as the first physician in history. He lived about 2980 BC during the reign of Pharoah Zoser of the Third Dynasty. As a member of the pharoah's court he was an architect, scribe, priest, and administrator as well as a physician. He designed the step pyramid at Saqqara. Over the centuries, Egyptians in need of healing flocked to shrines and temples erected in his honor. By 525 BC, he had become a full deity. In hieroglyphs his name means "to come in peace." An inscription to the deified, healing Imhotep reads: "Turn thy face towards me, my lord Imhotep, son of Ptah. It is thou who dost work miracles and who are beneficent in all thy deeds."[7]

Medical historians generally recognize the importance of Imhotep but do not comment on his race. According to Osler, he was "the first figure of a physician to stand out clearly from the mists of antiquity."[8] Sigerist introduces Imhotep as the architect of the step pyramid of Saqqara: "It is the oldest monument of hewn stone known to the world, and it was built by a man of genius, Imhotep, the first universal scholar, architect, engineer, statesman, sage, and physician."[9] Ackerknect also acknowledges the priority and importance of Imhotep but, like Sigerist, makes no mention of his race.[10]

The early Greeks knew Imhotep as Imouthes. They identified him with their later god of healing, Aesclepios. In early Christian Rome, Imhotep was identified with Jesus. Jesus replaced Imhotep, who was always represented as black. Massey writes concerning this representation:

Jesus, the divine healer, does not retain the black complexion of Iu-em-hetep in the canonical Gospels, but he does in the Church of Rome when represented by the little black bambino. A jewelled image of the child-Christ as a blackamoor is sacredly preserved at the headquarters of the Franciscan order . . . to visit the sick, and demonstrate the supposed healing power of the Egyptian Aesculapius thus Christianized.[11]

The few modern blacks who know about Imhotep still gain inspiration from him. He is the first personality discussed in Rogers' *World's Great Men of Color*.[7] In the middle 1950s black American physicians organized to combat racial discrimination in American hospitals and health care. They held a series of national conferences which they called the Imhotep Conferences.[12] By naming the conferences after Imhotep, the participants gave honor to his memory but also added cogency to their agitation. They correctly perceived the illogic of discrimination against physcans and patients because of their African origin when the Father of Medicine was of African origin.

In his biography of Imhotep, Hurry claims that Aesclepios, the Greek God of Medicine and present symbol of medicine in the western world, has usurped this position from Imhotep.[13] The claim can as well be made that Hippocrates (400 BC) has usurped the position of Father

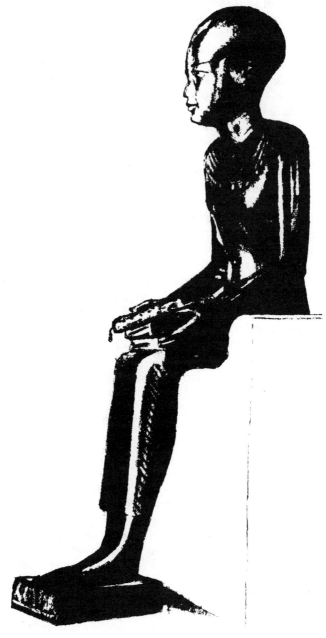

IMHOTEP

Egyptian "Father" of Medicine.   Newsome — Fig. 1

of Medicine from the African, Imhotep. More will be said about the relationship of Hippocrates to the blacks of Egypt.

Because the title of physician is not associated with Imhotep's name until "very late texts," Ghalioungui doubts that Imhotep was a physician.[14] He gives the distinction of having been the first physician in history to Hesy-Re (2600 BC). Hesy-Re was a scholar, a scribe, and Chief of Dentists and Physicians to the pyramid builders of the Third Dynasty.[15] Majno reproduces a panel showing Hesy-Re seated with the scribe's palette, ink container, and reed pen suspended on his shoulder.[16] Not keeping with the common Egyptian practice of wearing a head cloth or shaving the head bald for cleanliness, Hesy-Re reveals his woolly "Afro" hair. Considering the importance of writing to medicine today, it is not surprising, as the evidence supports, that the art of medicine developed first in Africa where the art of writing also developed at a very early date, if not the earliest. A conservative estimate of the date of appearance of east African hieroglyphs is 3500 BC. The material on which writing was performed was the processed African papyrus plant. The word paper derives from papyrus. Majno remarks that "papyrus probably influenced the history of medicine more than any ancient drug"[16]

Ghalioungui also gives us the name of probably the first woman physician, Preshet, a "chief" physician. For a documented, complete review of ancient Egyptian medicine, Ghalioungui is invaluable. However, he unfortunately maintains the modern tradition of never commenting on the race of the ancient Egyptians and of implying that they were not black. To say "modern tradition" is correct since this was not the practice of ancient writers on the Egyptians. More will be said about one of these important ancient writers later. In his book, Ghalioungui makes one reference to "Negroes" in a comment about hemoglobin S and resistance to malaria.[14] Since he makes a distinction between "Negroes" and the subject of his book, ie, the ancient Egyptians, the obvious implication is that the Egyptians were not "Negroes," i.e., not black. Sigerist implies the same by making a similar, incidental distinction between "Negroes" and the ancient Egyptians in a discussion of circumcision.[9]

It has been shown that blacks have contributed to the history of medicine by giving to the world its first physicians. Another contribution was that of producing the world's first medical knowledge and literature. When considering the invention of medicine in his essay "On Ancient Medicine," Hippocrates, although he does not say so, is referring to Egyptian medicine. He argues that the first medical knowledge was dietetics.[17] Dietetics was an early, major part of Egyptian medicine. The Greeks knew this also. Herodotus (450 BC) writes that "they (the Egyptians) have a persuasion that every disease to which

men are liable is occasioned by the substances whereon they feed."[18]
For Hippocrates, ancient medicine was Egyptian medicine. Hippocrates notes that dietetics may not qualify as distinctive medical
knowledge since all people who survive must discover it if they do not
already know it. However, because Hippocrates knew of the priority of
Egyptian medicine and its emphasis on dietetics, it is not surprising that
he called dietetics the first medical knowledge. Galen (200 AD), who
devotedly continued Hippocratic teachings, is simply expressing the
belief of his Master when he writes "the invention of medicine was the
experiences of the Egyptians."[19]

Ancient Egyptian medicine included more than dietetics. This we
know from the surviving, translated medical papyri. These documents
represent the oldest medical knowledge and literature. Two of the
most important among the several medical papyri include the Ebers
papyrus[20] (1500 BC) and the Edwin Smith papyrus[21] (original 2600
BC). The latter is kept at the New York Academy of Medicine. The
medical papyri include a considerable share of magic and religion but
also contain anatomy, herbal pharmacology, pathology, physical diagnosis, and what today would be called scientific medicine. The Ebers
papyrus contains chapters on intestinal disease, helminthiasis, ophthal-
mology, dermatology, gynecology, obstetrics, pregnancy diagnosis,
contraception, dentistry, and the surgical treatment of abscesses,
tumors, fractures, and burns. It also contains a section on the movement of the heart, the pulse, and diagnostic percussion. Ghalioungui
makes the following assessment of the Edwin Smith papyrus:

In fact, the Edwin Smith papyrus proved the existence of an objective and scientific
medicine, devoid of theories and magic, except in one case, and based on the attentive
and repeated observation of the patient, on bedside experience, and on a hitherto
unsuspected knowledge of anatomy.[14]

J. H. Breasted, the translator of the Edwin Smith papyrus, attributes
its authorship to Imhotep. Majno appraises the medical knowledge of
the Egyptians as revealed in the papyri:

(they) produced some excellent anatomoclinical correlations; probably the first tapes
and sutures; the beginnings of hemostasis by cautery; the beginnings of antisepsis with
copper salts . . .[16]

Before the translation of the medical papyri, Herodotus informed us
of the practice of scientific, although nonexperimental, observation in
Egypt:

The Egyptians have also discovered more prognostics than all the rest of mankind
besides. Whenever a prodigy takes place, they watch and record the result; then, if
anything similar ever happens again, they expect the same consequences.[18]

Column XI of the Smith papyrus, written about 1650 B.C. A red asterik (arrow) shows where the scribe had left out the words. "Thou shouldst say concerning him." He added neatly at the top of the page.   Newsome — Fig. 2

He also comments on the medical specialization apparent from the papyri:

Medicine is practised among them on a plan of separation; each physician treats a single disorder, and no more; thus the country swarms with medical practitioners, some undertaking to cure diseases of the eye, others of the head, others again of the teeth, others of the intestines, and some those which are not local.[18]

In addition to producing the earliest physicians, medical knowledge, and medical literature, there is a third important contribution of blacks to the ancient history of medicine. This contribution blacks made to Western medicine through their influence on Greek medicine. Wilson,[22] Saunder,[23] Luth,[19] Ghalioungui,[24] and others have noted the strong influence of Egyptian medicine on the development of Greek medicine. However, because they do not discuss the black identity of the ancient Egyptians, they miss the full significance and relevance of the ancient Egyptian-Greek relationship to the modern world.

Generally speaking, the Egyptian arts and sciences influenced the development of the Greek arts and sciences. Appreciation of the working of this relationship is necessary to understand the specific case of medicine. Also, in ancient times as today the development of medicine was linked to the concomitant development of the arts and, especially, the sciences. Herodotus writes that the following came into Greece from Egypt: "almost all the names of the gods,"[18] "solemn assemblies, processions, and litanies to the gods,"[18] astrology,[18] geometry,[18] the correct calendar, and astronomy.[18,25] Many of the well-known Greek philosophers and scientists went to Egypt to be educated and transported their acquired knowledge upon returning to Greece. These include Thales (600 BC), Solon (575 BC), Pythagorus (550 BC), Plato (375 BC), Eudoxus of Cnidus (360 BC) and others. This we are told by Isocrates[26] (400 BC), Diodorus Siculus[27] (50 BC), Strabo[25] (20 AD), Josephus[28] (75 AD), Plutarch[29] (100 AD), Diogenes[30] (200 AD), and Iamblichus[31] (300 AD). James,[32] ben-Jochannan,[33] and Christian[34] give complete, modern treatments of the Egyptian influence on the Greek philosophers. With the exception of Eudoxus, who was a physician, as well as a mathematician and astronomer, these sources are more informative about the travels and education of Greek philosophers than physicians. One of these philosophers, Pythagorus, played a major role in early Greek medicine which will be discussed here. It is reasonable to assume that many Greek physicians as well as philosophers studied in Egypt. Galen, who himself studied in Egypt, supports this assumption.[14]

Despite the absence of sources to affirm that Hippocrates studied in Egypt, there is ample evidence that Egypt directly and indirectly influenced him. Luth and Sudhoff support that the medical school at Cos with which he was affiliated was a branch of the Egyptian medical schools.[19] There are portions of the Hippocratic writings which are textual reproductions of Egyptian medical papyri. These include methods for the reduction of fractures of the clavicle and dislocation of the mandible.[14]

According to Hippocratic teaching, disease resulted from the imbalance of the four bodily humors: black bile, yellow bile, phlegm, and blood. Health was thought to be the balance or harmony of the bodily humors. The four humors represented physiologic opposites and were depicted on the Diagram of Opposites in symmetrical relation to the fundamental opposites of nature, ie hot (or fire), cold (or earth), moist, and dry.[16] According to Diodorus, the concept of the fundamental opposites of nature is Egyptian.[27] The origin of the concept of the four bodily humors is usually attributed to Hippocrates, but is Mesopotamian according to Sudhoff.[35] The belief in their possession of opposite qualities and the mechanism by which their imbalance produced disease is based on the ancient Theory of Opposites and Harmony. This theory, commonly attributed to Pythagorus, is Egyptian.[32-33]

Pythagorus was a major link through which blacks influenced Hippocrates and Greek medicine. The Egyptian Theory of Opposites and Harmony was adopted by Hippocrates from Pythagoreanism. This influence was indirect and secondhand but certainly real and deserving of recognition. Pythagorus was a disciple of the Egyptian priests and a disseminator of their teachings and culture among the Greeks.

Edelstein tells us that the principal concepts in the Hippocratic Oath are Pythagorean in origin. Edelstein writes: "Pythagoreanism then remains the only philosophical dogma that can account for the attitude advocated in the Hippocratic Oath."[36] Galimard[37] also traces elements of the Hippocratic tradition to Pythagorus. In addition to its selfless, noble spirit, the following are some of the features shared by the Hippocratic Oath and Pythagoreanism on which Edelstein bases his statement: (1) the division of medicine into dietetics, drugs (pharmacology), and cutting (surgery); (2) the belief in the superiority of dietetics and drugs to cutting; (3) the belief in the maintenance of secrecy among physicians about the Art.

Although Edelstein traces Hippocratic doctrine to Pythagorus, he does not trace the teachings of Pythagorus to the Egyptians. Yet, Pythagorus was a teacher of Egyptian knowledge and culture. Isocrates attributes the discovery of the art of medicine and philosophy to the Egyptian priests. Isocrates informs us that Pythagorus introduced philosophy into Greece after study among these priests. The instruction of Pythagorus included medicine, since, as will be shown, he sought to learn all that the priests knew to teach him. Also, among the ancients, philosophy and medicine overlapped. Isocrates is quoted in full because of his direct bearing on this discussion:

> And the priests, because they enjoyed such conditions of life, discovered for the body the aid which the medical art affords, not that which uses dangerous drugs, but drugs of such a nature that they are as harmless as daily food, yet in their effects are so beneficial that all men agree the Egyptians are the healthiest and most long of life among men; and then for the soul they introduced philosophy's training, a pursuit which has the power, not only to establish laws but also to investigate the nature of the universe.[26]

Shortly following the above, Isocrates mentions Pythagorus and his study in Egypt:

> On a visit to Egypt he (Pythagorus) became a student of the religion of the people, and was the first to bring to the Greeks all philosophy . . .[26]

'Some details are known about the life of Pythagorus. He went to Egypt seeking knowledge and wisdom on the advice of the then aging Thales, who admitted that the source of his own (Thales') wisdom was the Egyptians.[31] He brought gifts (three silver flasks) to the Egyptian priest.[30] He was a diligent student who was admired by his African teachers and, during the years of his visit, resided at several temples so as to learn from as many priests as possible.[29] Oenuphis of Heliopolis was one of his teachers.[29] During his several years in Africa (7 according to Diogenes and 22 according to Iamblichus), he learned the Egyptian language.[30,31] Although he may have taught some of his own ideas, this is not supported as he returned to Greece to teach "in a way perfectly similar to the documents by which he had been instructed in Egypt."[31] Most of the precepts which he taught he copied from Egyptian hieroglyphic texts.[29] After returning to Greece he went eventually to Croton, Italy where he established a Brotherhood which was an imitation of the Egyptian priesthood in dress,[18] practice, and philosophy.[27,29,32,34] His teachings included medicine and "dominated" instruction at the Greek medical school at Croton.[10,35]

The Egyptian influence on Pythagorus is apparent. It can therefore by asserted that the blacks in Egypt influenced and contributed to Greek medicine, Hippocrates, and the Hippocratic tradition through Pythagorus.

Three major contributions which ancient blacks made to the early history of Western medicine have been presented. Unfortunately, the writing of medical history is such that these contributions to medical history are never presented as the contributions of black people. The subject of the race of the ancient Egyptians is carefully avoided. One is correct in saying "carefully avoided." In this discussion, several modern medical historians have been cited. In the presentation of ancient medicine they all rely heavily in quotation and citation on Herodotus, the Father of History. They never, however, find occasion to include his comments about the physical appearance of the ancient Egyptians. This omission is particularly glaring in the invariable reference to the practice of circumcision in ancient Egypt, a fact of medical importance noted by Herodotus and associated with a comment about race. This writer will depart from the modern tradition and provide the quote here. Herodotus is referring to a colony of people called the Colchians who lived in western Asia near the Black Sea.

There can be no doubt that the Colchians are an Egyptian race . . . My own conjectures were founded, first, on the fact that they are black-skinned and have woolly hair, which certainly amounts to but little, since several other nations are so too; but further and more especially, on the circumstance that the Colchians, the Egyptians and the Ethiopians are the only nations who have practised circumcision from the earliest times.[18]

In another passage appearing shortly before his discussion of medical specialization in Egypt, Herodotus writes about the origin of the oracle at Dodona, Greece by a mythological talking black dove from Egypt:

Lastly, by calling the dove black the Dodoneans indicated that the woman was an Egyptian.[18]

Aristotle (350 BC), the Father of Science, makes the same observation as the Father of History, although with insult. Aristotle remarks that the Egyptians and Ethiopians were cowards because of their "excessively black color."[38] Complete treatments of the race of the ancient Egyptians and of the attempt of some modern scholars to conceal or misrepresent it are given by Diop,[39,40] Williams,[41] Jackson,[42] ben-Jochannan,[33,43] and the proceedings of the United Nations sponsored conference.[44]

In conclusion, one may ask what is the value of demonstrating black contributions to the history of medicine? The point has to be made that over the past few centuries through today the contributions of blacks to the history of medicine and to the history of civilization in general have been denied. This denial has been both spoken and unspoken. The influential Scottish philosopher David Hume very clearly expressed it, when in 1753 he wrote:

I am apt to suspect the Negroes . . . to be naturally inferior to the white. There never was a civilized nation of any other complexion than white, nor even any individual eminent either in action or speculation. No ingenious manufactures amongst them, no arts, no sciences.[45]

It is suggested that the persistence of such false beliefs through today underlies the reason many young black students "lack confidence in their scientific and mathematical ability and display disinterest in scientific, premedical subjects." Finally, knowledge of the contributions of blacks to the history of medicine may inspire young blacks to enter the profession and make further contributions.

Literature Cited

1. Norman JC: Medicine in the Ghetto. New York, Appleton-Century-Crofts, 1969

2. Sleeth BC, Mishell Rl: Black under-representation in United States medical schools. N Engl J Med 297:1146-1148, 1977

3. Relman AS: Minority admissions: Beyond Bakke, editorial. N Engl J Med 297:1175, 1977

4. Bayer AE: The black college freshman: Characteristics and recent trends. ACE Res Rep 7(3):1-98, 1972

5. Gardiner A: Egyptian Grammar. Oxford, Griffith Institute, 1976, pp 57, 449, 498

6. Manetho: Manetho Ptolemy Tetrabiblos, Waddell WG, Robbins FE (trans). In Loeb Classical Library. Cambridge, Mass, Harvard University Press, 1971, p 31

7. Rogers JA: World's Great Men of Color. New York, MacMillan, 1972, p 39

8. Osler Sir W: Evolution of Modern Medicine. New Haven, London and London, 1921, p 10

9. Sigerist HE: A History of Medicine. New York, Oxford University Press, 1951, Vol I, pp 228, 243

10. Ackerknect EH: A Short History of Medicine. New York, Ronald Press, 1955, pp 19, 45-47

11. Massey G: Ancient Egypt: The Light of the World. New York, Samuel Weiser, 1973, vol 2, p 754

12. Morais HM: History of the Afro-American in Medicine. Cornwell Heights, Pa, Publishers' Agency, 1970, p 143

13. Hurry JB: Imhotep. Chicago, Ares Publishers, 1978, p 88

14. Ghalioungui P: The House of Life: Magic and Medical Science in Ancient Egypt. Amsterdam, BM Isreal, 1973, pp 17, 38, 42, 66, 120

15. Quibell JE: Excavations at Saqqara (1911-12): The Tomb of Hesy. Cairo, Service des Antiquites de l'Egypte de l'Institut Francais, 1913

16. Majno G: The Healing Hand: Man and Wound in the Ancient World. Cambridge, Mass, Harvard University Press, 1977, pp 74, 140, 178, 179

17. Hippocrates, Adams F (trans). In Great Books of the Western World. Chicago, Encyclopedia Britannica, 1952, pp 1, 2

18. Herodotus: The Histories, Rawlinson G (trans). In Great Books of the Western World. Chicago, Encyclopedia Britannica, 1952, pp 49, 50, 60-65, 69, 70

19. Luth VP: Imhotep oder Asklepios: On the beginning of scientific medicine in Egypt and Greece. Hippocrate 34:826-827, 1963

20. Ebbell B: The Papyrus Ebers. Copenhagen, Levin and Munksgaard, 1937

21. Breasted JH: The Edwin Smith Surgical Papyrus. Chicago, University of Chicago Press, 1930

22. Wilson JA: Medicine in ancient Egypt. Bull Hist Med 36:114-123, 1962

23. Saunders JB: The Transition from Ancient Egyptian to Greek Medicine: Logan Clendening Lectures on the History and Philosophy of Medicine. Lawrence, University of Kansas Press, 1963

24. Ghalioungui P: The Relation of Pharoanic to Greek and Later Medicine. Bull Cleveland Med Lib 15:96-107, 1968

25. Strabo: The Geography, Jones HL (trans). In Loeb Classical Library. Cambridge, Mass, Harvard University Press, vol 8, 1967, pp 83, 85

26. Isocrates, Van Hook L (trans). In Loeb Classical Library. Cambridge, Mass, Harvard University Press, vol 3, 1946, pp 115, 119

27. Diodorus Siculus: Library of History, Oldfather CH (trans). In Loeb Classical Library. Cambridge, Mass, Harvard University Press, Vol I, 1968, pp 39, 41, 327, 335

28.   Josephus: The Life Against Apion, Thackerary H St J (trans). In Loeb Classical Library. Cambridge, Mass, Harvard University Press, Vol I, 1966, p 169

29.   Plutarch: Moralia, Babbitt FC (trans). In Loeb Classical Libary. Cambridge, Mass, Harvard University Press, Vol 5, 1962, pp 25, 27

30.   Diogenes Laertius, Hicks RD (trans). In Loeb Classical Library. Cambridge, Mass, Harvard University Press, vol 2, 1958, pp 321, 323

31.   Iamblichus: Life of Pythagorus, Taylor T (trans). London, 1818, pp 7, 9, 12, 13

32.   James GGM: Stolen Legacy. San Francisco, Julian Richards Associates, 1976, pp 68-72, 80, 139-142

33.   ben-Jochannan Y: Black Man of the Nile. New York, Alkebu-Ian Books, 1973, pp 313-339

34.   Christian P: History and Practice of Magic. Secaucus, NJ, Citadel Press, 1972, p 88

35.   Sudhoff K: Essays in the History of Medicine. New York, Medical Life Press, 1926, pp 67, 87, 104

36.   Edelstein L: Ancient Medicine. Baltimore, John Hopkins University Press, 1973, p 17

37.   Galimard P: Hippocrate et la Tradition Pythagoriciene. Thesis, Paris, 1940

38.   Aristotle: Minor Works, Hett WS (trans). In Loeb Classical Library. Cambridge, Mass, Harvard University Press, 1956, p 127

39.   Diop CA: The African Origin of Civilization: Myth or Reality: New York, Lawrence Hill, 1974

40.   Diop CA: The Cultural Unity of Black Africa. Chicago, Third World Press, 1978

41.   Williams C: The Destruction of Black Civilization: Great Issues of a Race from 4500 BC to 2000 AD. Chicago, Third World Press, 1974, pp 62-143

42.   Jackson JG: Introduction to African Civilizations. New York, University Books, 1970, pp 60-156

43.   ben-Jochannan Y: Africa: Mother of Western Civilization. New York, Alkebu-Lan Books, 1971

44.   The Peopling of Ancient Egypt and the Deciphering of the Meroitic Script. Symposium of the United Nations Educational, Scientific, and Cultural Organization, Cairo, Jan 28-Feb 3, 1974. Paris, UNESCO, Document SHC-73/CONF.812/4, 1974

45.   Hume D: Essays and Treastises on Several Subjects. London, 1753, vol. 1, p. 291

THE AFRICAN BACKGROUND OF
MEDICAL SCIENCE

Charles S. Finch

Summary: It has become increasingly clear that traditional African cultures
and civilizations knew and accomplished much more than has traditionally been
assumed. Even after we've "restored" ancient Egypt–a civilization that was the
fountainhead of science–to its true and natural place on African soil as an African creation, there is yet a profound reluctance to admit that Africa contributed
anything of substance to world science.

In this paper, the author hopes to show that traditional African physicians
evolved effective–even sophisticated–diagnostic and therapeutic modalities in
medicine which belie the notion that Africa was without a medical science.

Just as any discussion of the achievements of Western medicine harkens back
to Hippocrates and Galen, so any discussion of African medical achievements
harkens back to ancient Egypt. Newsome, among others, has shown what a debt
Greek medicine owed to the priest-physicians of Egypt.[1] Not only was the most
important Greek healing deity, Asclepios, identified with the legendary Egyptian
physician-architect-aphorist Imhotep but Hippocratic therapeutics had direct an-
tecedents in Egyptian medicine. The city-state of Athens used to import Egyptian
physicians, as did most of the kingdoms of the Near East, and in the *Odyssey*,
Homer says, "In medical knowledge, Egypt leaves the rest of the world behind."[2]

Like all African medicine, Egyptian medicine has baffled scholars because of
the complete interpenetration of "magico-spiritual" and "rational" elements.
Mostly, this magico-spiritual aspect has been downplayed or belittled. However,
at least one researcher concedes that healing, being a complicated psychic as well
as physical process, may be amenable to an approach that touches that hidden
area of the psyche beyond the reach of rational therapy.[3] Even modern medicine
concedes that as much as 60% of illness has a psychic base and indeed, the well-
known "placebo" effect of modern pharmaco-medicine arises from this.[4] We
moderns like to deride this magico-spiritual medicine but it can and does produce
startling results that we do not understand.

The Egyptians were writing medical textbooks as early as 5,000 years ago.[5]
This indicates not only a mature civilization but also a long period of medical development. Out of the hundreds and thousands of medical papyri that must have
been written, only 10 have come down to us, the most important being the Ebers
and Edwin Smith Papyri. These 10 papyri form the basis of most of what Egyptologists know about Egyptian medicine. It has been affirmed, however, that

much of the training and instruction of the healing priests must have been orally transmitted, as it is in the rest of Africa.[6] It is likely, therefore, that we have only a partial grasp of the true scope of Egyptian medical knowledge. Moreover, like their counterparts in the rest of Africa, the Egyptian priest-physicians often kept their best knowledge secret.

Egyptians physicians were instructed in the "per ankh" or "house of life" which served as a university, library, medical school, clinic, temple, and seminary. The numerous Greek philosophers who studied in Egypt, such as Pythagorous, Thales, and Plato, must have spent their time in a *per ankh*. In these centers of learning, there was no sharp demarcation between the fields of study; religion, philosophy, science, astronomy, mathematics, music, and hieroglyphics were all part of the same species of knowledge and were reflected in one another.

It is of interest that the Egyptians were alone among the nations of antiquity in the development of specialty medicine. In the Old Kingdom, the diseases of each organ were under the care of a specialist. In the later epochs, the specialists disappeared as the Egyptian physician began to function as a generalist. However, during Ptolemaic times, specialization came back into vogue, probably as a result of renewed interest in the archaic culture. Not until the 20th century did anything comparable in the sphere of medicine develop. Contemporary doctors are accustomed to believing that modern specialty medicine resulted from a progressive evolution of medical techniques and knowledge, hardly realizing that it is a throwback to the earliest form of Egyptian medical practice.

A study of ancient Egyptian diagnostic methods reads disconcertingly like a modern textbook on physical diagnosis. A physician summoned to examine a patient would begin with a careful appraisal of the patient's general appearance. This would be followed by a series of questions to elicit a description of the complaint. The color of the face and eyes, the quality of nasal secretions, the presence of perspiration, the stiffness of the limbs or abdomen, and the condition of the skin were all carefully noted. The physician was also at pains to take cognizance of the smell of the body, sweat, breath, and wounds. The urine and feces were inspected, the pulse palpated and measured, and the abdomen, swellings, and wounds probed and palpated. The pulse taking is worth noting because it indicates that the Egyptians knew of its circulatory and hemodynamic significance. Percussion of the abdomen and chest was performed and certain functional tests we still use today were done, i.e., the coughing test for hernia detection; the extension-flexion maneuver of the legs to test for a dislocated lumbar vertebra. Sometimes, the case required more than one consultation and the physician might, as is done today, embark on a "therapeutic trial" to ascertain the efficacy of treatment. It also seems that the Egyptians practiced a form of socialized medicine. All physicians were employees of the state and medical care was available to everyone.[7]

The extant medical papyri show us that the Egyptians had quite an extensive knowledge of anatomy and physiology. They understood the importance of pulsation and—4500 years before Harvey—knew someting of the structure and function of the cardiovascular system. They knew that the heart was the center of this system, had names for all the major vessels, knew the relation between heart and lung, and knew the distribution of the vessels through the limbs.[8] They had names for the brain and meninges (the covering of the brain and spinal cord) and also seem to have known the relation between the nervous system and voluntary movements. In addition, the ureters (the connections between the kidneys and the bladder) were known and named. Most writers state that the Egyptians' anatomical knowledge, while relatively sophisticated, was, by modern standards, rudimentary. They aver, for example, that the Egyptians attached no special significance to the brain.[9] But at least one researcher, utilizing sources entirely different from the papyri, contradicts this notion, asserting that their knowledge of neuroanatomy in particular was as detailed and advanced as that in modern times.[10]

The Egyptians were well-versed in many pathological syndromes. The identification of a disease necessitates acute and painstaking clinical observation, often over many years, and many of the ones described in the medical papyri are known today. Egyptian physicians understood the origin of paraplegia and paralysis from spinal cord injuries and recognized the traumatic origin of neurological symptoms such as deafness, urinary incontinence, and priapism. They described many syndromes of cardiac origin. They knew that excess blood in the heart and lungs was pathological which is consistent with what we know about congestive heart failure today. They also seem to have recognized the significance of heart palpitations and arrhythmias and gave a rather precise definition of angina pectoris:

> If thou examinest a man for illness in his cardia and he has pains in his arms,
> in his breast, and on one side of his cardia . . . it is death threatening him.[11]

The modern description of anginal pectoris can hardly improve upon this. The phrase seen in the Ebers Papyrus, "belly too narrow for food," seems to indicate an esophageal or stomach stricture perhaps from an inflammatory or ulcerating process. Egyptian physicians also knew that a weak heart adversely affected the liver, calling to mind the pathological enlargement of the liver which we know to be due to heart failure. Faintness due to a "dumb heart" was described which seems to be an allusion to a Stokes-Adams attack.[12] It is evident that the ancient Egyptian physicians had a fundamental grasp of the pathophysiology of many of the syndromes we know today.

Perhaps the most remarkable document among the medical papyri is the surgical Edwin Smith Papyrus, a compendium of Egyptian anatomical knowledge and surgical methods. It is in this papyrus that the remarkable descriptions of the traumatic surgical lesions and their treatment are found. We also find that the priest-physicians also recognized the signs and symptoms of sciatica, the sharp pain radiating down the leg caused by nerve compression in the lower spinal cord. Like many other peoples in Africa and the rest of the world, the Egyptians practiced trephination.[13] This operation, the forerunner of neurosurgery, involves boring a hole through the skull to the outer covering of the brain. This was done to remove fragments from a skull fracture compressing the brain, to treat epilepsy, or to relieve chronic headache. Today in Africa there are people who have undergone this operation with no apparent ill effects and there are skulls from ancient Egyptian graves with definite signs of healing around the trephination site, so it is clear that patients have survived this operation.

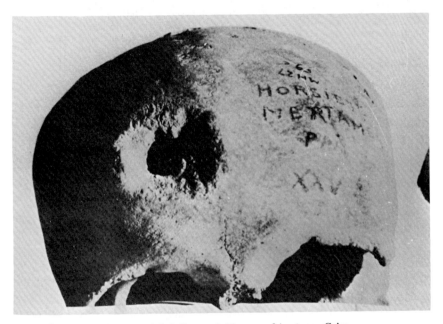

Fig. 1. *A trephine hole* or a healed skull wound. **Museum of Anatomy, Cairo Faculty of Medicine.**

As is seen very commonly in Africa, there was a separate guild of bonesetters in Egypt who treated fractures and dislocations. These specialists devised a completely effective method for reducing collar bone fractures which Hippocrates later used.[14] The Edwin Smith Papyrus also describes maneuvers for reducing dislocated jaws and shoulders. Long bone fractures were immobilized with tight splints and nasal fractures were treated by the insertion of stiff nasal packings into the affected nostril, a method also used today for uncomplicated nasal fractures.

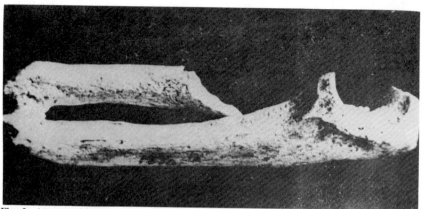

Fig. 2. *Amputated forearm bones* reunited by callus. Dr. Moeller-Christensen, Copenhagen.

Fig. 3. *Splints of wood* padded with vegetable fibre, surrounding a broken femur. Cairo Faculty of Medicine.

The Egyptians had perhaps three to four thousand years of experience dissecting and bandaging mummies and this must have had beneficial effects on surgical technique. They had an array of knives and scalpels to excise tumours and drain abscesses. They used red-hot metal instruments to seal off bleeding points and closed clean wounds with sutures or adhesive tape. They were unsurpassed as bandagists and used their techniques to control bleeding. Fresh meat was also used to stop oozing hemorrhage from surgical wounds. Like the ancient Chinese, they used molds from bread or cereals to treat wound infections. Modern penicil-

Fig. 4. *A collection of instruments*, including needles, a metal irrigator provided with a pout, tweezers, a small spoon, a spatula, and a strong hook such as would be used to evacuate the brain. The instruments are most likely embalming tools. Dr. Bietak, University of Vienna.

Fig. 5. *Circumcision operation* in progress. From the necropolis of Sakkara, VIth Dynasty.

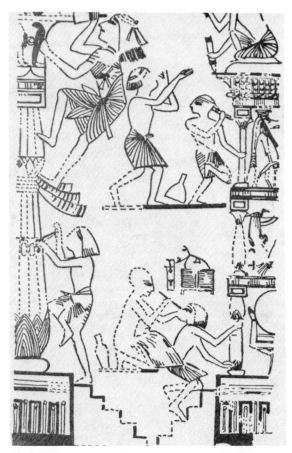

Fig. 6. *A person treats another workman's eye* by means of a
sticklike instrument (lower frame), either removing a
foreign body or instilling drops.

lin was extracted from a mold so the priest-physicians must also have been aware
of its bacteriacidal properties.[15]

Like all African peoples, the Egyptians had a large *materia medica*, using as
many as 1000 animal, plant, and mineral products in the treatment of illness.
Night blindness, caused by vitamin A deficiency, was treated with ox livers,
known to be rich in vitamin A. Poppy extract—the source of opium—was used to
treat colicky babies. Modern physicians use paregoric—whose active ingredient
is opium—for exactly the same purpose. Patients with scurvy—caused by vitamin C deficiency—were fed onions, a known source of vitamin C. Castor seeds,
the source of castor oil, were used to make cathartic preparations. Mandrake and
henbane, sources of belladonna alkaloids, were also known and used. The bella-

Fig. 7. *A mandrake root* **being offered to Akhenaten by his wife Nefertiti.**

donnas possess properties that stimulate the heart, decrease stomach motility, dilate the pupils, and cause sedation. The Egyptians dispensed their prescriptions as pills, enemas, suppositories, infusions, and elixirs in accurate, standardized doses, causing some to wonder if they had separate pharmacies and pharmacists.[16]

The Egyptians were also quite knowledgeable in handling obstetric and gynecological problems. They knew and treated uterine prolapse. They had means of inducing abortions and preventing conception. They even had an effective pregnancy test! A sample of a woman's urine was sprinkled on growing cereals; if the cereals did not grow the woman was considered not pregnant; if they did grow she was declared pregnant. Modern experiments have shown that a pregnant woman's urine has a permissive effect on the growth of barley in about 40% of the cases, demonstrating that there must have been some validity in the world's first pregnancy test.[17]

Our glimpse of the medical system of this ancient African civilization shows that it deserves its reputation as the best and most advanced of antiquity. Indeed, medicine as we know it today began in Egypt rather than Greece. A study of other African systems of medicine is more problematical, however, because of the absence of surviving written records. Thus, most of what we know comes from the testimony of European missionaries whose contemptuous view of traditional culture was most pointed when writing about traditional medical practices. Nonetheless, it can be shown that the best of the traditional healers in various parts of Africa acquired a startling level of proficiency and, contrary to comtemporary opinion, were not without a medical science.

It is pertinent to remember that Africa has been subjected to centuries of almost continuous political, social, and cultural disruption and that—among cultures that rely heavily on oral transmission of knowledge—a tremendous amount of knowledge has been lost. Thus, the state of traditional medicine today does not reflect the best of what the traditional doctors knew and surviving fragments of eyewitness reports—as shall be shown—indicate that they knew quite a lot.

Like ancient Egypt, all traditional African cultures had a magico-spiritual conception of disease. Thus in this setting, moral, social, or spiritual transgressions are likely to lead to illness because they create both individual and communal disharmony. Without the psycho-spiritual cure—without re-establishing this sensitive harmony—the medicinal cure is considered useless. The traditional practitioner is intimately acquainted with the psychic, social, and cultural nuances of his people and more than one commentator has acknowledged that the traditional doctor is often an expert psychotherapist, achieving results with his patients that conventional Western psychotherapy cannot.

Though there is no single paradigm of medical practice that applies to all of Africa, many of the essential features of the various traditional systems are comparable and even identical. Among the Mano of Liberia, for example, all children's diseases, all obstetrics, all of the "everyday" complaints are handled by women, particularly the elderly women; surgery, bonesetting, and special diagnostic and therapeutic problems are handled almost exclusively by men. This is a pattern that repeats itself throughout Africa.

The approach to the patient can vary in different parts of Africa. In some societies, where the doctor is credited with paranormal insight, the physician may arrive at a diagnosis and prescribe treatment without questioning or examining the patient since he is supposed to know what is wrong by virtue of his special powers. However, other traditional doctors affect an approach toward physical diagnosis closer to our own:

> Many Western-trained doctors concede that the traditional medical experts have a profound knowledge of the human body and anatomy. This is demonstrated by a usually careful diagnosis beginning with a history of the disease followed by a thorough physical examination . . . He palpates the different parts and looks for tender spots. He feels the beating of the heart, the position of the inner organs, checks the eyes and ears, and smells the mouth for bad breath.[18]

Most commentators have disparaged the traditional doctor's knowledge of anatomy and physiology. The Mano, however, have names for most of the major organs and know the difference between normal and abnormal anatomy.[19] Another author notes that the Banyoro of Uganda, renowned in the last century for their surgical skill, had a wide knowledge of anatomy.[20] A Hausa maneuver to test for impotence has been described:

> An individual is stripped and placed on a mat lying on his back, A pin or thorn is lightly rubbed over the inside of his thigh. If the scrotum or testicles do not move, the individual is considered impotent. There is a physiological basis for this procedure. The maneuver in effect tests the cremasteric reflex. The cremaster muscle contracts and pulls the testicles upward on stimulation of the inside of the thigh.[21]

This passage belies the notion that African doctors were without a knowledge of some of the body's physiological processes. Moreover, Mano physicians—reputedly without an understanding of the body's cardiovascular system—knew that the conditions of anasarca and ascites were due to fluid overload and treated accordingly with diuretic preparations. These interesting fragments do not by themselves admit of a sophisticated anatomical or physiological knowledge but they hint at a greater degree of knowledge—perhaps in past ages—than has hitherto been recognized.

Some case studies of cultures in east-central Africa have brought to light some remarkable evidence revealing the presence of scientific medicine there. The practice of carrying out autopsies on patients dying of unknown causes among the Banyoro of Uganda and the Likundu of Central Africa has been described. Almost always these were carried out to detect a possible witchcraft etiology but may well have contributed to a more extensive knowledge of anatomy than previously supposed:

> The procedures for autopsying bodies under the Likundu culture have been reviewed, not for the purpose of considering the beliefs that impelled such procedures but to indicate that in some areas autopsies were frequently carried out and that they involved searching in the body, a search which might be casual and superficial but which in other cases might be prolonged and exacting and involved opening up and examining a variety of organs. These are precisely the circumstances under which considerable knowledge of anatomy and pathology could be acquired by persons who, for any purpose, might wish to do so.[22]

Further, there is a report of a Banyoro king who commissioned a traditional doctor to travel around the countryside to investigate, describe, and search for a cure for sleeping sickness, which was ravaging the country at the time.[23] This clearly indicates that a spirit of clinical investigation did exist among Banyoro physicians and probably among other traditional practitioners as well. In many parts of Africa, treatments were devised for new diseases like venereal disease and scrofula that were imported into African and this would presuppose some form of clinical investigation and experimentation.

In some parts of Africa, it would seem that the traditional doctor had a firm grasp of some fundamental public health principles. In Liberia, the Mano developed an admirable quarantine system for smallpox. They were well aware of its contagiousness and set aside a "sick bush" for affected patients. This was situated well away from the village and the patient was attended by only one person; no one else was allowed to approach the area. The patient was put on a careful diet and was rubbed with topical anesthetic medications to prevent scratching which could lead to superinfection. When the illness ran its course, the area was burned. The "sick-bush" approach would do a modern epidemiologist proud. Of further interest is the centuries-old practice of smallpox variolation which is carried out all over Africa. During an epidemic, material from the pustule of a sick person is scratched into the skin of unaffected persons with a thorn. In the majority of instances, there is no reaction and the persons inoculated are protected against smallpox. In some cases, the inoculation will produce a mild, non-fatal form of the disease which will also confer permanent immunity.[24] Centuries before Jenner, Africans had devised an effective vaccination method against smallpox.

In the area of surgery, the best evidence indicates that some African surgeons attained a level of skill comparable, and in some respects superior, to that of Western surgeons up to the 20th century. As in ancient Egypt, the bonesetter guilds were separate from those of the traditional doctors and were renowned for their skill. Some commentators, observing the bonesetters of today, feel that this reputation was somewhat inflated and the bonesetters' results were less than optimum by Western standards.[25] Yet other reports cite techniques that led to highly satisfactory results. Mano bonesetters treated a patient with a thigh fracture by placing him in the loft of a house allowing the affected leg to dangle free with a heavy stone attached. This was a very effective traction method and once the fracture was reduced, it was immobilized with a tight splint.[26] In addition, the patient was encouraged to excercise a fractured leg and we know today that new bone is laid down more rapidly over the fracture site when there is some exercise of the limb. Bonesetters in other parts of Africa would dig a deep pit for the purpose of exercising traction on a fractured limb and in East Africa, the bonesetters reduced fractures and dislocations by manual manipulation and traction. These examples indicate that the bonesetters' reputation was not entirely undeserved.

In many areas, especially among warlike peoples, the traditional physician was particularly adept in treating traumatic wounds. One report describes the treatment of an open wound by the following method: plant juices with antiseptic properties were squeezed into the open wound, a red hot metal tip was used to cauterize bleeding points and burn away damaged tissue, the wound edges were closed with a tough thorn, an awl, and fibrous suture, and a fiber mat was wrapped tightly around the wound to prevent bleeding. The wound was never closed until the bleeding had been stopped.[27] In another documented instance, a native surgeon successfully resected part of a patient's lung to remove a penetrating arrow-head.[28] In the Congo, a native surgeon was seen using stiff elephant hairs to probe for and successfully remove a bullet.[29] In Nigeria, a man who had had his abdomen ripped open by an elephant was treated by the doctor by replacing the intestines in the abdominal cavity, securing them in place with a calabash covering, and finally suturing together the overlying abdominal wall and skin. Not only did the man recover but was soon back working on a road gang.[30] In the testimoney of one author:

> Witch doctors of many tribes perform operations for cataract. They squeeze the juice from the leaves of an alkaloid-containing plant directly into the eye to desensitize it, then push the cataract aside with a sharp stick. A surprising number of these cases turn out successfully.[31]

In East Africa, Masai surgeons were known to successfully treat pleurisy and pneumoritis by creating a partial collapse of the lung by drilling holes into the chest of the sufferer.[32]

It is pertinent to now consider one of the most remarkable examples of African surgery ever documented. This is an eye-witness account by a missionary doctor named Felkin of a Caesarean section performed by a Banyoro surgeon in Uganda in 1879:

> The patient was a healthy-looking primipara (first pregnancy) of about twenty years of age and she lay on an inclined bed, the head of which rested against the side of the hut, She was half-intoxicated with banana wine, was quite naked and was tied down to the bed by bands of bark cloth over the thorax and thighs. Her ankles were held by a man... while another man stood on her right steadying her abdomen .. the surgeon was standing on her left side holding the knife aloft and muttering an incantation. He then washed his hands and the patient's abdomen first with banana wine and then water. The surgeon made a quick cut upwards from just above the pubis to just below the umbilicus severing the whole abdominal wall and uterus so that amniotic fluid escaped. Some bleeding points in the abdominal wall were touched with red hot irons. The surgeon completed the uterine incision, the assistant helping by holding up the sides of the abdominal wall with his hand and hooking two fingers into the uterus. The child was removed, the cord cut, and the child was handed to an assistant.[33]

The report goes on to say that the surgeon squeezed the uterus until it contracted, dilated the cervix from inside with his fingers (to allow post-partum blood to escape), removed clots and the placenta from the uterus, and then *sparingly* used red hot irons to seal the bleeding points. A porous mat was tightly secured over the wound and the patient turned over to the edge of the bed to permit drainage of any remaining fluid. The peritoneum, the abdominal wall, and the skin were approximated back together and secured with seven sharp spikes. A root paste was applied over the wound and a bandage of cloth was tightly wrapped around it. Within six days, all the spikes were removed. Felkin observed the patient for 11 days and when he left, mother and child were alive and well.[34]

In Scotland, Lister had pioneered antiseptic surgery just two years prior to this event but universal application of his methods in the operating rooms of Europe was still years away. Caesarean sections were performed *only* under the most desperate circumstances and *only* to save the life of the infant. A Caesarean section to save the lives of both mother and child was unheard of in Europe nor are there records of such a procedure among the great civilizations of antiquity. As one commentator has said:

> The whole conduct of the operation as Felkin described it suggests a skilled long-practiced surgical team at work conducting a well-tried and familiar operation with smooth efficiency and unhurried skill . . . Lister's team in London could hardly have performed with greater smoothness.[35]

Not only did the surgeon understand the sophisticated concepts of anaesthesia and antisepsis but also demonstrated advanced surgical technique. In his sparing use of the cautery iron, for example, he showed that he knew tissue damage could result from its overuse. The operation was without question a landmark, reflecting the best in African surgery.

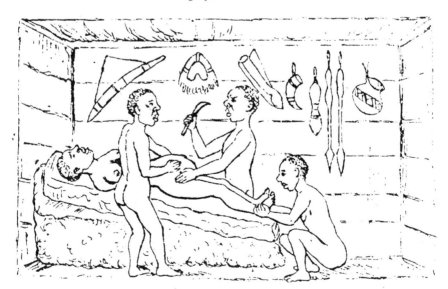

Fig. 8. Illustration from Dr. R.W. Felkin's description of the Caesarean section. *Edinburgh Medical Journal*, 1884.

African midwives possessed a good understanding of some fundamental obstetric and pediatric principles. Mano midwives pulled repeatedly at the breasts of women in labor, a maneuver which induces the release of oxytocin—a stimulator of uterine contractions—from the pituitary gland. They sometimes took laboring mothers upon their backs, walking around with them and shaking them. This undoubtedly had the effect of causing the cervix to dilate and the head

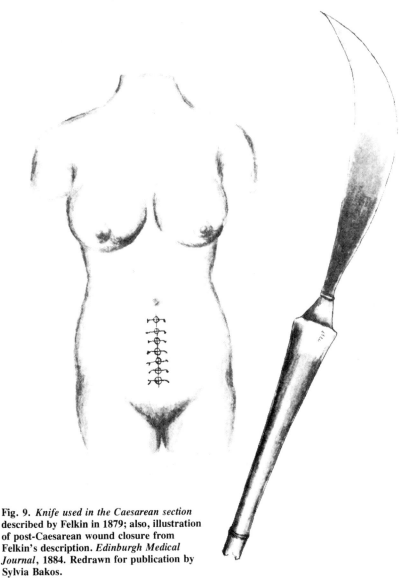

Fig. 9. *Knife used in the Caesarean section* described by Felkin in 1879; also, illustration of post-Caesarean wound closure from Felkin's description. *Edinburgh Medical Journal*, 1884. Redrawn for publication by Sylvia Bakos.

to engage, thus facilitating labor.[36] Some Bantu midwives were known to use Indian hemp during labor for its sedative properties. Newborn babies and infants were taken and exposed to the sun for a period of each day "to make them strong." One author attributed the rare occurrence of rickets among Mano children to this practice.[37] In addition, these women healers recognized the causes of malnutrition and retarded development, putting such children on special diets high in vitamins and carbohydrates with favorable results.[38]

Traditional African cultures have an abundant materia medica. The Zulus, for example, are reputed to know the medicinal uses of some 700 plants.[39] Ouabain, capsicum, physostigmine, kola, and calabar beans are just a few of the substances from the African materia medica that have made their way into the Western pharmacopeia.[40] The traditional midwives often have drugs that can induce abortion in the first three months of pregnancy and in Uganda, in an area where there is a high incidence of dystocia (retarded labor), the midwives have preparations which stimulate uterine contractions. "Fever-leaf" is used all over Africa to treat the recurring fevers of malaria. Certain Bantu-speaking peoples use the bark of *Salix capensis* (willow) to treat the musculoskeletal complaints of rheumatism.[41] This family of plants yields salicylic acid, the active ingredient in aspirin, a sovereign remedy the world over for musculoskeletal pains. Kaolin, the active ingredient in Kaopectate® is used in Mali to combat diarrhea. Caffeine-containing kola nuts are chewed all over Africa for their stimulating and fatigue-combating properties. To combat snakebite, plants containing ouain and strichnine are used. The former is a heart stimulant and therefore useful against cardiotoxic venoms and the latter is a nerve tonic, useful against neurotoxic venoms. In Nigeria, in 1979, the rootbark *Annona senegalensis* was found to possess strong anti-cancer properties.[42] Even earlier, in 1969, herbal preparations that were used in Nigeria to treat skin infections were found to have definite bacteriocidal activity against gram-positive bacteria, the very organisms that cause skin infections.[43] There was an interesting case in 1925 of an eminent Nigerian in England who was suffering from severe psychotic episodes not amenable to treatment by English doctors. A traditional doctor from Nigeria was summoned who was able to relieve the patient of his symptoms with decoctions made from a rauwolfia root.[44] The *Rauwolfia* family of plants is the source of modern-day Reserpine®, first used as a major tranquilizer to treat severe psychosis but now used mainly as an antihypertensive medication.

The list of effective drugs in the African pharmocopeia is too extensive to elucidate here but suffice to say that traditional doctors in Africa had and have effective remedies against intestinal parasites, vomiting, skin ulcers, rashes, catarrh, convulsions, tumours, venereal disease, bronchitis, conjunctivitis, urethral stricture and many other complaints.

There are at least two documented instances of Europeans benefitting from the ministrations of the traditional physician. In the last century, a Bushman doctor cured a European woman dying of sepsis that the European doctor could not treat. In Swaziland, a European doctor, dying of dysentery, was cured by a native physician.[45] Moreover, the native physicians in this area were so skilled at treating Typhoid Fever that the European doctors used their decoctions for the same purpose.[46]

This paper has attempted to show that the traditional doctors of Africa from the earliest times had a high level of medical and surgical skill, certainly much more than they have been given credit for. It is to be hoped that more substantive and careful investigations will be carried out among the traditional healers of Africa before Western-style medicine supplants them entirely.

Notes

1. Newsome, F: Black Contributions to the Early History of Western Medicine. *Journal of African Civilizations*, 2(1&2): 27-39, 9/80

2. Quoted in Sigerist, HE: *A History of Medicine: Primitive and Archaic Medicine*. New York, Oxford University Press, 1951, p. 325.

3. Ghalioungui, P: *The House of Life: Magic and Medical Science in Ancient Egypt*. Amsterdam, BM Israel, 1973.

4. A placebo is a pharmacologically inactive drug which the patient believes is active. In many illnesses, the mere act of believing in the efficacy of the medicine can give beneficial results in 40% or more of patients. Without this effect, faith healers would have gone out of business centuries ago. An interesting recent article is "The Placebo Effect" in the April, 1981 issue of *MD* magazine.

5. Sigerist, op. cit., p. 300.

6. Ghalioungui, op. cit., p. 30.

7. Sigerist, op. cit., p. 323.

8. Ghalioungui, op. cit., pp. 49, 51.

9. Reeves, C: Illustrations of Medicine in Ancient Egypt. *J. Audiov Media Med*, 3(1): 5, 1/80.

10. Schwaller de Lubicz, RA: *The Temple in Man*, trans. D. Lawlor, Brookline, Autumn Press, 1977.

11. Ghalioungui, op. cit., p. 123.

12. A modern medical textbook says this about Stokes-Adams attacks: "Syncopal (fainting) attacks . . . are common in Type II block, and they have the characteristics of all such syncopal attacks that are due to a *sudden cessation of circulation*." (emphasis mine) *Harrison's Principles of Internal Medicine*, Thorn, Adams, et. al., eds., New York, McGraw Hill, 1977, p. 1203. Compare this to an inscription in the Ebers Papyrus: "As to faintness: it is that the heart does not speak or that vessels of the heart are dumb . . ." Ghalioungui, op. cit., p. 217.

13. Ghalioungui, op. cit., p. 89.

14. Ibid., p. 42.

15. In *MD* magazine, March, 1981, p. 20, there is a short note on the Nubians of the Sudan who were known to be "remarkably free from infectious disease." Skeletal evidence has revealed the presence of tetracycline, a highly active antibiotic, in these people. Tetracycline is derived from the *Streptomycetes* family of fungi and it is assumed that it grew in the stored grains of these Nubian people living between 350 and 550 A.D. The report seems to doubt that a Tetracycline-like antibiotic was dispensed by Nubian physicians but this has by no means been ruled out.

16. Ghalioungui, op. cit., pp. 148-9.

17. Ibid., pp. 112-3.

18. Kiteme, K: Doctor Still Makes House Calls, *Ebony*, p. 116.

19. Harley, GW: *Native African Medicine*. London, Frank Cass, 1970, p. 41.

20. Davies, JN: Primitive Autopsies and Background to Scientific Medicine in Central Africa. *New York J Med*, 65:2831, 11/15/65.

21. Imperato, PJ: *African Folk Medicine*. Baltimore, York Press, 1979, p. 110.

22. Davies, op. cit., p. 2833.

23. Davies, JN: The Development of 'Scientific' Medicine in the African Kingdom of Bunyoro-Kitara. *Med Hist*, 3:54, 1959.

24. Imperato, op. cit., pp. 162-75.

25. Ibid., pp. 55-6.

26. Harley, op. cit., p. 95.

27. Ibid., p. 221.

28. Ibid., p. 222.

29. Ibid.

30. Ibid.

31. Thompson, EE: Primitive African Medical Lore and Witchcraft. *Bull Med Libr Ass*, 53:89-90, 1/65.

32. Johnston, H: *The Uganda Protectorate*. London, Hutchinson & Co., 2:750, 1902.

33. Davies, The Development . . ., pp. 50-1.

34. Ibid.

35. Ibid., p. 52.

36. See Ambulation Versus Oxytocin for Improved Labor. *Family Practice Recertification*, 3(11):11, 11/81.

37. Harley, op. cit., p. 64.

38. Ibid.

39. Bryant, AT: *Zulu Medicine and Medicine-Men*. Cape Town, C. Struik, 1966, p. 84.

40. Thompson, op. cit., p. 88.

41. Hewat, M: *Bantu Folklore*. Cape Town, T. Maskew Miller, 1906, p. 62.

42. Durodola, JI: Contribution of Traditional Medicine to the Chemotherapy of Cancer. Niger Med J, 9(5):616, 5-6/79.

43. Malcolm, SA, Sofowara EA: Antimicrobial Activity of Selected Nigerian Folk Remedies and Their Constituent Plants. *Lloydia*, 32:512-7, 12/69.

44. Aikman, L: Nature's Gift to Medicine. *National Geographic*, 146(3):428, 9/74.

45. Harley, op. cit., p. 250.

46. Hewat, op. cit., p. 79.

STEEL-MAKING IN ANCIENT AFRICA

Debra Shore

Summary: In our pilot issue of the Journal of African Civilizations *(Vol I, No I, April, 1979)* we began our survey of early African Science with an article by Peter Schmidt and Donald Avery *"Complex Iron-Smelting and Prehistoric Culture in Tanzania"*. The Schmidt-Avery discovery that Africans had produced carbon steel 2000 years ago startled the scientific world and opened a new chapter in African history as well as the history of technology. In this article, first published by the Brown Alumni Monthly *(December, 1978)* Debra Shore gives a lucid and informative account, based on interviews with the Brown University scientists themselves, of the background to this discovery.

In the September 22 issue of *Science*, two Brown professors announced what for those interested in the history of technology is a rather startling discovery. Assistant Professor of Anthropology Peter Schmidt and Professor of Engineering Donald H. Avery have found that as long as 2,000 years ago Africans living on the western shores of Lake Victoria had produced carbon steel in preheated forced-draft furnaces, a method that was technologically more sophisticated than any developed in Europe until the mid-nineteenth century.

Their finding was based on the recent reconstruction of a similar furnace by men of the Haya tribe in Tanzania whose ancestors had passed on their steel-making methods orally for centuries. They compared the steel produced in this modern re-enactment with evidence from archaeological excavation of early Iron Age furnaces located near Lake Victoria. Though separated by as much as 2,000 years, the construction of the furnaces and the composition of the steel were essentially the same. "We have found a technological process in the African Iron Age which is exceedingly complex," Schmidt said. "To be able to say that a technologically superior culture developed in Africa more than 1,500 years ago overturns popular and scholarly ideas that technological sophistication developed in Europe but not in Africa."

Strange bedfellows often seem the peculiar domain of universities. Take Avery and Schmidt, for example. Until several years ago, Don Avery spent most of his time in the laboratory studying superplasticity in alloys and thermo-mechanical processing of certain metals. Among his publications was a paper called "Some Remarks on the History of the Cutting Edge," for the Gillette Company. Historical anthropologist Peter Schmidt, for his part, had made sev-

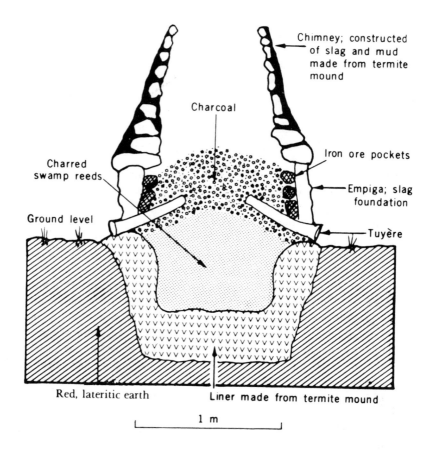

Chimney; constructed
of slag and mud
made from termite
mound

Charcoal

Iron ore pockets

Charred
swamp reeds

Empiga; slag
foundation

Ground level

Tuyère

Red, lateritic earth

Liner made from termite mound

1 m

An idealized profile of a Haya iron smelting furnace; this view is before the mixed iron ore and charcoal charge has been added. Note that the tuyeres are inside the furnace and therefore are conduits that preheat the air passing through them. Iron ore pockets are added inside the foundation blocks to roast iron ore for the next smelt.

eral visits to Tanzania over the last nine years to trace the history of the Haya people through their rich oral tradition. In the course of his work with the Haya, a Bantu-speaking people who live along the western shore of Lake Victoria, Schmidt was told of an ancient king who had climbed a pillar of iron to ascend to the heavens. He was shown the site of this "shrine tree," and archaeological investigation there confirmed what the elders had told him: this was a site on which steel had been produced as long as 2,000 years ago. But Schmidt, who saw some similarities between the stories he was told and his archaeological findings, did not understand exactly how they fit. So he enlisted the help of metallurgist Avery, who had long nurtured an interest in the history of technology and had once constructed an iron-smelting furnace on the ancient Hittite model—circa 1000 B.C.—in the basement of Barus & Holley. Theirs has proven a most fruitful collaboration. "Our work was written up recently in *My Weekly Reader*," Avery says. "I think it's the first time the engineering department has been written up there."

The Haya whom Peter Schmidt studied live in densely populated villages where they herd cattle, subsist on a banana and bean agriculture, and grow coffee and tea as cash crops. At one time, though, they were iron smelters. Archaeological surveys suggest that their ancestors had developed an organized, highly cooperative labor force necessary to prepare the materials for smelting iron, operate the furnace, and process the iron. Though the Haya no longer practice this craft—cheap, imported iron tools have been readily available for the last fifty years and coffee-growing offers greater economic rewards—Schmidt did find a group of blacksmiths and other old men who had smelted iron in the traditional way during their youth fifty to sixty years ago. But their knowledge, Schmidt wrote, "is threatened every day by the passage of time, by death, and by age-related infirmities occurring in this quickly shrinking group of expert smelters."

In 1976 Schmidt persuaded these elderly Haya smelters to construct a traditional furnace. Tests on the slag—fused refuse separated from metal in smelting—found at early Iron Age sites showed that it had been formed at temperatures of 1350° to 1400°C (about 2500°F). Schmidt and Avery hypothesized that preheating of the air blast by means of ceramic blowpipes inserted into the base of the furnace had been a prominent feature of ancient iron smelting. "We reasoned that higher combustion temperatures achieved by this preheating would have formed slag at temperatures similar to or higher than those indicated by our heat tests on prehistoric slag," they wrote in *Science*. "Preheating would permit the attainment of much higher furnace temperatures and better fuel economy than was obtainable in cold blast European bloomeries." Could the Haya replica achieve such temperatures and would the iron formed resemble the excavated fragments?

In appearance, a Haya furnace looks roughly like an inverted ice cream cone. A bowl about eighteen inches deep is dug and lined with mud made from the earth of a termite mound. "Termite mud turns out to be a very good refractory material," Avery says. "Termites have made their hills of material that won't absorb water, so they make them of bits of alumina and silica, grain by grain." The shaft, or cone, is made of old, refractory slag gathered from a site at which iron had been successfully smelted and of termite mud, and it stands five feet high. Eight blowpipes, or tuyères, about two feet long are inserted to varying depths at the base of the furnace, and eight drum bellows covered with goat skins are used to force air into the tuyeres. Swamp grass is burned in the bowl until the bottom of the furnace is filled with charred swamp reeds. These then provide a bed of charcoal—technically, "filamentary alkaline-coated carbon fiber"—that is readily wetted and penetrated by the molten iron slag.

For the smelt itself, the Haya produced charcoal over an open fire. "Charcoal is made each time for the smelt," Avery explains. "There is no charcoal industry supplying the iron smelters. The charcoal was then sifted and it was important to use sifted charcoal in making iron." The whole process, Avery says, had to be carried out in the traditional manner. Sifting charcoal was merely one aspect of this. The charcoal and iron ore are then added through the top of the furnace while air is continuously blown thrugh the tuyères for seven to eight hours. Temperatures in the blast zone of the furnace exceeded 1800°C (3275°F), some 200-400°C higher than temperatures observed during smelting experiments based on European archaeological evidence.

Following the smelt, the furnace is dismantled in order to remove the lumps of steel, called bloom, which form in the bed of swamp grass charcoal. The formation of carbon steel in the grass charcoal is a critical part of this process, Avery notes, as well as a feature that distinguishes this method from that used in Europe. Before the iron ore nodules mined by the Haya were placed in the furnace, they had been "roasted" in a pit with densely-packed wet wood. In the pit, due to limited O_2 access, a chemical reaction takes place in which carbon penetrates the iron ore—is essentially co-deposited internally much as chips are found throughout chocolate chip ice cream. When these pieces of "roasted" iron ore are added to the furnace, they melt in the high temperatures produced just above the tuyères. The molten iron silicate slag is drawn into the bed of grass charcoal. "The carbon infiltrates the slag, which then causes a chemical reaction, giving off carbon monoxide," he writes. "As this happens, large and very perfect crystals of iron grow in the slag to form a bloom . . . . Carbon steel results when carbon from the burned swamp grass is absorbed into the iron." Thus, two characteristics of the Haya smelting process are unique: the preheating of the air draft through blowpipes, and the formation of iron crystals, rather than by "the sintering of fine, solid particles" as in European smelting.

"It's a very unique and original process that uses a large number of sophisti-

In the center, ceramic blowpipes—called tuyères—are placed at the base of the furnace over the pit, which has been filled with charred swamp reeds and sifted charcoal. These blowpipes will serve as a conduit for the air forced into the furnace and preheat the air as it passes through them. At far right opposite, the furnace is constructed of large chunks of refractory slag cemented by termite mud. (Photo by Peter Schmidt)

cated techniques,'' Avery comments. ''This is really semi-conductor technology—the growing of crystals—not iron-smelting technology.''

In the course of their experiment, Avery said that four separate furnaces had collapsed—one right after the other. ''In this case we went to a diviner's hut. He told us that a man who had not been allowed to participate had hidden in the trees and had pointed his ass at the furnace, which would prevent it from smelting iron. It was determined that we had taken some shortcuts and had not built the furnaces in the traditional way.'' So, they abandoned the shortcuts—and had a successful smelt.

One year after the reconstruction of a furnace by Haya elders and the re-enactment of a smelt, Schmidt excavated thirteen early Iron Age furnaces at Kemondo Bay on the coast of Lake Victoria, one of the most complex early Iron Age industrial sites in Africa. The Kemondo Bay furnace pits had physical properties very similar to the reconstructed pit, including evidence that blow-pipes had been inserted inside the furnace. So the archaeological evidence bore out the oral history of the Haya, and the oral history had been passed down without major alterations for 2,000 years.

Schmidt suggests that similar furnaces were used by neighboring cultures—in Uganda, for instance—and that this level of technological complexity was not limited to East Africa. ''Further archaeological research is required to discover why such a complex technology grew up along the western shore of Lake Victoria,'' he writes. ''One possible hypothesis is that the heavy exploitation of forests (for charcoal and for agricultural purposes) may have triggered the development of an efficient, fuel-economizing technology. The widespread distribution of Early Iron Age industrial sites in West Lake, the manner of charcoal production and its ten-to-one weight ratio of wood to charcoal, and the need for five hundred pounds of charcoal all suggest that, if smelting was widely practiced in prehistoric times, then the impact of the technological system must have been severe. The decline of productivity may be linked to an overexploited forest resource base; the evolution of the fuel-efficient preheated furnace may be an adaptation by the local smelters to that depleted resource.''

This year (1978) Peter Schmidt is in Tanzania conducting further research funded by the National Science Foundation. Through his work, coupled with Don Avery's expertise in metallurgical analysis, Schmidt has gone a long way towards solving a problem he had not even meant to tackle: how iron metallurgy developed in sub-Saharan Africa.

TRADITIONAL AFRICAN WATERCRAFT:
A NEW LOOK

Stewart C. Malloy

Summary: In this essay, Stewart Malloy of the Oceanographic Sciences Division, Brookhaven National Laboratory, takes a new look at the watercraft of Western and Central Africa. This region once formed part of a great inter-locking trade network running from the Mediterranean to the Gulf of Guinea and from the West Coast to Lake Chad. The interaction of these diverse peoples through conquest, reconquest and trade offered countless opportunities for the diffusion of ideas on boats.

Malloy's survey, based mainly on observations well after the height of development of these societies, indicate that traditional African boat-building technology included both extension and expansion techniques used world-wide to make "dugouts" sea-worthy. He shows that the capacities of these boats for long-distance journeys have been underestimated.

There is a startling body of evidence of a linguistic, cultural, horticultural, social and archaeological nature which suggests continued contact between Africa and MesoAmerica in pre-Columbian times. In a recent book, *They Came Before Columbus*, Ivan Van Sertima (1977) presents forceful arguments for this contact with the New World based upon the lines of evidence suggested above. He offers new and re-examined facts indicating that contrary to popular belief, black Africans were neither sedentary nor timid about great travels upon land and the sea. Indeed, African peoples explored as much as they were explored. With these ideas in mind, I will attempt to present some observations on African watercraft upon which our African forefathers might have journeyed to MesoAmerica.

In examining any historical document on the peoples, culture, and technology of Africa, one must realize the framework and the biases in which the material was gathered or observed. It is no surprise then that we find a great degree of tunnel vision on the part of the early European explorers. Their voyages to and travels in Africa were financed and backed by their sovereigns, mercantile interests, and others whose designs were to exploit the continent. Therefore, the reader should realize that the journal writings of many European explorers may frequently underestimate African competence and capability in many areas, including naval and architectural achievements.

One of the earliest records of West African watercraft comes from the voyages of Cadamosto in 1455 (Crone, 1937). He found the coastal inhabitants of the Senegal River using three- to four-men dugouts for fishing and ferrying goods from place to place. About ten years earlier in 1445, Dinis Dias had visited the Senegal and West African coast and established trade with these coastal people. He documented the sighting of a number of these boats. Accompanying Cadamosto were several Africans who had been secured from the Senegambia region, taught Spanish and/or Portuguese in Europe, and who now were acting as interpreters on this and other voyages to the African coast.

Later on the Gambia River, the party of Cadamosto encountered decidedly larger African boats.

> On the return, there issued from the mouth of a stream which flows into this great river, three canoes (we call them *zopoli*) which from what I observed later, are all made of a single portion of a large tree hollowed out, fashioned like the little boats which are towed behind our ships....
> ...When our men had boarded their ship, they began to gesticulate and to make signs to the canoes to draw near. These slowed down, and approached no nearer. There were about twenty-five to thirty Negroes in each; these remained for awhile gazing upon a thing that neither they nor their fathers had ever seen before; that is, ships and white men, without showing any wish to parley, despite all that was said to them, they went about their own affairs.[1]

This reluctance on the part of the Africans to interact with the Portuguese may have reflected a language barrier, distrust due to earlier accounts of white men taking slaves, or simple disinterest. Whatever the reason it would contribute to the European ignorance of African boats at this and future times.

On the following day, an African navy attacked Cadamosto's expedition further up the Gambia.

> In a short time they rushed up. I being in the leading ship, split the canoes into two sections, and thrust into the midst of them: on counting the canoes, we found they numbered seventeen, boats of a considerable size. Checking their course and lifting up their oars, their crew lay gazing upon a marvel. We estimated on examination that there might be about one hundred and fifty at most....[2]

Still later on this fifteenth century voyage, the Portuguese were visited by more African sailors at the mouth of the Rio Grande.

> The next morning came out to our ships two canoes, which were similar to the ones already described, and in truth were of a great size; one was almost as long

as one of our vessels, but not so high; and in it were more than thirty Negroes; the other was smaller, having about sixteen men.[3]

These few recorded examples of pre-Columbian African watercraft illustrate the extremes in size and carrying capacity to be found in the coastal dugout between the Senegal and the Rio Grande at the middle of the fifteenth century. These vessels were used to transport from three to thirty-five people. The large number of boats found in one of the examples suggests that they formed part of a highly organized societal structure. As Basil Greenhill puts it:

> The undertaking of making a canoe is a considerable one. Suitable trees must be available near to the water, and the community concerned must have a good deal of time available for this kind of specialized work, for making a dugout frequently takes more time than building houses, or cattle pens or fencing fields. It is a kind of large-scale capital investment requiring a surplus of food production to enable the dugout makers to give the considerable amount of time demanded by the work. They must have reasonably efficient tools. It follows that to make such a big investment the community must be a prosperous one in a certain stage of development.[4]

It should be added that to make a planned Atlantic crossing these are precisely the societal conditions one would hope to find.

Although the most favorable embarking point for a trans-Atlantic crossing (Schwerin, 1970; Heyerdahl, 1963) from the west coast of Africa is the Senegambia area (Fig. 1), the impetus for such an undertaking or some of the technical and nautical skills needed may have originated from beyond the coast—particularly the Niger River and the environs of Jenne' and Timbuktu. Indeed the motivating force for European exploration of West Africa was to gain access to the gold trade and the merchandise coming from black Africa to the Mediterranean via Saharan caravans. These routes to the interior were Moslem controlled and effectively excluded Christian Europe. The Europeans hoped to come in through the "back door" via the West Coast to the interior and cut out the Moslem middlemen (Fig. 2). Most of this gold and slave trade centered around the Niger and its tributaries. Western and Central Africa was criss-crossed with a network of trade routes leading to the interior (Fig. 2). The trade communication between the West coast and the Niger existed ages prior to the coming of the Europeans. On one of the first voyages to Cantor on the Gambia in 1456-1457, Diogo Gomes was told of the trade routes to Timbuktu and Kukia (Crone, 1937).

With the demise of the great empires of Songhay and Mali culminating in the sacking of Timbuktu in 1591 (Bovill, 1968; Barth, 1857), the trade routes leading to the interior of Africa lost a major part of their importance. The two thousand six hundred miles of the Niger, its

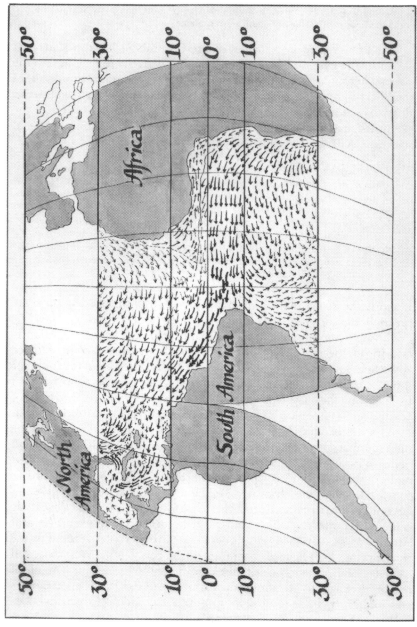

Average ocean sea surface currents from Africa to the Americas during the Northern Hemisphere winter (Latitude 30°N-30°S)   Malloy - Fig. 1

tributaries, and the Senegambia region saw smaller volumes of traffic and intercourse. As a result, there was a decrease in the trading caravans and fleets and a stagnation in innovative boat building similar to the death of the New England whaling industry. Thus the boats and riverine craft seen by the first outside travellers to this area represented traditional watercraft.

From the mid-fifteenth century the Portuguese, French, Spanish, and English were busily engaged in establishing trade entrepots and settlements along the west coast. Because of the climate, disease, the colonization of America, and African opposition, the Europeans by the eighteenth century were completely unfamiliar with the interiors of Africa. However, with this quickening pace of mercantile capitalism, the pressure was on the wealth beyond the coast. Our narratives on African watercraft begin anew at this point in history.

What did the interior of Africa have to offer the coast in terms of boat type and construction? To answer this question we turn to the diaries and journals of French, English, and German explorers of the late eighteenth century. These travellers provide us with excellent accounts of many of the watercraft in which they journeyed and observed.

African boats in the interior were as large or larger than those found on the coastal rivers. Mungo Park writing in 1796 noted that:

> ...they are therefore very long and disproportionately narrow, and have neither decks nor masts; they are however very roomy; for I observed in one of them four horses, and several people crossing over the river.[5]

In describing the events leading up to the death of Mungo Park during his trip to the Niger in 1805, Amadi Fatouma wrote that a certain canoe was large enough to carry one hundred and twenty people (Park, 1954).

About twenty years after the ill-fated adventures of Mungo Park, Rene Caillie trekked from Senegal through central Africa to Timbuktu during his four-year sojourn. Covering about 4,500 miles of territory of which 3,000 miles were unknown to Europeans, he wrote extensively about large African canoes.

> We arrived on the banks of the Milo (between Kankan and Boure') which I found very rapid and as broad again as when I first saw it. We crossed it, with our baggage, in a canoe about fifty feet long and exceedingly narrow; it was formed of two trunks of trees united lengthwise and fastened together with cords....[6]

On crossing the Dhioliba (Niger) from Cougalia to Jenne', Caillie' remarked:

> We crossed the river in a frail canoe, about thirty feet long, and very narrow made of a single trunk of the bombax....However, we succeeded in getting the asses on board; for the river was too wide for them to swim.[7]

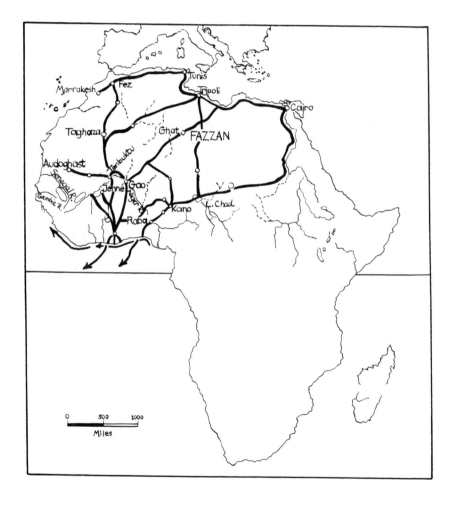

Major trade routes in central and western Africa between 1000 and 1700 A.D.
Malloy - Fig. 2

The most impressive boats, however, were to be found in the trade between Jenne' and Timbuktu. Caillie' describes a flotilla of nearly eighty large boats carrying on trade.

> A vessel of sixty or eighty tons burden is about ninety or one hundred feet long, twelve or fourteen abroad at midships and draws about six or seven feet of water.... In addition to their cargo, they frequently have on board forty or fifty slaves, half of whom remain on deck. The non-human cargo consisted of rice, millet, cotton, honey, vegetable butter, and other provisions of the country.[8]

Much farther to the south Richard and John Lander were attacked between Domuggoo and Kirree in 1832 as they sought to determine for England the course and termination of the Niger River.

> There was nothing to be done now but to obey; as for running away it was out of the question, our square loaded canoe was incapable of it and to fight with fifty war canoes, for such we found them, containing each above forty people most of whom were as well armed as ourselves would have been throwing away my own and my canoe men's lives very foolishly.[9]

At Brasstown above the Niger delta, the Landers described a Niger River trading vessel whose load is reminiscent of the boats that Caillie' travelled upon at Jenne'.

> The Brass canoe is extremely large and heavy laden; it is paddled by forty men and boys, in addition to whom there may be about twenty individuals, or more including a few slaves and ourselves—so that the number of human beings will amount to at least sixty.... It contains a number of large boxes or chests, which are filled with spiritous liquors, cotton, and silk goods, earthenware, and other articles of European and other foreign manufacturers, besides an abundance of provisions for present consumption.... In this canoe, three men might sit with ease abreast of one another. It has been cut out of a solid trunk of a tree, and draws four feet and a half of water, being more than fifty feet in length.[10]

While admitting to great size and capacity of some of the boats they saw, all of these explorers were critical of the craft they were obliged to use. For example, Mungo Park states:

> The canoe returned, when Demba Sego and myself embarked in this dangerous passage-boat, which the least likely motion was likely to upset. The king's nephew thought this a proper place to have a peep into a tin box of mine that stood in the forepart of the canoe and in stretching out his hand for it, he unfortunately destroyed the equilibrium, and overset the canoe.[11]

Caillie reported that:

> We crossed the Lin in a canoe, so ill-contrived that it would have upset; it was made of a crooked trunk of a tree, and was very narrow and leaky; every time we stirred, it inclined so much that water came in over the gunwale.[12]

It should be emphasized that this leaky unstable condition of some African watercraft did not necessarily reflect craftsmanship, but instead was the result of other factors. First, a number of these unsatisfactory boats were obtained after these early explorers had stumbled upon some village unannounced and unwelcomed. Their passage across a river was facilitated begrudgingly. On numerous occasions, they were denied use of an adequate vessel and had to settle for something less which they overloaded. Bartering for transportation in some communities resulted in the promise of a dugout from "downstream" or from the opposite bank. Upon delivery, however, the boat was found deficient. In other villages, where water transport and activities were uncommon, these travelers procured the only dugout available. Lastly, the tribute or fee paid to pass through some territory was deemed inadequate and thus the means of water transport provided reflected that dissatisfaction.

The dugout, past and present, has been the basic means of water transport on the African continent and elsewhere (Greenhill, 1976). From the preceding discussion on the encounters and uses of these age-old vessels by travellers to western and central Africa, I have mainly emphasized their size and river worthiness. The dugout is not simply a hollowed-out log of whatever dimensions. It is and can be a working template by which other seaworthy craft evolve. In discussing the evolution of modern boats, Basil Greenhill asserts:

> The fourth root was of much greater significance in the origins of boats than any of the first three. Far more types of boats owe their origin remotely to a hollowed-out log than to a raft, skin or bark boat, for the hollowed log is susceptible to almost limitless development while the very nature of the structure and materials used in rafts, skin and bark boats restricts their development in varying degrees.[13]

One interesting development of African watercraft found in the narratives of Mungo Park and then later in other journals is the jointed or joined dugout.

> The canoes are of a singular construction, each of them being formed of the trunks of two large trees, rendered concave and joined together, not side by side by end ways; the junction being exactly across the middle of the canoe.[14]

This boat was described in 1796 at Sego by Mungo Park as he prepared to ferry across the Niger. Such construction increases both the length and width of a boat (Fig. 3). These jointed boats were observed up and down the Niger also be Caillie, Lander, and Barth on their respective expeditions. One hired by Barth (1857) at Say hundreds of miles southeast of Timbuktu carried his three camels (Fig. 5A) across the Niger in 1853. It was about forty feet long and four or five feet across. A

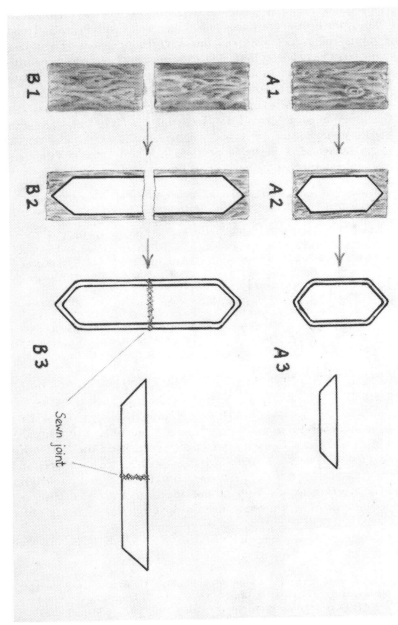

Diagram illustrating the increase in boat size and carrying capacity gained from the "jointed" dugout technique. Felled tree trunks (A1 and B1). Hollowing and shaping of trees (A2 and B2). Finished dugout and jointed boat (A3 and B3).

Malloy - Fig. 3

very similar boat (Malzy, 1946) was still being used in this region as late as 1938 by the Bozos. The Bozos joined their boats with hemp and made the joints waterproof with oakum or vegetable butter. Their large Djenne boats were 33 feet long, 4.95 feet wide and 2.5 feet deep and fitted with a woven straw cabin. The wide distribution of these jointed dugouts emphasizes that they were utilized over hundreds of miles on the Niger in central Africa having changed very little over centuries.

The dugout can be extended by fastening planks or stakes along the gunwale to increase its depth. An extension of the African dugout appears to have been effected before the Europeans penetrated the coast. The Landers observed at the town of Bajiebo on the Niger:

> We have seen today several large canoes, the bottom of which is made of a single tree and built up with planks to a considerable height. In many of them sheds, or houses as they are called, have been erected which are thatched with straw and in which fires are kindled, food prepared, and people sleep, and indeed live together. The roof is circular, and formed in much the same manner as the upper part of a covered wagon in England. These sheds are of the most essential service to the natives, as with their assistance, merchants are enabled to travel with some degree of comfort, with their wives and households several days journey up and down the Niger, without being under the necessity of landing except to purchase provisions, or whenever they feel inclined to do so. As the natives have nothing that equals or answers to pitch, hemp, or tar, they use staples for the purpose of repairing it and keeping the planks together when a canoe becomes leaky.[15]

This extended Nouffie boat appears to have had as its base a punt-like dugout of the type observed twelve days later at Zagozhi (Figs. 4A, 4B).

Probably the most unique boat or ship found in the interior of Africa and having its origin in the dugout was the large ninety to one hundred feet rope sewn plank vessels referred to earlier by Caillie. These deep draughted boats, built of five feet lengths of plank held together entirely by rope, had a deck as well as berths and cooking stove in the hold. From the construction details, they do not appear to have been built on a dugout foundation, however, the Caillie's referral to it as "canoe" suggests otherwise.

Barth describes another plank built boat on a tributary of the Shari flowing into Lake Chad (Fig.5B).

> The joints of the planks are provided with holes through which ropes are passed, overlaid with bands of reed, and are tightly fastened upon them by smaller ropes which are again passed through small holes stuffed with grass.[16]

The rope joined plank boats may have had local origins or may have been related to ancient bhum or dau of the Mediterranean and the Indian Ocean (Hourani, 1951; Greenhill, 1976).

Figure 4A — Sketch of punt-like canoe

Figure 4B — Extended boat derived from the punt

Large African watercraft observed by Henry Barth. Camel carrying boat on Niger at Say.   Fig. 5A

Plank built vessels seen at Kabara and Korome   Fig. 5B

None of the plank built boats mentioned in the narratives examined here possess sails. However if these crafts are related to the plank vessels of the Mediterranean, sails were definitely a part of their past. Local wind and river conditions may have rendered sails useless. For example the huge trading boats discussed by Caillie drew seven feet of water and were propelled by driving poles against the river bottom. These trading craft frequently ran aground (Caillie, 1968) and had to be pushed and dragged into deeper water. This shallow and narrow condition of the Niger between Jenne and Timbuktu may have prevented effective tacking with sails and thus they were omitted and finally forgotten in antiquity. Similarly, the Lake Chad reed boats are known to have originated from the ancient sail-powered reed ships of Egypt. Yet, the boats of Lake Chad are without sails and the very idea of sails on a "kaday" was scoffed at by the Buduma builders of the Ra I (Heyerdahl, 1971).

I have deliberately concentrated on the watercraft of Western and central Africa for this region once formed part of a great inter-locking trade network running from the Mediterranean to the Gulf of Guinea and from the west coast to Lake Chad. The interaction of these diverse peoples through conquest, reconquest, and trade offered countless opportunities for the diffusion of ideas on boats. This brief survey, based mainly on observations well after the height of development of these societies, indicates that traditional African dugout or boat building technology included both extension and expansion techniques used worldwide to make dugouts seaworthy (Greenhill, 1976).

Although additional research is necessary to verify that traditional western and central African watercraft in fact journeyed long distances upon the Atlantic Ocean, it is clear that the capabilities of these boats and their sailors have been underestimated.

NOTES AND REFERENCES

[1]G.R. Crone, *The Voyages of Cadamosto*, London, Hakluyt Society, 1937, p. 57.

[2]Ibid., p. 58.

[3]Ibid., p. 76.

[4]Basil Greenhill, *Archaeology of the Boat*, Middletown, Conn., Wesleyan University Press, 1976, pp. 130-131.

[5]Everyman Park, ed., *Travels of Mungo Park*, New York, E.P. Dutton and Co., 1954, p. 151.

[6]Rene Caillie, *Travels in Central Africa to Timbuctoo,* London, Frank Cass and Co., 1968, I, p. 287.

[7]Ibid., p. 443.

[8]Ibid., II, 9.

[9]Robin Hallett, *The Niger Journal of Richard and John Lander,* New York, Frederick A. Praeger, 1965, pp. 232-233.

[10]Ibid., p. 259.

[11]Park, *Travels,* 54.

[12]Caillie, *Travels in Central Africa,* I, 294.

[13]Greenhill, *Archaeology,* 129.

[14]Park, *Travels,* E.P. Dutton and Co., 1954, p. 151.

[15]Richard Lander, *Expedition to Explore the Course and Termination of the Niger,* London, J. Murray, 1832, p. 261.

[16]Henry Barth, *Travels in North and Central Africa,* London, Longman, Brown, Green, Longman and Roberts, 1857, III, pp. 293-294.

BIBLIOGRAPHY

Barth, Henry. *Travels in North and Central Africa.* 5 vols, London, Longman, Brown, Green, Longman and Roberts, 1857.

Bass, George F. *A History of Seafaring.* London, Thames and Hudson, Ltd., 1972.

Bovill, E.W. *The Golden Trade of the Moors.* New York, Oxford University Press, 1968.

Caillie, Rene. *Travels through Central Africa to Timbuctoo.* 2 vols., London, Frank Cass and Co., 1968.

Crone, G.R. *The Voyages of Cadamosto.* London, Hakluyt Society, 1937.

Defant, Albert. *Physical Oceanography.* Oxford, Pergamon Press, 1961.

Greenhill, Basil. *Archaeology of the Boat.* Middletown, Conn., Wesleyan University Press, 1976.

Hallett, Robin ed., *The Niger Journal of Richard and John Lander.* New York, Frederick A. Praeger, 1965.

Heyerdahl, Thor. "Feasible Ocean Routes to and from the Americas in Pre-Columbian Times," *American Antiquity,* 28, 4, 1963, pp. 482-488.

————————. *The Ra Expeditions.* Garden City, New York, Doubleday and Co., 1971.

Hornell, James. "The Sea-going Mtepe and Dau of the Lamu Archipelago," *Mariner's Mirror*, Jan. 1941, pp. 54-68.

Hourani, G.F. *Arab Seafaring in the Indian Ocean in Ancient and Early Medieval Times.* Princeton, N.J., Princeton University Press, 1951.

Hull, Richard. *Munyakare: African Civilization Before the Baturee.* New York, John Wiley and Sons, 1972.

Jett, Stephen C. "Diffusion versus Independent Development." in Riley, Kelley, Pennington and Rands (eds), *Man Across the Sea,* Austin, University of Texas Press, 1971, pp. 5-53.

Kehoe, Alice. "Small Boats on the North Atlantic." in Riley, Kelley, Pennington and Rands (eds.), *Man Across the Sea,* Austin, University of Texas Press, 1971, pp. 275-292.

Lander, Richard. *Journal of the Expedition to Explore the Course and Termination of the Niger.* London, J. Murray, 1832.

Malzy, P. "Les Bozos du Niger et leurs modes de peche." *Bulletin de l'institut Francais d'Afrique Noire*, 8, 1946, pp. 100-132.

Park, Everyman ed., *Travels of Mungo Park.* London, Everyman's Library, 1954.

Schwerin, Karl H. "Winds across the Atlantic." *Mesoamerican Studies,* No. 6, University Museum, Southern Illinois University, 1970, pp.

Van Sertima, Ivan. *They Came Before Columbus: The African Presence in Ancient America.* New York, Random House, 1977.

AN OUTLINE OF AFRICA'S ROLE IN
THE HISTORY OF PHYSICS

John Pappademos

Summary: *The choice of historical topics and figures found in current physics and physical science texts has the effect of reinforcing the racial stereotypes that denigrate the intellectual and scientific abilities of nonwhites. A survey of seventeen representative texts published since 1970 shows that "not once is a scientific discovery or discoverer identified as being of African orgin. No black scientist is pictured in any of these books nor is a single black credited with any contribution."*

Dr. John Pappademos, Professor of Physics, University of Illinois at Chicago Circle, who conducted this survey, begins the task of revising conventional assumptions about the role of Africans and other nonwhites in the history of physics by outlining some of their contributions.

I. How Physics Texts Distort the History of Physics

The overwhelming majority of students that take elective or required courses in physics or physical science in the U.S. learn of the history of physics through their contact with textbooks of physics as such, rather than by taking a course in the history of the subject. High school and college teachers of physics, while they may be expected to have read more widely about the history of physics than their students, are nonetheless influenced considerably in their concepts of the history of physics by the emphasis commonly given in physics textbook treatments of historical topics. Therefore the concepts held by a very large number of people (those who have taken a physics or physical science course in high school or college) concerning the history of physics are affected strongly both directly and indirectly by the views concerning the subject expressed in physics and science textbooks.

It is of interest to inquire as to whether it is possible that the choice of historical topics and figures found in current physics and physical science texts has the effect of reinforcing the racial stereotypes that denigrate the intellectual and scientific abilities of nonwhites. We have made a survey of 17 textbooks of physics and physical science issued since 1970 by leading U.S. publishing houses.[1-17] The texts were distributed among both calculus and non-calculus types, as well as some introductory physical science and/or astronomy texts (since courses in physical science and astronomy are frequently taught in physics departments). Both college-level and high school-level books were examined. The texts were selected at random except for the requirement that they be published since 1970 (in order that they would be likely to be in current use).

The results of this survey clearly support the view that currently used U.S. physics and physical science texts do indeed tend to reinforce racial stereotypes. This is indicated by the choice of pictures of people which appear in the various texts, the references to the contributions of identified individuals, and the references to the contributions of whole peoples (races, nations, or continents). Few pictures of non-white individuals are used and identified as contributors to the history of physics. Remarkably few references appear to the achievements of the scientists of Persia, the Near East, North Africa, Moorish Spain, China or India. A whole continent (Africa) is deleted from the history of physics: in all 17 books surveyed, not once is a scientific discovery or discoverer identified as being of African origin. No Black scientist is pictured in any of the books*, nor is a single Black scientist credited with any contribution. The picture of science in general and physics in particular that emerges from these books *without exception* is that the cradle of physics was in Europe and that it owes its present development entirely to scientists of the U.S. and Europe (rarely other than white males). As is seen in my survey, in ten [2,3,4,5,6,8,12,13,14,17] there was not a single instance of credit given to a scientist from a country other than the U.S. or Europe*. In these ten texts, no country (other than the U.S. or Europe) was even mentioned as having been the locale of a scientific discovery. Frequently, the work of U.S. or European physicists was praised and/or their work received extensive discussion; this mark of respect was not given to a single non-white physicist.

Another mark of respect is the inclusion of a picture or a portrait of a scientist. As shown in my survey, out of the 17 books surveyed, although there were 94 different scientists appearing in 186 pictures of scientists, Asian scientists were pictured only eight times, including Chandrasekhar, Raman, Yukawa, Ting, and three that were unidentified. There was not a single Black or Latino scientist pictured in any of the books.

* Altogether, 10 pictures of Blacks appear in the 17 books. Of the 10, eight are athletes or musicans[7,8,10,17]; the remaining two are unidentified[10,15].

* A reference to a scientist by name was not counted as a reference to a non-European or U.S. scientist unless the country of the scientist's origin was given, because a person reading the text who was unfamiliar with the name would not be expected to know that association. The notion that only whites have contributed to science is so prevalent that an explicit reference to a scientist's origin is not necessary in order for him or her to be assumed by most readers as being white U.S. or European.

We conclude from the above results of the survey that by neglecting the contribution of non-whites (particularly Blacks) the 17 texts belittle their contributions and effectively promote the view that the progress of physics owes little or nothing to the intellectual ability and labor of other than whites.

Several kinds of objections to the above criticism can be rather easily anticipated. One is that if Blacks and other minorities do not figure very largely in the history of physics as seen in introductory physics texts, it is simply a reflection of the fact that their contributions *have* been minimal. This objection, of course, merely reaffirms the position taken by the textbooks we have surveyed; we believe it is in many cases based on ignorance, and we make a start, at least, to deal with it in the following sections of this paper. Or another objection that might be made would run somewhat as follows: "The authors of a physics text do not intend, and have no obligation, to present a balanced view of the history of physics. Historical passages are inserted only at those points where the *physics* content and the historical insert can be appropriately joined. The author's first responsibility is to the physics content, not the historical content, and it is the former that determines which history is included and which is left out. For example, it is not Africans or Asians, but Galileo, Newton, or Archimedes who are frequently the first historical figures to be discussed in the mechanics section of a physics course; this is because they laid the foundations of the subject of the science of mechanics as it is universally taught today. This objection, which is a relative of the first, has as its unspoken premise a low opinion of the contributions of nonwhite peoples. It also assumes a narrow and almost tautologic definition of physics; namely, that physics is that which is taught in physics courses. One is reminded of Kuhn's paradigms[19]. In the following sections we will attempt to meet the objection by examining in a concrete way the contributions of at least some of the non-white peoples to the development of physics. Obviously, we do not attempt here to write a world history of physics, including the contributions of all peoples to its development. Such a task is far beyond the scope of this paper. But by citing just a few facts about the contributions of non-white peoples, we believe the nature of the distortion cited above will become evident. We devote our greatest emphasis to the contributions of native Africans and those of African descent (although barely scratching the surface even in this limited area), because these have been *totally* omitted in all the texts we have surveyed.

II. *Some of the Contributions of Africans and Other Non-White Peoples to Physics Prior to the Seventeenth Century*

We have seen that the commonly accepted version of the history of physics — at least that version which comes through from a reading of physics texts* — is a thoroughly "Europeanized" version. In this version, little or no acknowledgement is made of the basis laid by the peoples of Africa and the Near East for the later European achievement in science. An immediate consequence of this version is that it lends support and justification for the racist ideas of the superiority of white over peoples of color. Another consequence is that the causes that underlie the development of science in any human society, including the present, become mystified. It is a gross oversimplification and distortion of the history of physics to ignore the many millenia of development of human society that preceded the known European contributions to science (in ancient Greece). More than three thousand years of *recorded* history in Egypt, for example, preceded the Greek philosopher Thales of Miletos, who is cited as the first scientist in several of the books we have surveyed. As George Sarton has pointed out, "The understanding of ancient science has often been spoiled by two unpardonable omissions. The first concerns Oriental science. It is childish to assume that science began in Greece; the Greek "miracle" was prepared by millenia of work in Egypt, Mesopotamia, and possibly in other regions. Greek science was less an invention than a revival".[20] Sarton's statement is perfectly correct except for the fact that he makes the common error of classifying the Egyptian civilization as "Oriental" (Asian) rather than African; we will return to this point later.

The history of physics must surely go back to the very origins of human society, as evolving man began to solve the problems of gathering and producing food, shelter, and clothing. The first thought-out, dynamic experiments must have been done in relation to the development of throwing devices for spears, and in inventing the bow and arrow — the first device utilizing the principle of stored mechanical energy and converting it into kinetic energy.[21] The practical mastery of the principles of mechanics — the oldest branch of physics — grew as man learned to make flint weapons, tools, dwellings, boats, etc.

It is in this light that the total exclusion of Africans from the history of physics appears the most astonishing. Anthropological evidence shows that the origin of man is to be found in Africa. It was in Africa that man first started up along the tool-making path that distinguishes him from the lower forms of life. In the words of L.S.B. Leakey, "In every country that one is drawn into a conversation about Africa, the question is regularly asked by people who should know better 'But what has Africa contributed to world progress?' The critics of Africa forget that men of science are today, with few exceptions, satisfied that Africa was the birthplace of man himself, and that for many hundreds

---

* There are now available some books in English on the history of science which, to varying degrees, refute this version. See the Bibliography.

of centuries thereafter, Africa was in the forefront of all world progress".[22]

Because of the climate of Africa below the Sahara, which is generally unfavorable for the preservation of much archeological data, and because not enough archeological work has been done in sub-Saharan Africa, we know far too little about the history of science and technology in that region. However, evidence such as the Ishango bone tool handle[23] found in central Africa indicates the progress during the Paleolithic era being made in man's ability to use abstract mathematical operations. The importance of the Ishango bone has been emphasized by Bernal, who termed it the "oldest scientific document we have so far".[24]

After man first began to raise crops in Nubian Egypt some 17,000 years ago[25], a knowledge of astronomy became important in response to the needs of more accurate predictions of events affecting agriculture such as the seasons and the annual overflow of the Nile. As societies developed and trading advanced, knowledge of measurement, mathematics, conversion of units of area, length, volume, weight, time, etc. arose. Sometime after around 6000 B.C., as the agricultural settlements of the upper Nile spread northward to the delta, this knowledge became highly advanced as a brilliant urban civilization rapidly developed. Over the years, many prominent Western scholars have tended to characterize this ancient Egyptian civilization as essentially Caucasian. In Hollywood portrayals of famous Egyptians such as Cleopatra, white actors and actresses have been used and the practice continues. But among scholars today it is generally accepted that ancient Egypt was essentially an African civilization. It is now clear from a number of lines of evidence that to call the North African and Nile Valley peoples of ancient times "white" is merely a "latter-day mystification of the racialist sort", as Basil Davidson puts it[26]. The unmistakably African features of pictures and statues of a number of ancient Egyptian gods and Pharoahs such as Menes, the founder of the First Dynasty (see Fig. I) the god Osiris; the Pharoah Zoser (Third Dynasty); Cheops (Fourth Dynasty); Mycerinus (Fourth Dynasty); Mentuhotep I (11th Dynasty). and so on[27] bespeak the Black origin of the Egyptian civilization. A most convincing line of evidence is that of the written records of ancient historians such as the Greek Herodotos, who characterized the color of the Egyptians as black wherever the question of their color was mentioned and had no difficulty in seeing the close kinship between the Ethiopians and the Egyptians[28]. Another line of evidence indicating the kinship of the early Egyptians and other African peoples is linguistic: Diop[29] has studied the relation between ancient Egyptian and Wolof, the language

Narmer (or Menes). First Pharaoh of Egypt, who unified Upper and Lower Egypt for the first time. He is assuredly neither Aryan, Indo-European, nor Semitic, but unquestionably Black.

Pappademos — Fig. 1

of his own country (Senegal), finding much in the basic structure that is common. In this regard, Sarton's opinion is worth quoting[30]: "Con sider the Egyptian number words. The words for 1,2,3,4,5, and 10 are African, those for 6,7,8, and 9 are Semitic. What does that mean? It means the original linguistic stock was African, for surely the words for 1,2,3,4, and 5 are among the first to be needed and coined in any language; it also means...that the number base of the early Egyptians was five. Later contacts...introduced Semitic features into their language plus the base ten". Whether or not the introduction of the base ten was independently developed in Egypt, in lands south of Egypt, or was an Asian import remains to be seen, but at any rate the linguistic evidence alone would make it very difficult to argue for a European or Asian origin of the Egyptian civilization.

To assess the level of scientific development attained by the ancient Egyptians, we may turn to the opinions of the ancient Greeks, whose civilization developed thousands of years after that of the Egyptians. The Greeks generally viewed Egypt as the seat of scientific knowledge. Socrates, in the *Phaidros*, called the Egyptian god Thoth, (see Fig. 2) the inventor of writing, astronomy, and geometry[31]. Herodotos had a similarly high opinion of Egyptian science, stating that the Greeks learned geometry from the Egyptians[32]. It was Democritos of Abdera's boast that his own scientific abilities were unsurpassed in the world, not exceeded by even the Egyptian scholars[33]. The most brilliant of the Greek students of science, such as Thales of Miletos (c. 600 B.C.), Democritos, Pythagoras, and Eudoxos (408-355 B.C.) travelled to Egypt to study[34]. Seneca[35] tells us that Eudoxos had to go Egypt to study planetary motion; at that time Egypt must have been the world's leading center of astronomy. Pythagoras (c. 6th century B.C.) spent no less than 22 years in Egypt studying astronomy, geometry, and the mysteries[34].

It is small wonder that the achievements of the Egyptians would excite the admiration of the ancients. They still do today; the scope and precision of their monuments and pyramids would challenge the abilities of today's engineers, 5000 years later. The technological progress of the ancient Egyptians are of importance for any student of the history of physics, since it is well known that advances in theoretical physics not only give rise to technological progress, but are themselves stimulated by advances in technology. The Egyptians were centuries ahead of Europeans in mining, metallurgy (including metal alloying), metals fabrication (including making wire and rivets), glass-making, medical science (including internal medicine, anatomy, and surgery), development of complex irrigation systems, carpetry, etc.[36,37,38,39,40]. Although they apparently did not use iron or steel extensively until much later, there is evidence the Egyptians wre smelting iron and steel and even welding these metals as early as 1500-1200 B.C.[41,42]. The Egyptians were highly advanced in shipbuilding as well. The walls of the Temple of Mut in Asher depict an expedition of the Ethiopian King Piankhi (25th Dynasty) in which ships of up to 45 cubits (23.6 meters) were employed. The obelisk barges of Queen Hatshepsut (around 1500 B.C.) have been estimated[43] at 95 meters in length, with a beam of 32 meters and a deadweight of 2500 tons. Such a barge would dwarf Lord Nelson's flagship the H.M.S. Victory at the battle of Trafalgar (1803 A.D.) which was 56.7 meters by 15.87 meters, weighing 2162 tons. The two obelisks transported by these barges were 108 cubits (57 meters) high, each weighing 2400 tons. (They have since perished, perhaps destroyed by Hatsepshut's rival and half-brother, Thutmos III.) The barge was hauled by 30 tugboats, manned by almost 1000 oarsmen. Egyptian obelisks were of both religious and astronomical significance, about which more later.

With the burning of the great library of Alexandria (see below), and the plundering of Egyptian archeological sites over the centuries, much has been lost of the history of Egyptian science, and few names of ancient Egyptian scholars and scientists survive today. One such name is that of Senmut, the chief architect of Queen Hatshepsut, and another is that of Imhotep, King Zoser's chief advisor and architect (around 3000 B.C.). Imhotep was probably the world's first multi-genius. He was an astronomer, poet, philosopher, engineer, and world-famous physician. (He also was an astrologer, which was common among first-rank scientists as late as the time of Kepler, in 16-th century Europe.) His fame as a physician was so great that after his death he was apotheosized and worshipped as the god of medicine as late as the Christian era. Over 2000 years before Archimedes (who is usually stated to be the inventor of the lever) Imhotep must have been a master of physical principles such as the lever and inclined plane[44]. He designed the step-pyramid of Sakkara, the world's first large stone building.

To the Egyptians we owe the concepts of most of the fundamental physical quantities; distance, area, volume, weight, and time. Europe is indebted to Egypt for the invention of standards, units, and methods for accurate measurement of all of these quantities. (Two ancient Egyptian scales are shown in Fig. 3.) We have already alluded to the fact that the ancient Greeks recognized that the Egyptians were the inventors of geometry. The few papyri which have survived show that they (the Egyptians) could compute the areas and volumes of abstract geometric figures, including the circle's area accurate to 0.6%[45]. The Greeks and the Romans both continued to use the Egyptian methods of arithemetic, they being superior to their own for many types of calculations[46]. To the Egyptians we owe the idea of letting a symbol represent an unknown quantity in algebra. The symbol they used was their word "aha" (heap), and they used it in solving equations of the first and second degree[45]. More than once, the accusation has been made that the Egyptians knew nothing of scientific proof, their mathematics being nothing more than a collection of computational recipes. Gillings[47] has effectively answered that criticism, in showing how the problem statements of the papyri have general applicability. While most authorities agree that the Pythagorean theorem was known to the ancient Mesopotamians 2000 years before Pythagoras (Pythagoras is not known to have *proved* the theorem; he merely announced in [48], there has been controversy over whether it was known to the ancient Egyptians as well. In a forthcoming article in *Historica Mathematica*, Beatrice Lumpkin points out that not only is a knowledge of the Pythagorean theorem implied by problems presented in a papyrus dating from the 12th Dynasty (2000 B.C.) but the idea of the Pythagorean Theorem is implied by the Egyptian use of the double remen as a unit of length measure.

The scientific measurement of time started with the Egyptians. Based on their stellar observations, the calendar they developed as far back as 4241 B.C. is the one we use today, with only two minor

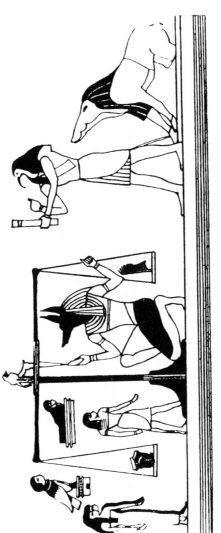

Fig. 2

The figure shows a balance being used to weigh the heart of a person, who has just entered the spirit world. The dog-head god Anubis is doing the weighing. The ibis-headed figure on the right who is recording the result of the measurement is Thoth, the god of wisdom. Since the two lever arms are about equal, it would seem that the heart in the left hand pan is only as heavy as a feather (pan on right). It is to be noted, however, that the feather was the Egyptian symbol for righteousness. The scene is from The Book of the Dead (c. 1500 B.C.), which was compiled from earlier writings called the Pyramid Texts dating to bout 2400 B.C.

Pappademos — Fig. 2

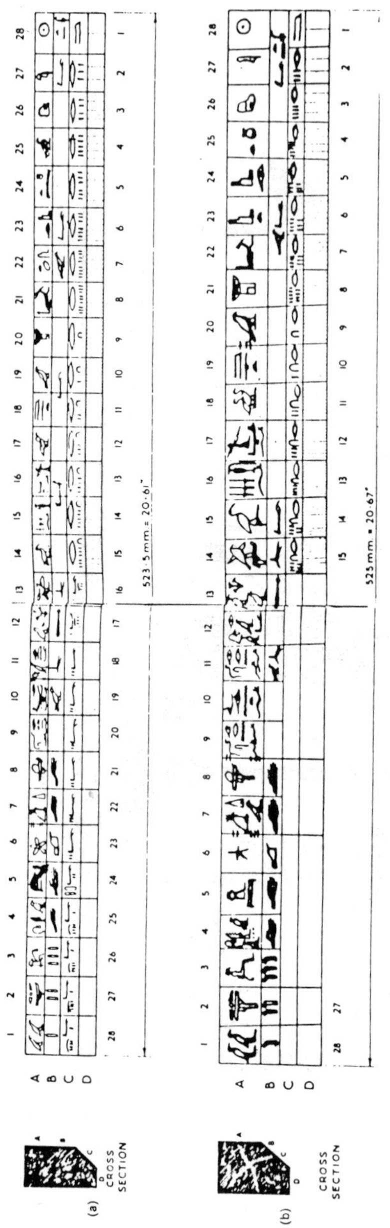

Fig. 3

Egyptian measures of length. The ancient Egyptian primary unit of length was the cubit — the length of the forearm. Thus the hieroglyphic sign for the cubit was the forearm and all sub-divisions of digits of fingers, palms, great and little spans and the foot can be seen in these cubit of Amenhotep 1 (a) and of his vizer (b) c. 1500 B.C.

Pappademos — Fig. 3

modifications. The Egyptian calendar year contained 365 days: 12 months of 30 days each, plus five festival days. Otto Neugebauer has termed the Egyptian calendar "the only intelligent calendar which ever existed in human history"[49]. This is because "the strictly lunar calendar of the Babylonians, with its dependance on all the complicated variations of the lunar motion, as well as the chaotic Greek calendars, depending not only on the moon but also on local politics for its intercalations, were obviously far inferior to the invariable Egyptian calendar. It is a serious problem to determine the number of days between two given Babylonian or Greek new year's days, say 50 years apart. In Egypt this interval is simply 50 times 365"[49]. It should be pointed out that unknown to the Europeans, the Mayan Indians had independently developed a 365-day calendar. However, it is the Egyptian one which is the parent of our own. The importance of the Egyptian calendar to science is emphasized by V. Gordon Childe, who has pointed out[50] that it is "the first recorded achievement of the application of numbers to accurately recorded observations."

To the Egyptians we owe the practice of dividing the day into 24 hours. Our modern practice of starting the day at midnight dates back to the Egyptians[51], as well as the origin of the names of the days of the week[52]. For measurement of smaller intervals of time, the Egyptians used sundials and water clocks as well as tables of star culminations and rising for nocturnal observation[53]. The most ancient sundial known is Egyptian, dating back to the time of Thutmosis III (15th century B.C.)[54]. The water clock was invented in Egypt, about 2000 B.C.[55] The water clock was still in use in Europe as late as the time of Galileo, who used one in his experiments on accelerated motion.

Not for nothing did the ancient Greeks view Egypt as the birthplace of astronomy. In Sarton's words[56], "The astronomic ability of the early Egyptians is proved not only by their calendar, tables of star culminations, and tables of star risings, but also by some of their instruments, such as ingenious sundials or the combination of a plumb line with a forked rod that enabled them to determine the azimuth of a star". Their astronomers were also aware of the precision of the equinoxes, as is indicated by the successive reorientation of the axes of a number of their stellar temples[57].

Finally, in connection with the measurement of time, it is appropriate to point out the religious and astronomical significance of obelisks. Obelisks, which were found all over Egypt, were a symbol of the sun-god Ra. The earliest known date to 3100 B.C.[58] From the shadows cast by the obelisks in the brilliant Egyptian sun, information relevant to timekeeping could be gained: the date of the summer solstice (our June 21), when the obelisk casts the shortest shadow, the

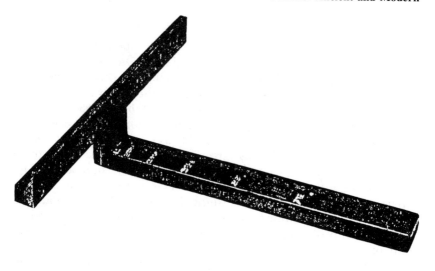

Fig. 4

Reproduction of an Egyptian shadow clock of about 1000 B.C. It was placed with the cross-bar in the east during the morning and in the west in the afternoon. The hours are marked by the symbols on horizontal scale.
                                                                    Pappademos —Fig. 4

winter solstice (our December 21) when the sun is lowest and the shadow the longest; and the dates of the vernal and autumnal equinoxes (March 21 and September 21), when the shadows fall along an east-west line at sunrise and sunset. (See Figs. 5 and 6) Clearly, the taller the obelisk, the longer its shadow and the more accurate the measurement. Therefore, the tendency seen in the history of Egypt to build ever taller and bigger obelisks may not have been due simply to the vanity of the Pharoahs. And of course it is not enough to simply make the obelisk taller. It has to be made bigger as well, in order to have sufficient structural strength. Thus the enormous size of some of the later obelisks, as indicated previously in this article.

During the 6th century B.C., Egypt came under the domination of Persia, and later was conquered by Alexander the Great. For more than seven centuries following Alexander's death in 323 B.C., centers of science and culture flourished in Alexandria (Egypt), in Syracuse, and in other locations around the Mediterranean. This was the period of Archimedes, Euclid, and others whose scientific achievements have been given just recognition — the so-called Hellenistic period. In this period, the leading center of science was in the African city of Alexandria, where the world's first university was established. What is

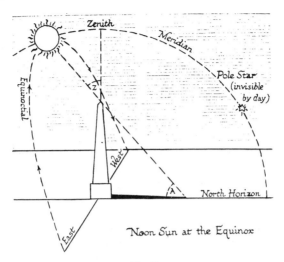

Fig. 5.

The noon or shortest shadow of the Obelisk or shadow clock points due north towards the celestial pole.
At the equinoxes (March 21st *and* September 23rd) *the sun rises due east and sets due west, and*
the observer is at the centre of its semicircular track, called the equinoctial or celestial equator.

Pappademos — Fig. 5

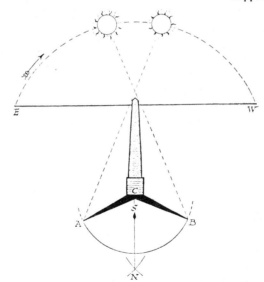

Fig. 6 — FIXING THE MERIDIAN IN ANCIENT TIMES

The method of equal altitudes was used to get the direction of the north point exactly. The points at
which this shadow just touched a circle traced on the sand around the shadow clock shortly before and
afternoon were noted, and the arc was bisected.

Pappademos — Fig. 6

perhaps not so well-known is the multinational and multiracial character[59] of Alexandria and the other centers of culture during this period. It is known that the conquering Greeks in Egypt practiced a policy of assimilation; many of their generals married Egyptian women and adopted the Egyptian religion. Diogenes Laertios, the third century Greek biographer, speaks of a black Ptolemaios of Alexandria[60]. Frequently it is taken for granted that because the great scientists of Alexandria like Euclid (author of not only the classic work on geometry but a book on optics as well), Heron (author of works on mechanics), and Claudios Ptolemaios (author of what was to remain the Bible of astronomy for fourteen centuries) were Greek, because they wrote in Greek and in some cases even had Greek names. Whatever their nationality, it was natural that they should write in Greek, for that was the language of science at the time; also, during that time Hellenization of names was common among other nationalities[61]. Practically nothing is known of Euclid other than that he lived in Alexandria around 300 B.C.; nothing is known of Ptolemy (Claudios Ptolemaios) either, other than that he flourished in Alexandria between 127 and 151 A.D.[62] It is interesting to note that the calendar reform usually attributed to Julius Caesar (in 45 B.C.)was actually done with the scientific advice of a famous Egyptian scientist Alexandria, Sosigenes[63,64]. There is strong evidence[65] that Hero (1st century A.D.) was actually an Egyptian, not Greek. Hero is best known for his invention of numerous devices based on principles of mechanics; Hero's Fountain, the first steam engine, etc., but he also wrote works on theoretical principles of mechanics and optics as well. (Fig. 7 illustrates Hero's engine, the first steam engine) More than sixteen centuries before the famous French physicist Fermat, who is always credited with the discoverer of the principle of least time in optics, Heron used the principle of least optical path to explain reflection.[66].

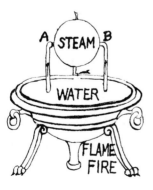

"*Fig. 7. Hero's Engine — the first steam engine. Steam from the boiling water rises through the vertical pipes and enters the spherical steam chamber at A and B. A and B serve as pivot points about which the chamber revolves, driven by the reaction from the steam escaping through the two small nozzles. The design of this famous engine, which undoubtedly served as the inspiration for engines built during the Industrial Revolution in Europe centuries later, is still used today in physics lecture demonstations and other applications.*"

Pappademos — Fig. 7

During the period following the fall of the Roman Empire, a cultural and scientific decline set in Europe that was to last for centuries; however, the spread of Islam in the East, North Africa, and in Spain was accompanied by the establishment of great centers of learning in Baghdad, Basra, Tunis, Cairo, Cordova, and other places. It is interesting to note that an important scientific event of 1054 A.D. — the super nova explosion — is not known to have been recorded in Europe, but was recorded by the Chinese and by Ibn Butlan, an Egyptian physician[67]. It was in this period that the Mohammedans founded universities, four hundred years before the first European ones. Our custom of wearing the academic cap and gown dates from these Mohammendan universities[68]. It was in this period (10th-11th century A.D.) that the great physicist Alhazen lived in Egypt. He gave a scientific explanation of refraction, reflection, focusing with lenses, the pinhole camera, spherical aberration, and binocular vision. He built spherical and parabolic mirrors, and was the first to calculate the height of the atmosphere using a correct conception of air pressure[69]. Alhazen's works were studied by Roger Bacon, Kepler, and in fact practically all students of science in Europe.

It is difficult to overemphasize the importance of the scientific work in Arabic for the emergence of European science in the medieval period. The systematic translation of Arabic works into Latin were first introduced to Europe by Constantine the African, and became highly sought after by aspiring young European scientists of the day. Constantine, the African, was also the first professor of the first European university (Salerno, c. 1000 A.D.)[70]

We have here mentioned only two of the Arab, Persian, African, Jewish, and scientists of other nationalities who wrote in Arabic. Space forbids us to mention more. Taton[71] lists 102 outstanding scientists and scholars of this period in which Arabic was the universal scientific language.

If the contributions of the Arab, Jewish, Persian, Indian, and Chinese to science during the medieval period are virtually ignored in U.S. textbooks of physics, still less is anything said of what was happening in the African civilizations south of the Sahara. Universities had been founded at Timbuktu and Jenne in the Empire of Mali (13th century A.D.)[72] A veritable revolution in Iron Age technology was sweeping across Africa, introducing profound social changes.[73] Recent research has shown that over 1500 years ago, Africans in what is now Tanzania were making carbon steel in blast furnaces superior to anything in Europe at the time. As P. Schmidt and D. Avery put it, "This knowledge will help to change scholarly and popular ideas that technological sophistication developed in Europe but not in Africa"[74].

III. *Africans in the More Recent History of Physics*

We have shown that since the dawn of human history, the genius of African peoples has contributed to the development of science. Now we come to the so-called "Classical" and "Modern" periods of physics — periods in which at first Europe, and later the U.S. and Europe, became the centers of scientific progress. Space does not permit us here to detail the enormous price Africa has had to pay to make it possible for capitalism in Europe to make such rapid progress in the 17th through the 19th centuries, stimulating scientific advances. Discussions can be found in the excellent works of DuBois[75] and by Walter Rodney[76]. Suffice it to note that the rape of Africa through the slave trade alone continued for about four centuries (1445-1870), and it has been estimated that in that time there were ten million slaves landed alive in the Americas, Atlantic Islands, and Europe. (This estimate is a very low one, frequently used by apologists seeking to minimize the effects of the slave trade in holding back the development of Africa)[76]. Thus, in the lifetime of Sir Isaac Newton (1642-1727), while he pondered the laws of motion and gravitation, at least two million able-bodied men and women were forcibly taken from Africa. The number of deaths and injuries through the war and in the process of transporting the slaves must have been many times that figure. Sometimes the connection between the slave trade and European technological development was very direct; West Indian slave owners directly financed James Watts' famous steam engine, for which he expressed his eternal gratitude[77]. These facts may give just an inkling of why European scientific and technological progress has been so rapid, while Africa's has been held back. But Black men and women have continued, in spite of all obstacles, to play a part in physics and in science. Here in the U.S., where our data are more readily accessible, we know of many who have overcome the almost impossible barriers of racism to play a part in physics. Yet the references, the pictures, and emphases of the 17 books we surveyed give the impression that Black men and women played no part in the recent history of physics. Only a little research is needed to convince oneself that this statement is false[78]. Among Blacks living in the U.S. who have made important contributions to physics, the following are just a few: Meredith Gourdine (1929-), best known for his pioneering work in electrogasdynamics and who now heads his own research and development company in New Jersey; James Harris, co-discoverer of the transuranium elements 104 and 105; George Carruthers, designer of the far UV camera/spectrograph which was used in the earth's first moon-based observatory (Apollo 16) and which was later used to photograph Comet Kohoutek from Skylab 4; Earl Shaw, a sharecropper's son from Clarksdale, Mississippi, who is now a physicist at Bell Laboratories and who, in 1970, was the co-inventor of the spin-flip tunable Raman laser; Walter Massey, the scientific director of the leading energy research center in the U.S. (Argonne National Laboratory); and Shirley Jackson, who did research in the theory of elementary particles for two years at Fermilab and is now a scientist at Bell Laboratories.

Although a number of references to white contributors to progress in technology were found in the 17 books surveyed, no mention was made of outstanding Black inventors such as Lewis Latimer (1848-1928), who patented a process for making carbon filament for light bulbs, helped install the carbon filament lighting system in New York, Philadelphia, Montreal, and London, joined the Edison research organization and wrote the book *Incandescent Electric Lighting* which became a guide for lighting engineers[79], Norbert Rillieaus, who revolutionized the sugar refining industry, and many more.

IV. *Conclusion*

As we close this discussion of the seminal role played by African peoples in physics and other fields of science from ancient times up to the present, it is appropriate to confront a prevalent slander against African science that is probably as old as racism itself. One version has it that ancient Egyptian science (or in more recent times, the contributions of Black inventors like Latimer, McCoy, Matzeliger, etc.) may be science, but not *pure* science (implying that it somehow takes intellectual abilities of a higher order to work in the field of "pure" science, or that one has to be motivated by abstract intellectual curiosity to work in "pure" science). Another form taken by this tale has been that the science (physics, astronomy, mathematics, etc.) of the ancient Egyptians was purely *practical* in character, with no evidence of the abstract thinking and generalization characteristic of true science; it was the "abstract spirit"[80] of the Greeks which gave them the right to be called the first true scientists. These myths are again basically "latter-day mystifications of the racialist sort", to use Davidson's phrase. No "abstract spirit" is possessed by people of one race but not by another. Whether in paleolithic times or in the physics research laboratories of today, science has always possessed a two-fold character; on the one hand, it is impelled by an intellectual curiosity, and requires abstract thinking; on the other hand, scientific activity ultimately arises from the basic productive life of mankind, in response to very practical needs. Examples of this in physics are well-known: Carnot's Theorem, which sets a theoretical upper limit for the efficiency of any heat engine and which is directly related to the Second Law of Thermodynamics, was discovered by an engineer while trying to learn how to improve steam engines. It is hard to imagine how Newton's laws of mechanics would have been discovered in the absence of *both* (a) intellectual curiosity and (b) the stimulus provided by the needs of gunnery and navigation in the period of the rise of European trade, colonization, and capitalist production.

The ability to conceptualize, to think abstractly, to generalize, to discover new laws of physics, is shared by peoples of all races, and Africans take second place to no one in their record of accomplishment in this aspect of human cultural life.

Acknowledgement

It is a pleasure to acknowledge my debt to Ibrahim Sundiata, Beatrice Lumpkin, Dalvan Coger, and Harold Rogers for fruitful discussions during the course of this work. I am especially grateful to Linda Nelson for her help in getting data about Black physicists.

REFERENCES

1. Apfel & Hynek, *Architecture of the Universe*, Menlo Park, Cal., Benjamin/Commings, 1972.
2. Blackwood, Kelly, and Bell. *General Physics (4th ed.)*, New York: Wiley, 1973.
3. Carr & Weidner, *Physics From the Ground Up*. New York: McGraw-Hill, 1971.
4. S. Gartenhaus, *Physics*. New York: Holt, Rinehart, and Winston, 1975.
5. D. Halliday & R. Resnick, *Fundamentals of Physics, Revised Printing*. New York: John Wiley, 1974.
6. Hood, *Physics: A Modern Perspective*. Altanta: Houghton-Mifflin, 1975.
7. H. O. Hooper & P. Gywnne, *Physics and the Physical Perspective*. New York: Harper & Row, 1977.
8. J. Kane & M. Sternheim, *Life Science Physics*. New York: John Wiley, 1978.
9. J. Marion, *General Physics with Bioscience Essays*. New York: John Wiley, 1979.
10. F. Miller, Jr., Th. Dillon, and M. Smith, *Concepts in Physics* (2nd ed.). New York: Harcourt Brace Jovanovitch, 1974. (High-school level).
11. Sears, Zemansky, & Young, *College Physics (4th ed)*. Reading, Massachusetts: Addison-Wesley, 1975.
12. G. Shapiro, *Physics Without Math*. Englewood Cliffs, N.J.: Prentice-Hall, 1979.
13. Smith & Cooper, *Elements of Physics (4th ed.)*. New York: McGraw-Hill, 1979.
14. Stehle, *Physics: The Behavior of Particles*. New York: Harper & Row, 1971.
15. R. Stollberg & Faith Hall, *Physics: Fundamentals & Frontiers* (Revised ed.). Boston: Houghton Mifflin, 1975. (High-school level).
16. Tilley & Thumm, *College Physics*. Menlo Park: Cummings, 1971.
17. P. Tipler, *Physics*. New York: Worth Publishers, 1976.
18. This was Madame Curie, in Ref. 16, p. 31.
19. T. S. Kuhn, *The Structure of Scientific Revolutions (2nd ed.)*. Chicago: University of Chicago Press, 1970.
20. George Sarton, *A History of Science, Vol I*. New York, W. W. Norton, 1952, p. ix.
21. J. D. Bernal, *The Extension of Man: A History of Physics Before the Quantum*. Cambridge, Mass.: The MIT Press, 1972, p. 40.
22. L. S. B. Leakey, *Progress and Evolution of Man in Africa*.
23. Claudia Zaslavsky, *Journal of African Civilizations, 1 No. 2* (November 1979)
24. J. D. Bernal, op. cit., p. 25.
25. Wendorf et al., *Science* (September 28, 1979).
26. B. Davidson, *Africa in History*. (New revised edition) New York: Collier Books, 1974, p. 10.

27. Cheikh Anta Diop, *The African Origin of Civilization*. New York: Lawrence Hill & Co., translation published 1974.

28. Herodotos in: *The Greek Historians*. New York: Random House, 1942 (Rawlinson translation), pp. 115, 130, 131.

29. Cheikh Anta Diop, *Parente Genetique de l'Egyptian Pharaonique et des Langues Negros Africaines*. IFAN, Dakar, 1977. An English translation of this work is now in preparation. Also see his The African Origin of Civilization (prev. cited), pp. 153-155.

30. G. Sarton, op. cit., p. 23.

31. Quoted in Sarton, op. cit., p. 116.

32. Quoted in Sarton, op. cit., p. 115.

33. Quoted by Sarton, op. cit., p. 116. The quotation's source is a work by Clement of Alexandria (155 A.D.-220 A.D.), one of the fathers of the Christian church. Clement also shows the barbarian (foreign-jp) origins of Greek philosophy and almost every other act. Clement's work has been translated by William Wilson (2 vols.): Edinburgh, 1867-69.

34. G. Sarton, op. cit., pp. 170, 200, 441.

35. Quoted by G. J. Allman, in: *Greek Geometry*. Dublin, 1889, p. 133.

36. G. Sarton, op. cit., pp. 40-50.

37. D. A. Fisher, *The Epic of Steel*. New York: Harper & Row, 1963, p. 36.

38. H. H. Coghlan, *Notes on the Prehistoric Metallurgy of Copper and Bronze in the Old World*. Oxford: Oxford University Press, 1951, P. 95.

39. ibid., p. 95.

40. R. J. Forbes, *Metallurgy in Antiquity*. Leiden: 1950, p. 105.

41. H. H. Coghlan, *Notes on Prehistoric and Early Iron in the Old World*. Oxford: 1956, p. 135.

42. ibid., p. 66.

43. B. Landstrom, *Ships of the Pharoahs*. New York: Doubleday, p. 129.

44. C. G. Fraser, *Half-hours With Great Scientists: The Story of Physics*. New York: Reinhold Publishing Corp., 1948, p. 11.

45. G. Sarton, op. cit., pp. 35-40.

46. Sir William Dampier, *A History of Science* (4th ed.). Cambridge: 1949, p. 42.

47. R. J. Gillings, *Mathematics in the Time of the Pharoahs*, Cambridge, Mass.: MIT Press, 1972, pp. 232-233.

48. G. Sarton, op. cit., p. 10.

49. O. Neugebauer, *The Exact Sciences in Antiquity*. New York: Harper, 1962, p. 81.

50. V. Gordon Childe, *New Light on the Most Ancient East*. New York: Praeger, 1953, p. 3.

51. Hanbury Brown, FRS, *Man and the Stars*. Oxford University Press, 1978, p. 1.

52. Giorgio Abetti, *The History of Astronomy*. New York: Henry Schumann, 1952, p. 21.

53. Rene Taton (ed.), *History of Science: Ancient and Medieval Science*. New York: Basic Books, 1957, p. 39.

54. Rene R. J. Roh, *Sundials: History, Theory, and Practice*. University of Toronoto Press, 1965, p. 5.

55. Alexander Pogo, "Egyptian Water Clocks". Isis *25*, 403-425 (1936), with illustrations.

56. G. Sarton, op. cit., p. 30.

57. Giorgio de Santillana, in the preface to Norman Lockyer, *The Dawn of Astronomy*. Cambridge, Mass.; The MIT Press, 1964, p. ix.

58. Harrison J. Cowan, *Time and its Measurement*. Cleveland: The World Publishing Co., 1958, p. 18.

59. Frank M. Snowden, Jr., *Blacks in Antiquity*. Cambridge, Mass.: Harvard University Press, 1970.

60. Diogenes Laertios, x, 16-21, as translated by R.D. Hicks. Loeb Classical Library, 1925.

61. M. Hadas, *Hellenistic Culture*, New York: Columbia University Press, 1959, p. 35.

62. René Taton, op. cit., p. 319.

63. G. Sarton, *A History of Science: Hellenistic Science and Culture in the Last Three Centuries B.C.* Cambridge, Mass.: Harvard University Press, 1959, p. 322.
64. René Taton, op. cit., pp. 213, 264.
65. James Gow, *A Short History of Greek Mathematics.* New York: G.E. Stechert & Co., 1923, p. 285.
66. René Taton, op. cit., p. 300.
67. K. Brecher et al., *Nature*, Vol. 273, pp. 728-730 (June 29, 1978).
68. J. D. Bernal, op. cit., p. 11.
69. *World Who's Who in Science*, lst ed., Marquis Whos's Who Inc., 1968.

70. *Encyclopedia Brittanica*, 14th ed., article on "Universities".
71. Rene Taton, op. cit., p. 399.
72. B. Davidson, op. cit., pp. 82-87.
73. ibid., p. 72.
74. P. Schmidt and D. Avery, "Complex Iron Smelting and Prehistoric Culture in Tanzania", Science (September, 1978). Reprinted in *Journal of African Civilizations 1*, No. 1, April, 1979.
75. W.E.B. DuBois, *The World and Africa*, enlarged ed. New York: International Publishers, 1965.
76. Walter Rodney, *How Europe Underdeveloped Africa.* Bogle-L'Ouverture Publications, 141 Coldershaw Road. London W. 13, 1972. Also published by Tanzania Publishing House, P.O. Box 2138, Dar es Salaam, 1972, p. 105.
77. ibid., p. 96.
78. John Henrik Clarke, "African-Americans in Science and Invention — A Bibliographical Guide", *Journal of African Civilizations 1*, No. 2 (November, 1979).
79. John Henrik Clarke, "Lewis Latimer, Bringer of the Light", *Journal of African Civilizations Vol. 1*, No. 2, 73-81 (November, 1979).
80. G.J. Allman, *Greek Geometry.* New York: Arno Press, 1976, p. 7.

BIBLIOGRAPHY

1. J.D. Bernal, *The Extension of Man: A History of Physics Before the Quantum.* Cambridge, Mass.; The MIT Press, 1972. Also, by the same author, see *Science in History* (3 vols.). Also from MIT Press.
2. W.E.B. DuBois, *The World and Africa,*, enlarged ed. New York: International Publishers, 1965.
3. R. J. Gillings, *Mathematics in the Time of the Pharoahs.* Cambridge, Mass.: The MIT Press, 1972.
4. John G. Jackson, *Introduction to African Civilizations.* New York, 1970.
5. *Journal of African Civilizations* Vol. 1, No. 2. The entire issue is devoted to African science and technology.
6. Walter Rodney, *How Europe Underdeveloped Africa.* Bogle L'Ouverture Publications, 141 Coldershaw Road. London W. 13, 1972. Also published by Tanzania Publishing House, P.O. Box 2138, Dar es Salaam, 1972.
7. J. A. Rogers, *Africa's Gift to America.* New York; Helga M. Rogers, 1961.
8. George Sarton, *A History of Science* (Vol. I). New York: W.w. Norton, 1952.

THE ANCIENT AKAN SCRIPT:
A REVIEW OF *SANKOFA*, BY NIANGORAN-BOUAH

Willard R. Johnson

Summary: This article previews work of the Ivorian professor, Niangoran Bouah, who has shown that the so-called Akan "gold weights" are really a kind of encyclopedia that preserves in miniature the objects and ideas of their ancient culture. Letting the data and the Akan royal officials speak for themselves, he corrects former notions that these objects were merely artistic devices, or at best, either weights or mnemonic aids for citing proverbs. Bouah shows that the objects preserve all the symbols of the ancient Numidian or Libyan writing system, plus some extra symbols. Bouah shows that the Akan people may have contributed to, and not simply borrowed from, the ancient civilizations of Northeast Africa. The article also argues that writing need not have had a single origin, and that black Africans in ancient Nubia and Egypt probably invented its major components.

The book that is discussed in this article concerns the small brass objects that have widely come to be called "Ashanti Gold Weights," and that often take the form of figurines of animals, plants and other objects, or that bear markings and patterns that Western observers have generally considered to be merely artistic and esthetic decoration. This book argues that these symbols are actually relics of the ancient writing of the Akan people (of which the Ashanti are one among many groups), a writing very similar to the script that was used in the Saharan area of what is now Libya. The Akan people, who are now located along the West African coast in the Ivory Coast and Ghana, are known to have migrated from this Saharan area hundreds and hundreds of years ago. The book indicates that these objects are not best thought of as "weights" at all, because only a very small proportion of them were used in the process of weighing gold, which is what the Portuguese saw them used for and from whom we have derived the designation. Actually they seem to have been the way the Akan people recorded their body of knowledge, perhaps at the time of their migrations from the desert. They represent a miniaturization of the world and constitute a kind of encyclopedia.

The book's author sets his task out in the *Avant Propos*, "to know if black Africans ever knew (had) writing in the way that term is generally understood." He does not argue that they invented it on their own, although important arguments on that issue are also provided here. Nor

PH. 5 à 16 — Exemples
de symboles figurant
sur les poids akan.

Akan symbols represented on the "gold weights." From Niangoran-Bouah's
Sankofa, *reviewed by Willard R. Johnson (M.I.T.)*   Johnson - Fig. 1

does he argue that it is a complete writing system or a completely *alphabetic* system, or show how fully to read the writing if that is what this is. Of course, other writing systems are known to have been invented among Africans, but they are all attributed by European scholars to either outsiders or very recent origins, after contact in fairly modern times with fully developed European writing systems. This book may be dealing with one of Africa's very early writing systems.

The book's basic approach is to let the data, the cultural objects of the brass Akan "gold weights," speak for themselves as much as possible, and for the author's informants, royal Akan officials, also to speak for themselves. His major contribution is to have *listened* enough to get the point, and to have so arranged the data for our own perusal as to allow us to see the point, or the basis for the point, in the evidence itself. This is what allows this author to avoid the mistakes that virtually hundreds of previous observers of the "gold weights" made—to start with their own assumptions and end up missing the point.

The author quotes some of his informants about what the metal pieces are and what they are used for, rather than asking the traditional question "tell me about these gold weights?" It turns out that only a small subset of them actually are for weighing gold. The informant says, "These pieces represent the things that were known ('etats de conscience'—state of knowledge) to our defunct sovereigns, their memory; the *dja* (the packet in which they are wrapped) is our paper, our universe, our world;" that is, it contains a symbolic representation of what is important to their world. The author also portrays these cultural patterns in their own classificatory scheme: those things that live in the air, on the land, in the sea; material creations and non-material creations; things created by God and those created by Man. And, he gives something of the classifications within such groupings.

He defines the Akan people.

He defines writing: "representation of speech and thinking by suitable symbols." There is no insistence here, nor need there be, that it be alphabetic.

A lot of the work, in terms of number of pages, consists of photographs of groupings of the pieces and a number of charts of writing scripts and symbols. These convey the idea of the types and variety of African writing, and their similarity to each other or to the ancient Egyptian and Saharan (Tifinagh, Numidian, etc.). He quotes Theophile Obenga and others to make it clear that there is every reason to believe that there are historical reasons for the resemblance.

The display of the charts also allows the reader to get the idea that the other African symbols might have served the same function as the Egyptian. If one can accept that such symbols *were* elements of *writing* for the Egyptians, then why must they be considered by Western skeptics as simply mnemonic devices to help griots recite the traditional lore for the Akan. The author notes Jean Gabus's observation that almost all the elements of writing, including syllabaries, are known in African writing systems (although alphabetic is not specifically mentioned). (J. Gabus, *175 Ans d'Ethnologie a Neuchatel*. P. Attinger S.A. Neuchatel 1967.)

Bouah displays page after page of photos of the metal pieces grouped to reveal the combination of symbols into related and more complex arrangements. He relates the role of writing to the sociological pattern of organization, and lays out the functional conditions needed for the operation of a writing *system*—use of identical symbols over a widespread area, and combination of the symbols in some way, use of symbols that are found in other parts of the culture, use of symbols that lend themselves to decipherment or interpretation, and presence of a common language by those using these symbols. All of these conditions are met by the Akan.

Bouah's identification of about one hundred thirty-five (135) basic symbols in this collection is itself an accomplishment of great significance. This is the heart of the analysis of the study, from the point of view of establishing the basis for the full decipherment of the writing. Publication of his work would be worth it for this chart alone.

Both in his text, and in the way he simply presents the evidence, by groupings of the pieces, one is able to see how logically one arrives at the identification of the basic symbol elements. He also gives a basis for understanding the way in which symbols became more complex. by adding additional loops to the spiral, for example e @ @ ; thus using similar forms to make symbols that might have different meanings.

The various possibilities of the process of interpretation are spelled out, although not their specific product. There is the possibility, amply demonstrated in the arrangement of the groups of pieces, of presenting the signs in strict symmetry, or in strict opposition, on one face of the metal base, or several, in association with particular groupings of other symbols or not, or in the absence of a combination of certain of the symbols. All these configurations are probably meaningful. That they are not chance occurrences are, again, made plausibly evident simply by the way he displays the photos of the pieces, in groupings carefully arranged to reveal progression to more complex combinations.

There is presented in this material even the basis for philosophical speculation. For example, in showing the basic principles of construction for the "swastika" symbol, as a combination of the male and female principle,—and considering that this symbol is considered by the Akan to be the most important one—he gives the idea that the culture itself emphasizes dialectical thinking, the conception of reality as the combination of opposites. This idea is reinforced by much of what we know from other aspects of not only Akan culture, but Black African (and much of "brown" or "hamitic" African) culture as well.

There are places of seemingly abrupt switches in theme, for example where he takes up the symbols among peoples in Surinam, but the divergence is only apparent, because the Surinam peoples are also Akan, and the point is to show that despite the separation over centuries of time and many miles, the cultural pattern of design and use of these symbols is very similar.

The author's arrangement of the material carefully gives the reader a basis for understanding, even without explanation, that the individual brass pieces themselves do fit the individual symbols together in diverse arrangements. The complex patterns can be thought of as doing what a word or a phrase does, arranging the individual symbols (e.g., the alphabetic letters of our system) into a pattern that is decipherable.

As to the manner of reading these pieces, again, he lets the culture speak for itself instead of imposing his own "incisive analysis" on it. An informant says, "the ancients attended veritable public séances of collective reading and explication of the texts. On each figurine there is engraved a complete text which in our day have become cryptograms."

Occasionally, the distribution of the photographs among the pages is simply to fill out empty spaces on the page. It in no way detracts from the understanding of an *interested* reader.

The author displays an example of the symbolic representation on one of the flat writing-bearing "weights" of a figurine from a three dimensional weight. This is an important example of his technique of letting the data speak for themselves. Here you see that objects often associated with particular sayings or proverbs get represented, sometimes rather abstractly, on the flat weight pieces. And his explicatory text then carries even more significance, as he calls the African culture a "civilization of the image" (that is, of abstractions, or metaphors). As an informant says, "The ideas (of this civilization) the thoughts (precepts) and even the institutions are represented by images of known objects. Behind the image there is a whole literature relative to politics, law, morals, religion and economics. Often the material image has no formal connection with the idea or the thought symbolically expressed."

Occasionally in the book there is a photo or bit of text that could fit virtually anywhere in the book. That does not prevent it from adding insight into how the Akan culture works. In this case it conveys the idea that the specific signs acquire a textual meaning when they become affixed to the metal base; the sign might be taken for itself, as a mere design, when standing alone. You have an example of the occurrence of one of the specific symbols as an object unto itself, without the typical flat base onto which it is normally inscribed or embossed. This supports the idea that the sign is a thing unto itself, different from the "weight" on which it is embossed (an important idea when dealing with designs that appear often to be decorations).

The section that follows carries the argument forward. When not on the base, the symbol may have no more meaning than say the appearance of the single letter "I" does. But on the base it becomes a message. Thus, where symbols occur on these metal pieces that are the same as or similar to ones used elsewhere in the culture, with known ideogrammatic content, such as the symbols of particular proverbs or complex ideas, one might at least hypothesize that they have the same meaning. Then, when they appear in combination, they may represent the combination of proverbs or complex thoughts such that in these new combinations they acquire additional meanings that go beyond the sum of the parts. Thus one of the metal pieces with a very complex assortment of such symbols might represent quite an elaborate text. It is unfortunate that this book does not give us the translation of any such complex text on the metal weights, although it presents the known ideograms that are more widely used in the culture. It is quite possible that the knowledge of the writing on the "weights" is now lost, or that the informants have not yet decided to reveal it. We should note that Marcel Griaule worked for fifteen years with the Bambara sages before he was given any very full philosophical explanation of the symbols and ceremonies of that culture.

I think the book's discussion and use of the Saharan rock paintings of chariots is very helpful, most importantly to demonstrate something about what African culture had been subjected to by many Western scholars. The double standard and reversed logic often comes through in their analyses, the chariot becomes an object of cultural diffusion—pure and simple. Therefore there is no significance to its appearance in Africa, thus reinforcing the widespread assertions that Africans invented neither the wheel nor writing. In this book the author refers to traditional western analyses of the Saharan "chariot people" rock paintings. These analyses argue that, from the way the horses are depicted in their gallop, these paintings must represent displaced Mycenian culture. That the paintings occur in an area of Africa, with other paintings of Africans, is of no account in terms of cultural attribution. In these western accounts neither the style of the chariot itself, nor its manner of harness, is taken into account—these have no Mycenian semblance. It is curious, then, that such analysts are sure that the paintings represent "diffusion."

The book compares Western treatment of the chariot rock paintings to the frequent occurrence of similar logic in the analysis of Egyptian painting; where the Egyptian art shows the invading "Sea People" as light skinned people with blue eyes, it is taken by the typical Western analyst as proof that these were Nordic peoples, but where the same Egyptian art shows the Pharoahs as very dark, or even black skinned people, with thick lips, broad or fleshy noses, and elongated builds, this is taken as mere artistic convention of no significance in identifying the Egyptians. So, in our day, millions of Americans can file by the relics of a black teenage boy, Tutankhamen, and think they are looking at the glories of European achievement.

When will we be rid of this kind of "scholarship" and the uses to which it is put? And when will we be rid of the reactions of this sort of reviewer to our efforts to negate that "scholarship."

The author of this book considers the Saharan chariots, with their script-like symbols, in the context of other Saharan symbols from the rock paintings, and along with the ancient scripts from that area. The script symbols show up on the Akan "weights." It is not by accident, says the author, that the Akan are in the same cultural boat with the Saharans. The author does not make his main purpose an assertion of Akan invention of these symbols. On the other hand, neither is it his purpose to deny that possibility!

The author shows in photographs, charts, and quotes, that a number of the cultural objects depicted by the ancient Saharans are among those to be found among West Africans, especially the Akan today. He also shows that although the ancient Saharans used a number of items that are widespread in Africa, such as certain styles of masks, there are no distinctive ancient Saharan features that are mixed into the art, dress, dance, music, or language of West Africans. Thus, perhaps the influence went the other way. Evidence that would support such a possibility, which is advanced here only as an hypothesis, is the fact that *all* of the ancient Saharan writing symbols are found among the Akan "gold weight" symbols, but not vice versa. Who then was the more inventive? One could say that the Akan added on some symbols, or that the Saharans dropped out some of them they didn't need (that didn't correspond to their sounds, perhaps). Mauny[1] has shown, according to the author, that the Saharan scripts were neither Asiatic nor European. Why not African then?

Mauny also draws on an earlier article by M.R. Paris in referring to African sallabaries: "However, in certain cases one wonders if one doesn't have veritable alphabetic inscriptions of symbols of the sort we

[1]R. Mauny, *Gravures, peintures et inscription rupestres de l'Afrique de l'Quest.* IFAN, Dakar, 1954.

have in Black Africa (among the Dogon, Bambara, Baule (read Akan) weights...)." (Paris, Recherche sur l'origine des marques de tribus (feux), Bulletin d'IFAN, Dakar, 1953.) In prepublication discussions in the United States Bouah's work has been criticized unjustly under the assumption that it was his major argument that the Akan *had* to have invented this writing. Such criticism ignores Akan migration from an area close to the Ancient southern Saharan regions. They might have learned it there. But, they might also have brought it there, or invented it there.

Moreover, I am not so sure that it is accepted wisdom that the invention of alphabetic writing occurred just once in history. If that is *accepted* among present day scholars of this subject, it must once again represent a gross glossing over not only of the evidence, but even of the previous analyses. It may well be that Akkadians were the first to develop a complete alphabetic system, although they did not fully rely on it, and that the Hittites took it even further in that direction. But it is certain that the Egyptian system of hieroglyphs included alphabetic elements from the oldest preserved texts on, which certainly occurred by the time of the first dynasty and is attributed to even earlier times, which would be as late as 3200 B.C. and perhaps earlier. Lionel Cassel, in *Great Ages of Man: Ancient Egypt,* says that "the oldest surviving hieroglyphs— dating from around 3100 B.C.—(his date is controversial) represent a fully developed written language." He goes on to say that although they "never evolved an alphabet as we know it, they set aside symbols for every consonant sound in their speech." Maurice Pope in his *The Story of Decipherment* states (p. 102) "the simple uniconsonantal signs are already present in full force in the earliest Egyptian writing that we have." About pre-cuneiform, he could only say that it "*seems* to have already possessed *phonetic* signs" (let alone uniconsonantal). The emphasis here was added.

Going to a more specialized source, Sir Alan Gardiner in his *Egyptian Grammar* notes that Egyptian hieroglyphic writing occurs by at least 3180 B.C. and many put it hundreds of years earlier. He notes that phonograms are one of the two basic types of hieroglyphs, and that alphabetic signs are one of the three types of phonograms. That vowels were not written does not prohibit these forms from being considered alphabetic, nor should they imply that the Egyptians never really had the idea of alphabet because they didn't rely on it entirely. Gardiner notes: "The reason for the Egyptian omission of the vowels is not far to seek. It is characteristic of the family of languages to which Egyptians belongs that one and the same word presents different vocalizations according to the forms that it assumes and the contexts in which it appears; thus the ideogram for 'house' ⊏⊐ pronounced par (from paru) in isolation, may well have represented *per when followed by a genitive and *pra (yyu) in the plural. Such a variability of the vowels could not fail to engender the feeling that the consonants were all that mattered..."

This reliance on the consonants is rather characteristic, although not definitive, of the semitic languages, such as Arabic (to this day) Akkadian, Hebrew, Phoenician, etc. Those systems, while developing the alphabetic elements more thoroughly than did the Egyptians, did not eliminate entirely the non-alphabetic elements. *The Funk and Wagnalls Encyclopedia,* 1972, pp. 320-322, for example, state, after describing logoramic systems, syllabic systems and alphabetic systems of writing: "in actual fact, writing systems do not exist in these pure forms. Elements from one type of system are almost always found incorporated in another, an example is the number of logograms (where signs represent complete words) used with the modern alphabetic writing systems...The Akkadians, for example, adapted the syllabic portion of the Sumerian logo-syallabic system to their own language, but retained the logograms."

In any case, consider this: the oldest hieroglyphs are found neatly carved on shist tablets, and soon thereafter you find them in superbly sculpted stone statuary, followed by their occurrence on towering step pyramids, and grand stone temples, the stones of which are so perfectly dressed that one can hardly push a hair between them, today, nearly five thousand years later. From nearly the earliest examples you find pictographs so superbly proportioned, so artfully done, with details often inlaid in semi-precious stone, and very precious (for those days) glass, that they remained the standard for three thousand years. And these occurred in Egypt from almost exactly the same date as the oldest surviving pictographic representations of speech in the Sumerian (proto-Sumerian) area. But how are the latter done? By cuneiform stylus in mud tablets, preserved in temples of mud brick, that have become, today, mounds of mud. By what chain of logic are we to reach the conclusion that it *must* have been the mud markers, and not the stone carvers, that *invented* the writing?

Who is being ridiculous, the author of this book or an American scholar whose reaction to this work, according to Bouah, was to assert that "Europeans did not invent writing, but adopted it from Southwest Asian semites, and that the Africans—even Egyptians—did the same." Were the Egyptian hieroglyphs not even writing, let alone alphabetic writing? There is not the slightest shred of evidence that the Egyptians derived their hieroglyphs from Asia. Maurice Pope (*The Story of Decipherment,* p. 182) states a basis for the *reverse* direction: "The primary phonetic signs of Egyptian hieroglyphic are consonantal in value and about twenty-four in number. It has therefore often been thought that the ancestors of the semitic scripts was consciously created *from* Egyptian (emphasis added) by borrowing these signs and these alone." He repeats the usual pattern of Western scholars, however, by saying although this is possible, he *prefers* for no obviously good reason, to think that the Greeks, working of Phoenecian forms, developed the alphabet "by accident."

Clearly the Egyptians had writing, and with alphabetic elements. So did the Sumerians, Akkadians and the later Asiatic groups. They might have invented it independently, or not. There is only the question "which came first, the Egyptian or the Asian?" The oldest surviving example of written Sumerian, in Pre-Cuneiform pictographs of the crudest form, dates from 3100 B.C. (Samuel N. Kramer, *Great Ages of Man: The Cradle of Civilization*, p. 131). Even Narmer's Pallette, in finely carved shist, and not the oldest of the Egyptian, dates from 3180 to 3200 B.C.! (assuming it was carved in his own time).

Moreover, Dr. Bruce Williams of the University of Chicago, working on artifacts discovered by Dr. Keith Steele, has now shown that to the South of Egypt, in the land of Nubia or Cush, that place from which had come the Egyptians' Gods according to a number of the hieroglyphic texts, there were the symbols of royalty—Horus, and the White Crown— already in use two hundred years or more *before* the first Egyptian dynasty. If these important symbols had their origin in the South, perhaps so also the pictographs that became hieroglyphics.

Who is being ridiculous, the author of this book, or those who charge that "blacks never invented writing." Were the Egyptians not black? Are we back to that? There is evidence galore of not just the "blackness" of the typical Theban stock, but of even blacker southern stock among the Egyptians; black like the Galla, the Masai, the Foulah, the Nubians; black perhaps even like the Dinka and the Shilluk.

And what is the significance of one critic's assertion that writing developed in Western Asia by *Semites.* Why is it so important for anyone to make *that* point? Is it to imply that there are no black African Semites?—not the Amharas? or Tigrinya? Are they trying to make the Egyptians out to be semitic? That line of argument is now dead. Where do the Sumerians fit into that picture?; neither their language, nor that of the earlier Ubaidians, was semitic! The Akkadians were semites, yes, and came quickly to submerge the Sumerians in a semitic Babylonia; but, that was later.

How willing are white scholars to actually relate all peoples in a global history? How willing are they to include Africans, not just Asiatic nomads who may have penetrated Africa, but good old brown skinned hamites like the Thebans, the browner Nubians, the browner still Galla, or the Akan, in that world history, as the *initiators* and *influencers* of civilization they seem in fact to have been.

A sense of shrinking markets for books about black contributions to civilization, and some of the attitudes and legacies that I have referred to in this article have made it difficult for Professor Niangoran-Bouah to find a publisher in the United States. Happily, the Italian firm of Giancarlo Serafini will bring not only this work on the writing and mathematical symbols that are preserved on the "weights" but all the other aspects of their role in Akan society. This will amount to three volumes, to be published in both English and French. They should open up many new vistas for research into African civilization and its relationship to our own.

Willard R. Johnson
Professor of Political Science
M.I.T.
Cambridge, MA

THE ANCIENT MANDING SCRIPT

Clyde-Ahmad Winters

It is usually assumed that writing was introduced into West Africa by the Arabs. But this view is unfounded because, due to the demands of trade, scripts were invented by African trader-groups in ancient times. This was especially true of the Mande or Manding-speaking peoples who are recognized as the inventors of several scripts.

It appears from the evidence that these writing systems were not recent creations. They were derived from a proto-Mande script invented thousands of years ago by the ancestors of the Mande when they lived in the Sahara at the time it was fertile. This proto-Mande script was used by the ancient Mande to write or engrave inscriptions throughout the Western Sahara. This script was a syllabary similar to the Vai script.

Although D. Dalby,[1] a well known British linguist, is of the opinion that the Manding scripts are of recent origin, I have shown in many articles that this view is incorrect.[2] An ancient invention of the Mande scripts is not a new theory. In 1899, M. Delafosse, one of the earliest scholars to write on the Vai script, noted the Vai tradition for its ancient origin.[3] Prof. K. Hau, in a very interesting article written in 1973, discussed the possibility of the Mande script being invented long ago by traders to keep their business records. "We cannot even guess when this occurred," she wrote, "but it is of great importance to note that almost all the people . . . who possess writing systems, whether syllabic or 'ideographic,' employ languages which belong to the great Mande language family of West Africa."[4]

These scripts, like others, were created by the demands of long distance trade. They were created by merchants to help them keep records of their business transactions and were only later used as a means of preserving religious doctrines and writing obituaries. These written scripts came into being in Africa as a result of the growth of trade centers. These served as the major terminal points for goods supplied by people who usually lived in small villages and practiced agriculture, herding and mining part-time. Among the Mande *Kuma* (which means the word) is considered sacred. As a result, written amulets have long been recognized as containing magical power.

The Mande have long been involved in long-distance trade. The Niger bend area has been important in the transshipment of trade items from the North and gold from the South, long before the Arabs arrived in North Africa.[5] Many of these goods were carried along chariot routes which met at the Niger bend.

The chariot trails led from Garama in the Fezzan, which converged at Ahaggar and went through Adrar des Ifora, to Gao on the Niger bend. Another road ran from Morocco, 300 miles island, parallel to the Atlantic coast. It crossed the Adrar of Mauritania and turned inland in a wide sweep reaching the Niger bend near Timbuktu.

The archaeological evidence suggests that copper and gold were the early items offered in trade by the Mande. According to a Vai tradition told by a Vai prince, his people mined gold early and brought their syllabary with them when they moved to their present place of habitation.[6]The Mande languages consist of two groups, known to scholars as the *Mande Tan* and *Mande Fu*, after the word for 'ten': *tan* (*tam, tamu*) or *fu* (*pu, bu*), which occur in the various languages. The speakers of the Mande Tan group live mainly in the north. These are the culture bearers of the historic Mande speakers. They are the Soninke cluster, which includes SoSo, Azer, Sarakhule, Khesonke, Bozo, Vai and Dialonke. These people are credited with the founding of Ghana. The second group, *Mande Fu*, includes the Malinke-Bambara-Dyula cluster.[7]

There is a diversity of opinion concerning the age of the Mande languages, but Greenberg[8] has suggested that around 7,000 years BP (Before the Present) the Niger-Congo (*N.C.*) group, which includes the Mande languages, began to break up. They were practicing a neolithic culture as indicated by the Proto-*N.C.* words for cow, goat and cultivate.[9]

The Mande speakers were part of the ancient *Maa* or Fish Confederation.[10] The *Maa* confederation included the ancient Egyptians, Elamites, Sumerians and Dravidians, in addition to the Mande and other Niger-Congo groups.[11] I call these ancient people that lived in the Sahara the Proto-Saharans. At this ancient date, between 8,000-4,000 BP, the Sahara was much wetter.

The proto-Saharans spoke common languages and had common cultural elements. For example, they had common pronouns:

Common Pronouns

Language	1st Per. Singular	2nd Per. Singular	3rd Per. Singular
Egyptian	'ink	ntk, ntt	ntf
Manding	na, n	i	a, e
Dravidian	an, naa, na	i	a
Elamite	u	nu	ri
Sumerian	ga, gal	za, zu	ene

Language	1st Per. Plural	2nd Per. Plural	3rd Per. Plural
Egyptian	inn	nttn	nten
Manding	alu		
Dravidian	ani	a, ar	aru
Elamite	un	nun	r:ir
Sumerian	men	zu, ne	ene-ne

Common Cultural Traits

Language	Chief	Writing	City
Dravidian	cira, Ca	cārrū	ur(u)
Elamite	Sunki, Salu	*talu	
Sumerian	Sar	—	ur
Nubian	Sirgi	Hor/Sor	
Ubaid	Sar		ur
Manding	Sa	Sebe	furu

During the proto-Saharan period they had domesticated cattle in the Western Sahara. This was as early as 5,000 BC, indicated by the appearance of painted slabs portraying cattle with rope leads around their necks.[12] At this time the people practiced a mixed pastoralist-sedentary culture, indicated by the discovery of abundant pottery and grinding stones at habitation sites throughout the Western Sahara.

The Proto-Mande occupied an area extending from the western Sahara to the Fezzan in southern Libya. The Mande influenced the style of western Mediterranean pottery. Archaeologists recognize that Western Mediterranean ware was derived from Western Saharan styles, and that eastern saharan styles have affinities to Middle Nile ware. But, according to J.B. Clark, even with slight variations, there was ''a general cohesion'' between the Saharan-Sudanese styles.[13]

McCall is of the opinion that the Mande speakers were established early in the southern Sahara.[14] Welmers[15] has suggested 3,000 BC or earlier for the separation of the Mande speakers into Eastern and Western branches.

Beginning around 2,000 BC a dry period returned to the Sahara, which has continued up to the present. It was during this period that the Mande began to migrate to their present areas of habitation. Around 2000 BC the Mande founded Karkarichinkat and Dar Tichitt.[16] In the Fezzan in the fertile valley between the Ubari Erg and the Erg of Murzuq, in oases spread from El Abiod to Tin Abunda, the Garamantes/Garamande/Mande tribe lived. This was the earliest Mande Empire known to Europeans. The capital city of the Garamantes was located at Jerma.[17]

In the western Sahara, Dar Tichitt was an important Mande site in antiquity. Here between 1,500-300 BC the Mande built their cities and cultivated bulrush millet.[18] Munson suggests that the Dar Tichitt cities were the forerunners of the Soninke empire of Ghana, on the strength of the fact that, in oases in the vicinity of the ruins of Dar Tichitt, the people speak Azer, a Soninke language.[19] The Mande communities in Mauritania at Dar Tichitt and those in the Fezzan communicated with each other by chariots. These carried goods across long established chariot routes which extended from the Niger bend to North Africa.[20] To pull their chariots, the ancient Mande used ponies, which are still found in the Sahilian region.[21]

Due to the demands of the Transsaharan trade the Mande invented their own script. This proto-Mande script was also used by other members of the *Maa* confederation including the Egyptians, Sumerians, (proto-) Elamites and the Dravidians of the Indus Valley.[22] The Mande have left numerous inscriptions throughout the Western Sahara in the Air, Mauritania and Morocco. These inscriptions engraved on rocks were obituaries and/or talismanic burial sites.

The proto-Mande script was probably invented sometime before 4,000 BC, because by 3,100 BC the proto-Saharan tribes separated. In the western Sahara, wherever these ancient signs are found, the Mande totem sign Kangaba often appears. The earliest Mande inscriptions found so far were located at Oued Mertoutek which has been dated to 3,000 BC by Wulsin.[23] These signs are identical to the Mande inscriptions located in the Grotte de Goundaka.[24]

The ancient Mande wrote on stone, wood and dried palm leaves. Ink was made from soot and liana.[25] The Bambara claim that they once carved their royal inscriptions/archives on tablets of wood.

Using the Vai syllabary but reading the signs in Malinke-Bambara I have been able to decipher the proto-Mande inscriptions found in the Western Sahara. The proto-Mande script has around 200-350 signs and around 40 different forms. It is not an alphabetic script as many scholars assume. It is syllabic. Due to the early date assigned to the Oued Mertoutek site, we can infer that the Manding had writing long before the Phoenicians arrived in north Africa circa 1,200 BC. Up to this day the Manding writing is used by members of the Manding secret societies.[26]

The inscriptions are read from right to left or top to bottom. The language was written in a syllabary due to the high frequency pf disyllabic roots of the kind: CVCV (Consonant/vowel/consonant/vowel) CVN (consonant/vowel/nasal) or CVV (consonant/vowel/vowel). The monosyllabic roots of CV seem often to be the result of the reduction of disyllabic roots.

In the Manding scripts the same sign can be used to represent different phonetic sounds. Therefore we find several characters which represent different phonetic values: $\longrightarrow$ *mbe* "act, deed," *ke* "to cut," *fo* "to make furrows with plough."

Although Malinke distinguishes nine vowels, we find, in the inscriptions soon to be discussed, only six vowels used in the syllabary: a, e, e, è, o, ò. The labiovelar consonants *kp* and *gb* occur in most of the inscriptions, e.g., *gbé* $\perp, \times$ "to hunt, purity, etc" and *kpe* $\vdash, \because, \mathsf{M}$ "to thrust, to push in."

The most common syllabic forms in those *American* inscriptions which I have shown elsewhere to be related to the African, are monosyllabic. They consist of CV types: *Ba* ⅃⅂ "mother," *ka* ϟ "to cut"; *go* ᑫ,ᗫ "river"; *di* ♀ "to give." The other common type is syllabic nasal: *n/m*, e.g., *ngbé* ╳ 'favorable.'' There is also the CCV form, as in *gbe* ╳,⊥ "pure, to hunt, etc." The CVV form occurs but it is rare and usually results from the writing of two characters to form a new character, thus: *ga a* I› "this hearth."

Compound nouns are not much in use in the script. But derivative nouns and adjectives are formed by suffixes, which may have originally been independent words: *di* "give," *di-la* /⊬♀ "giver" or *tege* "cut," *tege-na* I ⅄⊏ "cutting tool."

The major suffixes used in the inscriptions were *ka* ϟ the suffix of possession, or nationality, which is joined to a name or serves to form names and verbs; *la* /⊬ a suffix to augment value joined to certain pronouns; *to* ⊓⊓ a locative suffix, as well as *bi* + the affirmative suffix, which denotes action that is either completed, continuous, or repeated. Other affirmative suffixes which denote action are *ye* ⊬ and *nu* ⊞ ⍝ . *Nu* also features as a habitation sign.

The personal pronouns are all written in the second and third person singular, *i* | or *a* › respectively, The first person singular forms for *ne* and *ni* are sometimes shortened to *n'*.

The most common verbs in these texts are *bè* ⅄,⊊ "to lie down, to sink"; bwè ⊤ "to put down, to free; *ka* ϟ and *ta* O "to go"; *gā* ∂ "to warm, to cook";*fo* ⊤ "to speak"; pé :, M " thrust, to push in" and *tā* O "fire."

The attributive verb "to be" can be expressed in the Manding text as either *ye* ⊬ or *bé* ╥ —*a ye fi-ma* "he is back," *a ye lu ka gbe* ╳ ϟ ∩ ⊣ › "he has cut the family hearth well." In most cases I have used the *bé* form in my transliteration of the text, as well as *ye*. The verb of negation is usually the word *té* but in the inscriptions I found that a form of the word *tī* Γ was used instead.

The major nouns found among the inscriptions deal with death (⋌⌝) and burial customs, or agriculture. Some are talismans. There is much use of the sign *kyu/tyu* ⅢⅠ ⊔,∪,⋐,☼ "large hemisphere sepulchre or coffin." The term *gyo* ||,∃ for "talisman or cult" is also used.

In agriculture we frequently find the following signs: *gé* ⋊ "to sprout"; *kyè* ⌓ "beans (kidney)"; *kā* ϟ "Maize"; *gyī* ∿∿ "water"; *gbà* ⊗ "land of tillage"; *ku* ⊙ "yam";*fo* ⊤ "make furrows with a plough"; *Pé* :,ℇ "strike the ground", or *pwe* M,: "flat land, level land"; *mè* |||,... "surface, area"; *pi* ᗷ "plants in the ground"; *dé* ⊣,⅄ "land of inundation." Other nouns deal with habitation sites: *ga/gba* ⊗, I, ⅂ "hearth"; *yu* ∩ *nu* ◫,⍝ *lu* ⊓,Y,⋀,⊣,1 *su* ⋌ ⊬ "family habitation."

PROTO-MANDE SIGNS

$+,\times$ *ngbe*, favorable, purity

////   *gyu*, foundation, take root

$//,=$ *gyo*, talisman, amulet

∪,⊔   *yu*, hemisphere, sepulchre

⊔⊔   *to*, the abode

╫╫   *kyu*, coffin

⊙   *ko*, ridge, back, word, to say, behind, river, in the absence of

W,:   *pè*, flat lands, to fix, to hit

∧   *fe*, vacant

○   *ta*, place

...   *mè*, area

⊡   *mbo*, residue

⊕   *da*, landmark, wild terrain

⊥   *ga*, hot, hearth, habitation of family

⊥   *naa*, to come, to be pleasant, to bring

ı⁄   *su*, dead, home, night

Z,ζ *kaa*, to cut, term of respect, to go

⊗   *taa ngbe*, place of righteousness

⊗   *gba*, hearth, glow, terrain of cultivation, to plant

||| *sè*, realize

Υ,○   *taa*, place

$+,\times$ *gbe*, lay down, purity

•   *lii*, indeed

—   *ii*, thou, you

▭   *kpo*, superlative of white, clean

$\maltese$, $\propto$ *gè*, to sprout

$\wedge$ *tii*, to break

References

1. D. Dalby, "A Survey of the indigenous scripts of Liberia and Sierra Leone: Vai, Mende, Loma, Kpelle and Bassa," *African Language Studies* 8, pp. 1-51. 1967.

2. Clyde-Ahmad Winters, "The influence of the Mande scripts on ancient American writing systems," *Bull. de l'IFAN*, t39, ser. B no. 2, pp. 941-967. 1977.

3. M. Delafosse, "Vai leur langue et leur systeme d'ecriture," *L'Anthropologie*, 10, 1899.

4. K. Hau, "Pre-Islamic writing in West Africa," *Bull. de l'IFAN*, ser. B, no. 1, 1973.

5. S.K. McIntosh and R.J. Mcintosh, "West African Prehistory," *American Scientist*, vol. 69 (1981) pp. 602-613.

6. K. Hau, "African writing in the New World," *Bull. de l'IFAN*, t40, ser. B, no. 1, (1978) pp. 28-48.

7. M. Houis, "Les groupes linguistique Mande," *Notes African* 82, (IFAN) pp. 40-41.

8. J. Greenberg, "Historical inferences from linguistic research in Sub-Saharan Africa," *Boston University Papers in African History*, vol. 1.

9. D.F. McCall, "The cultural map and time-profile of the Mande-speaking peoples," in C.T. Hodge (ed) *Papers on the Manding*, Indiana Univ., Bloomington, 1971.

10. L. Desplagnes, "Notes sur les origines des populations Nigerienne," *L'Anthropologie* 17, (1906) pp. 525-527.

11. C.A. Winters, "The genetic unity of Dravidian and African languages and culture," *Proc. of the First International Symposium on Asian Studies (PFISAS) 1979*, Asian Research Service, Hong Kong, 1980; Winters, "Are the Dravidians of African Origin?," *PFISAS 1980*, Hong Kong, 1981; Winters, "The African influence on Indian Agriculture," *Jour. of African Civilization*, vol. 3, no. 1 (April, 1981) pp. 100-11; Winters, *Lectures in Africana: Kushite Diaspora*, (self-published) 11541 South Peoria, Chicago, Ill., 1982; Winters, "The Harappan script deciphered: Proto-Dravidian writing of the Indus Valley," *PFISAS 1981* Hong Kong, 1982.

12. McCall, Ibid., p. 39; Mc Intosh, Ibid., pp. 606-607.

13. H. Alimen, *Prehistoire de l'Afrique*, (Paris, 1955) pp. 195-202; 209-210.

14. McCall, Ibid., p. 38.

15. W.E. Welmers, "The Mande Languages," *Report on the Ninth Annual Round Table Meeting on Linguistics and Language Studies*, Georgetown, 1968.

16. P.J. Munson, *The Tichitt tradition*, Unpub. Ph.D. Thesis, Univ. of Ill., 1971.

17. Winters, "African influences on Indian Agriculture," p. 103.

18. Ibid., p. 103.

19. P. Munson, "Archaeological data on the origins of cultivation in the southwestern Sahara and their implications for West Africa," in *Origins of African Plant Domestication* (eds) J.R. Harlan, et al, The Hague: Mouton, pp. 187-209; and Munson, 1971.

20. C.A. Winters, "Manding scripts in the New World," *Jour. of African Civilizations*, vol. 1, no. 1 (1979) p. 83, Winters, "African influences on Indian Agriculture," *J.A.C.* vol. 3, no. 1, p. 103.

21. McCall, pp. 61-63.

22. Winters, "The Harappan script deciphered: proto-Dravidian writing of the Indus Valley," p. 926.

23. F.R. Wulsin, *The Prehistoric Archaeology of Northwest Africa*, Papers of the Peabody Museum of American Archaeology and Ethnology, Harvard University, vol. 19, no. 1, 1941.

24. L. Desplagnes, *Le Plateau centrale Nigerien*, Paris, 1907; and R. Mauny, *Tableau geographique*, Dakar, 1960.

25. Hau, Ibid., 1978.

26. Winters, "The influence of the Mande scripts on ancient America," pp. 942-45.

BLACK AMERICANS IN THE FIELD
OF SCIENCE AND INVENTION

Robert C. Hayden

SUMMARY: *By 1913 it is estimated that as many as one thousand inventions were patented by black Americans. These patents represented inventions in almost every field of industry. Robert Hayden, author of three books on black inventors and inventions, discusses some of the outstanding black inventors of the nineteenth century:-*

Elijah McCoy (automatic lubrication for steam engines) Jan Matzeliger (first machine for mass-producing shoes) Granville Woods (35 patents for electro-mechanical devices, bringing about improvements in telegraphy, telephones, automatic cut-offs for electrical circuits and electric motor regulators) Lewis Latimer (inexpensive cotton-thread filament which made electric light practical for homes) Garrett Morgan (first automatic stop-light and a smoke inhalator mask) Norbert Rillieux (vacuum evaporator for turning cane juice into white sugar crystals) Lewis Temple (movable harpoon head which revolutionized the whaling industry).

Hayden also introduces us to three 20th century inventors - Frederick McKinley Jones (movable refrigeration unit that transformed the food transport industry) Otis Boykin (the control unit in artificial heart stimulators and an electrical device used in all guided missiles and IBM computers) and Meredith Gourdine (a pioneer in energy conversion, inventor of many products and processes based on the use of electrogasdynamics technology.)

A discussion of the roles of black Americans who were inventors must of necessity be considered against the American social order as a background. It is within this larger societal and cultural context that black people's experiences occurred, evolved, and were conditioned. Inventors who were black are first and foremost products of their unusual American experiences as black people. From the outset, as a people, they were regarded as being "different," and their subsequent treatment was contingent almost solely upon this condition. While these inventors were inextricably a part of an outgoing struggle for full equality, they bore the added task of their thrust for full recognition of their contributions to society as creative personalities.

Historically, black inventors functioned in several identifiable roles in America. Some of the early roles evolved on the basis of the needs of society at a given time. Hence, the need for skilled craftsmen to do skilled work, ranging from painting, silver and goldsmithing to household building, was considerable. This condition existed in America during the 18th century. The genesis of black participation in the craft and inventive traditions of America might be traced from those nameless black craftsmen who helped produce the artifacts required for life in colonial America, to the identifiable personalities of the early and late 19th Century.

Before the end of the Civil War, noteworthy inventions by blacks were not numerous. For most slaves the foremost question was how to gain their freedom. Those with intelligence and vision used their minds to devise plans and to interest others in gaining freedom from slavery. Many free black people worked to save those blacks in bondage. They did so by developing their literary and speaking ability rather than by becoming machinists, engineers, or inventors.

During this same period most of the labor and mechanical industries of the South were carried on with slave labor. Bits and pieces of history show that many of the simple tools of the day were designed by slaves. They invented various pieces of equipment to lessen the burden of their daily work. None of these, however, could be patented by the United States Patent Office. Worthwhile ideas perfected by blacks were forever lost because of the attitude of the federal government at the time.

In 1858, Jeremiah S. Black, Attorney General of the United States, had ruled that since a patent was a contract between the government and the inventor, and since a slave was not considered a United States citizen, he could neither make a contract with the government nor assign his invention to his master. Thus it has been impossible to prove the contributions of many unnamed slaves whose creative skill has added to the industrial growth of our country.

Jo Anderson, a slave on the plantation of Cyrus McCormick, is said to have made a major contribution to the McCormick grain harvester. Yet, he is only credited in the official records as being a handyman or helper to McCormick.

In 1862, a slave owned by Jefferson Davis, President of the Confederacy, invented a propeller for ocean vessels. With a model of his invention the slave showed remarkable mechanical skill in wood and metal working. He was unable to get a patent on his propeller, but the merits of his invention were reported in many southern newspapers. The propeller was finally used in ships of the Confederate Navy.

The national ban on patents for slaves did not apply to those made by

"Free Persons of Color." So, when James Forten (1776-1842) perfected a new device for handling sails, he had no trouble getting one. From his invention he was able to earn a good living for himself and his family. This was also true of another black, Norbert Rillieux, whom I will discuss further along in this paper.

It is believed that Henry Blair was the first black American to be granted a United States patent. He received his first patent in 1834 for a seed planter. In 1836, Blair received his second patent on a corn harvester. In both cases he was described in the official records as "A Colored Man."

Following the Civil War, the growth of industry in this country was tremendous. Much of this was made possible from the inventions of both blacks and whites. By 1913, an estimated one thousand inventions had been patented by black Americans in such fields as industrial machinery, rapid transportation, and electrical equipment.

Let's look at the inventions made by black people after the war when legal slavery ended and fewer obstacles stood in the way. Industrial opportunities were generally available to everyone. There was a freer market and the records prove that blacks had just as much inventive ability as whites. It is interesting to see how the inventions of black people have been received.

Since Blair received his second patent, the United States Patent Office has never kept a record of whether an inventor was black or white. However, on two different occasions the patent office has sought this information. The first inquiry was made in the year 1900 by the Patent Office for the United States Commission that was preparing an exhibit on black Americans for a fair in Paris. The second was made in 1913 at the request of the Pennsylvania Commission planning a Freedom Exhibit in Philadelphia. In both cases the Patent Office sent out several thousand letters to patent lawyers, large manufacturing firms, and to the various newspapers edited by black men. The people who received the letters were asked to inform the Commission of Patents of any patents granted by the office for inventions by black people. The letter sent out by the Patent Office in 1900 read as follows.

Department of the Interior
United States Patent Office
Washington, D. C.

January 26, 1900

Dear Sir:

This Office is endeavoring to obtain information concerning patents issued to colored inventors, in accordance with a request from the United States Commission to the Paris Exposition of 1900, to be used in preparing the "Negro Exhibit."

To aid in this work, you are requested to send to this Office, in the enclosed envelope, which will not require a postage stamp, the names of any colored inventors you can furnish, together with the date of grant, title of invention, and patent number, so that a list without errors can be prepared.

You will confer a special favor by aiding in the preparation of this list by filling in the blank form below, and sending in any replies as promptly as possible. Should you be unable to furnish any data, will you kindly inform us of that fact?

Very respectfully,

O.H. Duell
Commissioner of Patents

The replies were numerous. The information showed that a very large number of blacks had contacted lawyers. Even so, many were unable to get patents because they lacked the necessary funds to apply for them. Some had actually obtained them but the records of most lawyers were poorly kept and so the names and inventions of many blacks were lost.

Patents were often taken out in the name of the lawyer. A large number of black inventors allowed this because they felt that the racial identity of the inventor would lower the value of a patented invention. Yet more than a thousand patents were fully identified by the name of the inventor, date, patent number and title of invention as being owned by blacks. These patents represented inventions in nearly every branch of industrial arts such as household goods, mechanical appliances, electrical devices and chemical compounds. In the beginning, agricultural and home utensils were most common. But gradually the black inventor widened the field of his efforts. Here is just a small part of a list of black inventors in the United States. The entire record included nearly 190 inventors and 370 inventions. Some of the people received more than one patent.

Inventor	Invention	Date	Patent Number
Beard, A.J.	Car Coupler	11/23/1897	594,059
Brooks, C.B.	Street Sweepers	03/17/1896	556.711
Burr, J.A.	Lawn Mower	05/09/1899	624,749
Butler, R.A.	Train Alarm	06/15/1897	584,540
Campbell, W.S.	Self-Setting Animal Trap	08/30/1881	246,369
Ferrell, F.J.	Valves for Steam Engine	05/27/1890	428,671
Grant, G.F.	Golf Tee	12/12/1899	638,920
Headen, M.	Foot Power Hammer	10/05/1886	350,363
Lee, J.	Bread Crumbing Machine	06/04/1895	540,553
Matzeliger, J.E.	Shoe Lasting Machine	09/22/1891	459,899
McCoy, E.	Lubricator for Steam Engines	07/02/1872	129,843

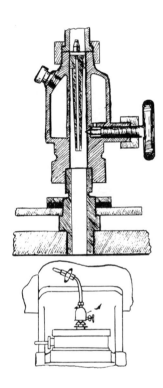

Graphite Lubricator — *Elijah McCoy invented a graphite lubricator for use on railroad locomotives with superheated engines. It provided a continuous flow of oil without clogging the engine. (Patented April 20, 1915)*   Hayden - Fig. 1

(McCoy received 25 patents for different types of lubricators between 1872 and 1899.)

Murray, G.W.	Fertilizer Distributor	06/05/1894	520,889
Purvis, W.B.	Paper Bag Machine	01/28/1890	420,099
Sampson, G.T.	Clothes Drier	06/07/1892	476,416
Winters, J.R.	Fire Escape Ladder	05/07/1878	203,517

The most significant black inventors following the Civil War were Elijah McCoy, Jan Matzeliger, Granville T. Woods, Lewis H. Latimer, and Garrett A. Morgan.

Let's look at each of these men in a bit more detail.

Elijah McCoy's invention was the lubricating cup that fed oil to machinery while it was still running. One industry that benefitted from this invention was the railroad industry. McCoy was born in Canada of runaway slave parents, and came to the United States after the Civil War. His basic invention, a "Drip Cup," ended countless complaints of waste and cost by making it unnecessary to stop and restart engines in order to lubricate them. McCoy opened the Elijah McCoy Manufacturing Co. in Detroit, Mich., in order to develop and market his inventions, working with such intensity that from 1873 to 1899 he received 25 patents for different types of lubricators. The confidence inspired by the reliability of his lubricating devices was such that the phrase "the real McCoy" was coined in regard to machinery that contained the McCoy device, and this phrase became a part of our language.

Jan Matzeliger is the inventor who revolutionized the shoemaking industry. Matzeliger was born in Dutch New Guinea and came to America in 1876. Operator of a stitching machine at the Harney Brothers Shoe Factory in Lynn, Mass., he studied the motions of hand-lasters in the hope of devising a machine to replace the hand-making of shoes. He worked for six months on a model, constructed a full-size working machine, and refused an offer of $1,500 for it. A third machine was completed and patented March 20, 1883; the Consolidated Hand Method Lasting Machine Co. was formed, and Matzeliger began working his fourth machine. When he died at the age of 37, his patent was purchased by the United Shoe Machine Co. of Boston.

Granville T. Woods, sometimes called the "Black Edison," held over 35 patents on electro-mechanical devices which he sold to American Bell Telephone, General Electric, and Westinghouse Air Brake. He lived between 1865 and 1910. More than a dozen inventions by Woods improved the electric railway systems. In addition to his electric railway works, Woods had other electrical inventions to his credit. They included improvements in telegraphy, telephone instruments, auto-

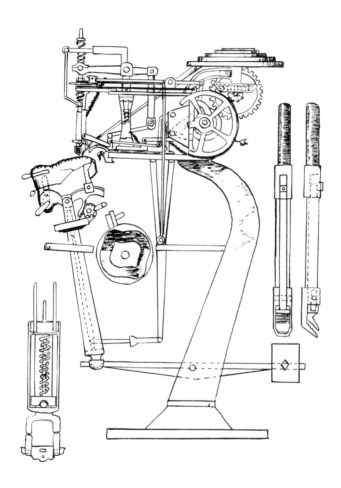

Shoe-Lasting Machine — *Jan Matzeliger built this lasting machine which was a breakthrough for mass-producing shoes. Because of his race, it was called "The Nigger-Head Machine." (Patented September 22, 1891)*

Hayden - Fig. 2

matic cut-offs for electric circuits, and electric motor regulators. His most noteworthy electrical invention was his induction telegraphy. This system was designed to send telegraphic messages to and from a moving train. His work attracted universal attention from technical and scientific journals both in this country and abroad.

Lewis Latimer, born in Chelsea, Mass., in 1848, studied electrical engineering and draftsmanship. He was employed by the patent firm of Crosy and Gould where, as chief draftsman in 1870, he made the drawings for Alexander Graham Bell's telephone. With the firm of Hirman S. Maxim he invented production techniques for making carbon filaments for their lamps. In 1878 Edison asked Latimer to work with him on a filament for the electric light bulb; on October 19, 1879, In Menlo Park, N.J., Latimer's inexpensive cotton thread filament passed the test which made electric light practical for homes. From 1896 to 1911 he was cheif draftsman of the Board of Patent Control of General Electric and Westinghouse, and later wrote the first textbook on incandescent lighting.

Garrett Morgan, inventor of the first automatic stop signal, was born in Paris, Tenn., in 1875 and moved to Cleveland, Ohio, in 1895 where he invented a belt fastener for sewing machines in 1901. His invention of a smoke inhalator won him first grand prize at the Second International Exposition of Sanitation and Safety (1914), and two years later, wearing his smoke mask, he dramatically rescued a score of workmen trapped in a tunnel under Lake Erie, and was awarded a gold medal for heroism by the City of Cleveland. He patented his stop light in 1923, then sold the patent rights to the General Electric Company for $40,000.

In addition to the works of these post Civil War inventors, there are two who lived and worked before the Civil War that should be mentioned -Lewis Temple and Norbert Rillieux.

Rillieux's invention revolutionized the processing of sugar. In 1846 he received a patent for a multiple-effect vacuum evaporator that turned sugar cane juice into a fine grade of white sugar crystals. Rillieux's process was more effcient and economical than any other method and basically his process is still used throughout the sugar industry today.

Norbert Rillieux was born a slave in New Orleans in 1806. Educated in Paris, France he taught there and published several papers on the steam engine and steam economy. Returning to Louisiana he became the most famous engineer in the State because of his invention. Rillieux's process was used throughout Louisiana, later adopted in Cuba and Mexico, and eventually adopted in Europe when it was applied to the sugar beet industry.

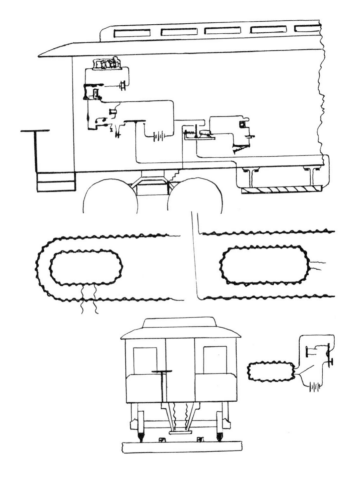

Railway Induction Telegraph — *Granville Wood's patent for his Railway Induction Telegraph System made travel much safer for it helped to eliminate many train collisions. (Patented November 29, 1887)*   Hayden - Fig. 3

Lewis Temple was a blacksmith who lived in New Bedford, Massachusetts from 1830-1854. As a blacksmith he fashioned whaling harpoons for the 19th Century New England whaling industry and he invented a harpoon that revolutionized whaling in this country. Before Temple's invention the barbed head of the harpoon was no match for the twisting and turning strength of a whale. Frequently whales pulled free from the hook of the harpoon. Temple fashioned a movable harpoon head — one that toggled at right angle to the shaft and "locked" into the whale's flesh. Temple's toggle harpoon became the universal harpoon and it is still used today in some parts of the Carribean.

In 1926, Clifford Ashley, an authority on whaling, wrote — "It is safe to say that the 'Temple Toggle' was the most important single invention in the whole history of whaling. It resulted in the capture of a far greater proportion of whales that were struck than had before been possible.

I would like to share with you something of the lives and work of three more contemporary, 20th Century inventors — Frederick McKinley Jones, (1893-1961); Otis Boykin (1920-   ) and Meredith Gourdine (1929-   ).

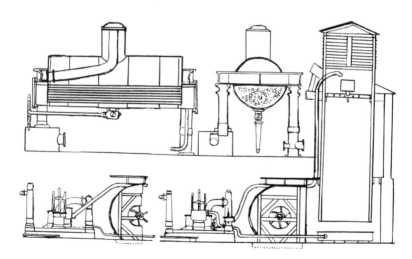

The Rillieux Evaporator — *A series of vacuum pans, or partial vacuum pans, have been so combined together as to make use of the vapor of the evaporation of the juice in the first, to heat the juice in the second and the vapor from this to heat the juice in the third, which latter is connected with a condenser, the degree of pressure in each successive one being less.... The number of sirup pans may be increased or decreased at pleasure so long as the last of the series is in conjunction with the condenser. (Patented December 10, 1846)*

Hayden - Fig. 4

Frederick McKinley Jones invented the first practical truck refrigeration unit that helped to change the food transport industry in this country. A portable refrigeration unit invented by Jones was on the battlefields of Europe during World War II and it helped to save many lives since blood serum for transfusions, medicines and foodstuffs could be kept readily available under a cooling system.

Jones was born in 1893, was an orphan for most of his boyhood and never had anything more than an eight grade education. He worked as an automobile mechanic as a teenager, built racing cars, and served in World War I where he studied electricity and electronics. He arrived in Hallock, Minnesota after the war and became employed first as a farm machinery mechanic and later as a technician for a company that manufactured motion picture film equipment and other cinema supplies.

One day in the early 1930's Jones learned that a friend of his boss who was in the trucking business had lost a shipment of poultry when the ice blocks melted before reaching the marketplace. Jones quietly began working on an air cooling unit for trucks. He was successful and in 1949 he received a U.S. patent for his air cooling unit.

During his lifetime, Frederick Jones was awarded more than 60 patents: 40 were for refrigeration equipment alone. Others were for portable X-ray machines and sound equipment techniques for motion pictures. Jones also patented many of the special parts of his air cooling machines; the self-starting gasoline engine that turned his cooling units on and off, the reverse cycling mechanism for producing heat or cold, and devices for controlling air temperature and moisture.

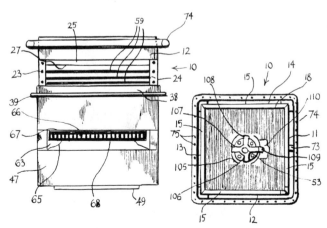

The Jones Removable Cooling Unit — *It transformed the food transport industry in this country. (Patented July 12, 1949)*   Hayden - Fig. 5

At fifty years of age, Frederick Jones was one of the outstanding authorities in the field of refrigeration in the United States. In 1944 he was elected to membership in the American Society of Refrigeration Engineers. College graduated scientists and engineers welcomed the chance to work and learn from him. During the 1950's he was called to Washington to give advice on problems having to do with refrigeration. He was a consultant to both the Defense Department and the United States Bureau of Standards.

Today on the expressways and main routes in every city you will see food transport trucks with refrigeration units over the cabs bearing the Thermo King Corp. The company, which manufactures these refrigeration units used to keep food cold and frozen until it reaches the supermarket, is in business today because of the inventive genius of Frederick McKinley Jones.

Otis Boykin born in Dallas, Texas in 1920 attended Fisk University and Illinois Institute of Technolgy (1946-47), but was discovered in 1941 while working as a parcel post clerk. Boykin is credited with devising the control unit used in artificial heart stimulators; with inventing a tiny electrical device used in all guided missiles and I.B.M. computers, plus 26 other electronic devices, and an air filter. Thirty-seven resulting products are now being manufactured in Paris and distributed throughout Western Europe. Since 1964 Boykin has been a private research consultant for several American companies and three firms in Paris.

Physicist and energy system engineer Meredith Gourdine has pioneered in the development of electrogasdynamic systems and the practical application of the energy converson process. In 1966 the U.S. Department of Interior, Office of Coal Research, awarded Gourdine over $600,000 to perfect a model generator that used a low grade coal to directly generate 80,000 volts of electricity. The generator had no moving parts and did not use steam.

Gourdine was born in Livingston, N.J. in 1929 and received his Doctorate Degree in Engineering Science from California Institute of Technology. In 1952, while still a physics student at Cornell University, Gourdine went to the Olympic Games in Helsinki and won a silver medal in the broad jump.

After earning the Doctorate at Caltech in 1960 Gourdine worked for the Aeronautical Division of Curtiss-Wright Corp. and it was here that he rediscovered an 18th Century energy conversion method and from it developed his bold new ideas in the field of electrogasdynamics. Failing to sell his generator to his employer, he raised $200,000 and founded his own research and development firm, Gourdine Systems, Inc.

He has invented a number of products and processes based on the use of electrogasdynamics technology — a process concerned with the inter-action of charged particles with a moving gas stream. Through this inter-action very high voltage can be produced from a low voltage originally generated. The phenomenon has been known to scientists since the late 1700's. The trouble was that no one could figure out how to harness the principle to generate enough electricity to make it practi-cal — especially for modern needs.

Gourdine Systems has moved from research and development in electrogasdynamics to four major application areas: energy conversion; paint-spraying systems; air pollution control; and printing.

The Gourdine direct high voltage electricity generation using pulver-ized coal and air in a combustion chamber located at the mouth of a coal mine could mean a new source of cheap electrical power.

Air pollution control in urban areas using principles of the Gourdine direct energy conversion process has been developed. In essence, dust particles are ionized and driven by a moving air stream to a collection point. The company has already developed methods for control of industrial, residential, automotive and diesel exhausting into the atmosphere.

In printing Gourdine's electrogasdynamics technology research has been used to deal with problems related to non contact printing processes.

The Gourdine electradyne coating or painting system uses a gun to emit particles charged by an applied potential of 6 kV. A portion of the kinetic energy in the moving air stream or in the particles themselves is utilized to raise the particles to high potential. The charged particles apply themselves to the nearest ground plane which is the work piece to be coated.

The applications of electrogasdynamics developed by Gourdine have the potential of affecting the lives of generations of people to come. And, as we continue to struggle with the energy problem, the work of Mere-dith Gourdine cannot be overlooked.

The solving of problems in any human society is a function not only of accumulating knowledge but of innovative thinking by particular individuals. It is people who must draw upon the resources of tradition as a springboard for inventiveness in the various sciences and technologies.

Were it not for the existence of black men of genius, our own modern day society would be a far less promising enterprise, whether looked at in terms of sheer physical well-being or in general terms of expanding horizons which make any society a much richer place in which to live. Blacks are advancing the frontiers of knowledge in virtually every new specialty of the sciences and technologies, from novel new approaches to engineering science to unprecedented new ways of interpreting our past. The genius of black men is today being employed by the National Aeronautics and Space Administration, with three blacks being recently named to the Space Shuttle Program, and by such humanitariun agencies as the World Health Organization. Blacks are writing treatises for many learned publications and conducting exciting new research at both predominately white and predominately black colleges and universities.

Such activity, of course, is no recent phenomenon as I have tried to illustrate in this paper. Most people have associated the black man's genius with the technological achievements of George Washington Carver (whose work with the peanut, soybean and sweet potato contributed so importantly to agriculture and industry) or with the medical contributions of Dr. Charles Drew, a pioneer in the field of blood plasma preservation. Unfortunately, what few have seemed to realize is that Carver and Drew are only two of literally dozens of black scientist-inventors and scholars whose genius has contributed to our society as we know it.

LEWIS LATIMER—BRINGER OF THE LIGHT

John Henrik Clarke

Summary: *Lewis Latimer was an outstanding member of that group of nineteenth century American inventors who helped to make America's twentieth century industrial revolution possible. Latimer solved the problem of transforming electric current cheaply into light through the invention of a durable filament for the electric bulb.*

Clarke looks at his inventions against the background of his times and touches upon his friendships with Maxim, the inventor of the machine-gun, Graham Bell (for whom Latimer drew the design of the first telephone) and Edison, for whom he worked and to whose pioneering probes in electricity Latimer brought a new illumination.

The collective contribution of Black Americans to science and inventions is so extensive that it is not possible to live a full day in any part of the United States, or the world in general, without sharing the benefits of their contribution. Yet, the genius of the Black American imagination, that influences every aspect of life in the United States is generally unknown to most Americans. The life of Lewis Howard Latimer (1848-1928), one of the many pioneer Black inventors, is a good example of the point I am trying to emphasize.

The contribution of African people to the making of the Americas, and the Caribbean Islands, extends far beyond forced labor. Before the Revolutionary War period and after, a class of skilled craftsmen developed among the Blacks who were brought to the slave plantations of what is called the *new world*. In South America, in The Caribbean Islands, and in the United States, these craftsmen often made the weapons that were used in the slave revolts. Some of them used their skill to make enough money, working after hours and on Sunday, to buy their freedom. Early in the nineteenth century small communities of Black freedmen had developed in New York City, Boston, Philadelphia, Chicago and other less populated cities in the Northern and Eastern parts of the United States. The first recognized Black inventors and skilled craftsmen came out of these communities.

In his book, "Great Negroes Past and Present," the Afro-American historian, Russell L. Adams calls attention to the fact that "Black Americans have made significant contributions to science despite the general absence of at least two basic conditions for scientific work: freedom from full-time pressures for personal survival, and a stimulating cultural environment. Slavery, segregation and cultural isolation have been the lot of most blacks in the United States. Nevertheless, scattered throughout the early history of Afro-Americans are individuals who made contributions of a scientific nature for the benefit of all."[1]

Lewis Latimer was an outstanding member of that group of American inventors whose work, started in the nineteenth century, helped to make America's twentieth century industrial revolution possible.

According to Russell L. Adams, Latimer was a product of the post-Reconstruction Period, when a sizeable number of Blacks began to study the biological sciences with the establishment of Howard University's School of Medicine in 1876, and the founding of Meharry Medical School in Nashville, Tennessee the same year. Lewis Latimer was a contemporary of other great Black inventors such as: Norbert Rillieux (1806-1894), who revolutionized the sugar refining industry; Elijah McCoy (1844-1929), who devised systems for the automatic lubrication of machinery and Granville T. Woods (1856-1910), who became known as the Black Thomas A. Edison, because of his contribution to the development of electrical equipment.

Lewis Howard Latimer was one of the great pioneers in the development of electricity. To him goes the honor of having solved the problem of transforming the electric current into light through the invention of the incandescent light. Latimer became an associate of the pioneer inventor Thomas A. Edison in 1878. He invented a carbon filament for the Maxim electric bulb and was assigned to supervise the installation of electric lighting of streets for New York, Philadelphia, London, England, and several other cities in the eighteen eighties.[3]

Lewis Howard Latimer was the only Afro-American member of the Edison Pioneers, a group of distinguished scientists and inventors who worked for Thomas Edison. Edison's teamwork approach in solving scientific and technological problems created a good atmosphere for the continuous development of the diverse talent of Lewis Latimer. The Edison laboratories in Menlo Park and West Orange, New Jersey, were forerunners of the present day industrial research centers.

For a number of years Latimer was also associated with Alexander Graham Bell, for whom he drew plans for the first telephone and assisted in preparing the patents. Near the end of his career he was chief draftsman for the companies, General Electric and Westinghouse. Lewis Howard Latimer was one of the most distinguished of the pioneers who

Lewis H. Latimer

Courtesy of the Lewis H. Latimer Foundation   Clarke - Fig. 1

started with Thomas A. Edison. He is the author of the book, "Incandescent Electric Lighting: A Practical Description of the Edison System" (1890).[4]

Early in his career Lewis Latimer worked in an office where applications for patents on inventions were reviewed and processed. In this atmosphere he was stimulated to begin the basic work on inventions of his own. One of his first inventions was patented on February 10, 1874. It was a "Water Closet for Railroad Cars."

After Thomas A. Edison invented the incandescent electric lamp in 1879, Lewis Latimer began the research that led to an improvement in the incandescent light. On September 13, 1881, Latimer and Joseph V. Nichols received a patent for their "Electric Lamp." Part of the description of the patent states:

> Our invention relates to electric lamps in which the light is produced by the incandescence of a continuous strip of carbon secured to metallic wires and enclosed in a hermetically sealed and thoroughly exhausted transparent receiver; and it relates more especially to the method of mounting the carbons or connecting them with wires.

In January of 1882, Latimer received what he considered to be his most important patent, a "Process for Manufacturing Carbons." This was again an improvement on the carbon filaments that were used in Edison's lamps. Latimer's carbon filaments lasted much longer.[5]

This gentle man is one of the unsung heroes of the great age of American invention. Among the little known facts of his life is that he was also a poet and an essayist. The full impact of his life and works must be considered in the light of the times during which he lived. He was never out of touch with his time. Though he is not known as a writer, his private papers show that he was concerned with every aspect of his developing country, and the role that his people were playing in shaping it. His life spanned three troublesome eras in the history of race relations in America: The Slavery Period, The Reconstruction Period, and The First Quarter of the 20th Century.

These periods contributed the main elements that went into the making of what would later be called "The Black Revolution."

Lewis Latimer, the son of a fugitive slave, became one of the men who created the electric industry. He was a draftsman, poet, inventor, musician, author and artist, good family man, a good citizen, and a great unsung American. His life proves what is possible in America despite drawbacks and handicaps. It also points up the fact that if America is to survive as a nation, it will have to make better use of the talent of its many ethnic minorities.

The story of Lewis Latimer began when it was legal for one person to hold another in bondage. His father was a slave in Virginia. He escaped and found his way to Boston, where William Lloyd Garrison, Frederick Douglass, and other abolitionists secured the funds needed to purchase his freedom. That is how Lewis came to be born in Chelsea, Massachusetts in September, 1848.[6]

When he was ten years old his father disappeared suddenly, leaving his mother with four children. He was sent to a Farm School for boys and was later joined by his brother William. The two boys planned their escape from the farm and were finally successful. Back in Boston they went to work to help support their family. At the age of fifteen Lewis enlisted in the Union Navy during the Civil War. He saw action on the James River when his brothers were fighting with the land forces. After the end of the war he returned to Boston to seek work.

After some effort and many disappointments Lewis Latimer found a job as office boy in a firm named Crosly and Gage. There he was draftsman making drawings of things that other people wanted to build. At once, he knew what he wanted his life's work to be. He bought a set of second hand drafting tools and started to read every book he could find on the subject. When he had confidence that he had mastered his tools he asked his employer to let him do some drawings. At first his employer did not take him seriously. When he finally got his chance he made the best of it and was given a desk and a raise in pay.

The office where he worked was located near the school where Alexander Graham Bell was a teacher. Lewis Latimer and Alexander Graham Bell became close friends. They often met and talked about their work and their families. Bell's father had invented the sign language that enabled deaf and dumb people to communicate with each other. Bell had come to America to teach the language. His wife was a deaf mute. In trying to invent a device that might enable his wife to hear him, Alexander Graham Bell perfected a machine which he named the telephone. He asked Lewis Latimer to make a drawing of his invention in order to patent it. This was not an easy job. Latimer had to draw each part of the device and describe how it worked. Finally, the work was finished and Bell got his patent in 1876.

In 1879, Lewis Latimer met Herman Maxim while doing odd jobs for a machine shop in Bridgeport, Connecticut. Maxim was amazed to see Latimer doing the work of a draftsman and said that this was the first Black draftsman he had ever seen. Herman Maxim, who had invented the machine gun was at this time Chief Engineer and Electrician for the United States Electric Lighting Company. He hired Lewis Latimer as a draftsman and as his secretary. Under the guidance of Maxim, Latimer learned all he could about the then young, electric industry. He began experimenting in order to improve some of the electric devices of his day.

In 1881, he invented and patented the first electric lamp with a carbon filament. He also invented a cheap method for making the filaments. His innovations and lighting were a sensation for his day and some of his inventions are now on display at the Smithsonian Institute in Washington, D.C.

Maxim and Charles Wilson raised money to set up factories to manufacture some of the inventions of Lewis Latimer. His lamps lit up railroad stations in Canada and other countries. He learned French so that his instructions could be clearly understood in the French-speaking areas of Canada. During the late 1870's he married Mary Wilson and was made a gift of a honeymoon in London by the company who employed him. It was a business honeymoon. While in London on his honeymoon he was assigned to inspect some of the new electric factories in that country.

In London, Lewis Latimer supervised the production of carbon filaments, using the method he had invented. The London businessmen who were in charge of the Maxim-Weston Electric Light Company were not accustomed to being told what to do by one of their employees. Now they were being told by an employee who was Black. In spite of the unfriendly atmosphere, Latimer completed his assignment.

Mr. and Mrs. Latimer returned to New York in 1882, and helped to light up New York City, in many ways. After working a short while with an old friend, Charles Weston, in New Jersey, he established the Westinghouse Company and asked Latimer to continue as his employee. The major assignments in the new company went to Latimer such as lighting the Equitable Building and the Union League Club. He supervised some of the first electric lighting on the streets of New York City.

In 1883, a company formed by Thomas A. Edison sent for Latimer and asked him to join their engineering department. Soon he was transferred to their legal department. Some Wall Street interest from their General Company also used the services of Latimer. The two giant electrical companies at the time were General Electric and Westinghouse. They organized a Board of Patent Control and appointed Latimer Chief Draftsman and expert legal witness for this board. During this time he travelled widely gathering evidence against companies who ill-used the patents of Westinghouse and General Electric.[7]

By now, he had two girls, Louise Rebecca and Emma Jeanette. Latimer had a happy family life.

Out of his admiration for Thomas A. Edison and his leadership and genius in the electrical industry, Latimer wrote the first textbook on the electrical lighting system in 1890.

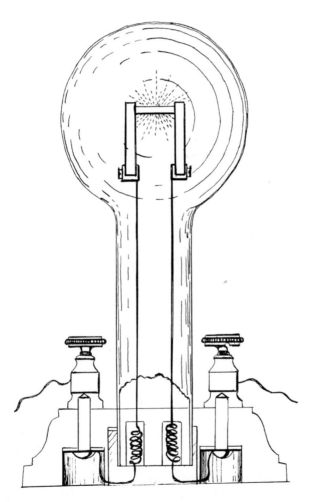

*The first drawing made by Lewis H. Latimer of his invention of the first
practical electric light bulb (1880).*   Clarke - Fig. 2

Since the 1870's, he had been involved with the Civil Rights Movement and his friend, Richard Greener, one of the outstanding Black intellects of the 19th century. In 1906, Latimer was asked to go to the Henry Street Settlement to teach a class in mechanical drawing. His students were recent immigrants to America. Because of the language barrier the assignment was interesting and challenging. Latimer had to teach mechanical drawing and English at the same time. He recalled while teaching this class that William Lloyd Garrison and other abolitionists were some of the busiest men in the world, yet they found time to help his father, a fugitive slave. He also recalled his long friendship with the great Frederick Douglass and rededicated himself to helping any American who needed him.

In 1918, Latimer received what he considered to be the greatest thrill of his life. An organization was formed for the men who were described as "the creators of the electric industry." He had been asked to become a Charter Member of this group of men. They were called The Edison Pioneers. Every man in the group had worked with Thomas Edison.

Lewis Latimer lived to see many of the students in his class of immigrants become distinguished Americans.

Lewis Latimer was concerned about the plight of the disadvantaged people in America, irrespective of color. His interest in his own work did not prevent him from devoting time to the cause of Civil Rights, as the following statement from a letter written in 1895 shows:

> ...Because there is no separation of the colored Americans from those of the white American, and it is our duty to show our country, and to the world, that we are looking to the interests of the country at large, when we protest against the crime and injustice meted out to any class or condition of our citizens.

The recent discovery of two of Lewis Latimer's relatives and his papers indicated something of his early life and his long and happy life with his wife, Mary, and their two daughters. This man born of slave parents was one of the best informed and one of the most imaginative of American inventors. He lived a life worthy of emulation by American youth. His numerous letters including the correspondence between him and Frederick Douglass proves that he was forever concerned with the plight of his own people who during the latter part of his life were still suffering from disfranchisement and second-hand citizenship. He died in Flushing, New York, on December 11, 1928, on the eve of the great Depression.

On May 10, 1968, a public school in Brooklyn, New York, was dedicated to the memory of Lewis Latimer. It is now known as The Lewis H. Latimer School.

NOTES AND REFERENCES

1. "Great Negroes, Past and Present," by Russell L. Adams, Afro-Am Publishing Company, Inc., Chicago, Ill., 1969, pp. 61-64. Also see: "Lewis Howard Latimer: Black Inventor," produced by The Thomas Alva Edison Foundation, Detroit, Michigan, 1973.

2. "The Story of Lewis Latimer: Manual and Study Outline," by M.A. Harris, Negro History Associates, New York, NY, 1964. Also see: two other books by the same writer and publisher: "Black Inventors: The Revolutionary Period," and "Early American Inventors, 18th and 19th Centuries."

3. "Eight Black American Inventors," by Robert C. Hayden, Addison Wesley Publishing Company, Inc., 1972, pp. 78-92.

4. "Incandescent Electric Lighting: A Practical Description of the Edison System." D. Van Norstrand Company, New York, NY, 1890. Also see: "Black Pioneers of Science and Invention," by Louis Haber, Harcourt, Brace and World, New York, NY, 1970, pp. 49-60.

5. "Black Innovations," by Dr. Irene Diggs, Institute of Positive Education, Chicago, Ill., 1975, pp. 1-9.

6. "Harlem, What Teachers, Parents and Children Should Know About Our Community." Prepared by Beryle Banfield for The Anniversary Bulletin Committee of P.S. 175, Manhattan, New York, NY, 1965, pp. 79-81. Also see: "Black Pioneers of Science and Invention," by Louis Haber, Harcourt, Brace and World, Inc., New York, NY, 1970, pp. 49-60.

7. "The Hidden Contributors: Black Scientists and Inventors in America," by Aaron E. Klein, Doubleday and Co., 1971, pp. 97-108.

SPACE SCIENCE:
THE AFRICAN-AMERICAN CONTRIBUTION

Curtis M. Graves and Ivan Van Sertima

The first Space Shuttle Orbiter, which should be launched within the next year, will open a whole new phase in space exploration, the most exciting and rewarding phase since America's moon landings a decade ago. It will not only open new windows upon the vast universe but windows within the science and life of our own planet, illuminating our medicine, our communication systems, our manufacturing industries. The spin-off of benefits from space science may, in fact, revolutionize our daily lives.

For space exploration is not, as so many believe, the costly adventure of a few in pursuit of a fascinating but barren knowledge. The practical value of these exploratory probes is already becoming clear. The scientific enterprise it promotes may solve many problems unrelated to space itself. We are now mapping, for example, new sources of Earth's minerals with the all-seeing eye of our satellites. We learned more about our Earth and the total solar system in a 48-hour encounter with Jupiter than we had learned in the whole history of the universe. We are beginning to unlock secrets of matter that may someday solve the frightening problem of energy. We may eventually place behind us, as we thrust forward into time and space, the nightmare of our dwindling resources. Man, therefore, is not building a network of dream observatories above the clouds to distance himself from the human anguish beneath.

African-Americans are as much involved in this new scientific adventure and enterprise as they were involved in the science of earlier centuries (see Journal of African Civilizations Vol I, No.2). The nature and scope of their contributions to this field is startling. It is impossible to deal with it comprehensively in a single article. Here, however, we attempt to bring to public attention, and in a layman's language, some of these contributions. Curtis Graves, Chief of Community and Education Services Branch, National Aeronautics and Space Administration, in conversations with Ivan Van Sertima, Editor of *J.A.C.*, introduces us to a few of the African-Americans, working at NASA or on loan to NASA, who have made important contributions to space science and aeronautical research. The selection of those who appear in this introduction were made by the editor and he bears full responsibility for important omissions.

MAJOR FREDERICK D. GREGORY

Major Frederick D. Gregory will be the first black astronaut pilot in the history of space flight. He is a research test pilot for the U.S. Air Force. He has flown more than 40 different aircraft, ranging from helicopters to fighters, and has been involved with aircraft and simulation evaluation and testing for the Airforce and NASA for more than seven years. He is a Member of the Society of Experimental Test Pilots, a graduate of the U.S. Naval Test Pilot School and holds BS and MSA degrees.

MAJOR GREGORY

He was loaned to NASA three years ago to fly research missions. One of the missions he has flown is the ground-based microwave landing system. He was the person that field-tested it and sold it to the Airport Association and, about five years from now, this system, which was built by Bendix Aircraft and tested by Gregory, will be the system that will be used world-wide to land airplanes. It's a computer-based system that works on the micro-wave. Markers are set up some distance away from the landing field which coincide with devices on the plane. These markers send microwave messages to the plane to tell it to go high or low or right or left so that the plane will literally be landing by honing in to instruments on the ground.

Most airplanes at present make instrumented landings but the whole thing is done with the pilot controlling instruments aboard the plane rather than turning control over to devices on the ground. In the future, with the micro-wave instrumentation landing system, the pilot can just press a button and the airport will land the plane for him. For instance, if you're a pilot coming in to National Airport in Washington, and, because of the wind direction, ground-control decided to make you go around the other side, to come in the other way, a switch will be handled by ground-based computers which speak to the computer on your plane and give it directions on how to come in on the microwave system.

The system that is now in use on 747's — the jumbo jets — is similar in some respects. They are the only commercial planes at the moment which have the automatic landing system. This is geared to the altimeter on the plane (the instrument that measures the distance of the plane from its point in flight to the ground). The signals that come from the ground base, however, are radio waves whereas in the new system it will all be done by micro-wave. Every commercial plane will have this system 5-6 years from now because all the airports in the world are moving to this microwave landing system. Gregory was one of the people who pioneered in setting it up. He was part of the team that put it together. He field-tested it and sold it.

For field-testing it, they built a plane with a second cockpit inside where Gregory sat, blind to the outside. (See Figure 2)

Gregory — Fig. 2

The TCV AIRCRAFT (tested by Major Gregory) is used to demonstrate new concepts of airborne control systems of advanced design, particularly approach and landing systems for future use at airfields in the U.S. and abroad.

They flew the plane from the second cockpit. They put two pilots up front to make sure nothing went wrong but Gregory flew it with nine observers from the International Airport Association on board to prove that the system was superior to the foreign systems. It could land planes with hands off.

Anyone could be the pilot in such a system which practically eliminates human error in landing operations. You just set the computer and put the record in and there is a diagram of the landing system of the airport. Every airport would have its diagram and you could just stick this diagram into the computer and the computer does the rest for you. It would land the plane, along with the ground-based systems which tell you whether you're on track or not. The test plane landed everytime without a problem and nobody had to touch anything.

Yet this is a small thing compared to what he has done in terms of redesigning cockpits for aircraft. Gregory was on loan to NASA to do aeronautical research and while he was there he redesigned and built cockpit redesigns for commercial planes. He has several patents on file of cockpit redesigns.

Among the designs of Gregory is a "single-hand" controller that combines both throttle power control as well as control over roll and pitch. This can enable the pilot of an aircraft to perform several functions with one hand, thus freeing the other for more "positive aircraft control." Aircraft control, in the usual type of airplane, requires that roll and pitch be controlled with one hand and the throttle (or power-stick) with the other. Several cockpit functions — gear, flaps, radios, systems etc — require the action of the pilot and so divert his attention from the main task.

The introduction of a controller that allows complete and precise airplane control *with one hand free* could improve the pilot's ability to manage the critical systems. Gregory has designed such a singlehand controller, known as the SSTC (Side-Stick Throttle Controller — see Fig. 3). This has been evaluated by test pilots at NASA's Langley Research Center. It was found to be acceptable under rigorous testing and in some cases a suitable alternative to conventional controls. Some aspects, however, need further investigation, (such as the problem of hand fatigue in conventional controls, which can be eliminated with the SSTC).

Gregory — Fig. 3 — Sidestick Throttle Controller

A single-hand roll, pitch and power controller designed by MAJOR FREDERICK GREGORY. An alternative to two-hand operated conventional controls in airplanes.

Gregory has the major responsibility for cockpit redesign aboard the Space Shuttle. He is the technical monitor for the astronauts and he is redesigning the cockpit on the new shuttles that will be flown in the eighties. The first shuttle cockpit is already in place but they have found problems with it already and it is Gregory's responsibility to re-do the cockpit and come up with a new design that will give the pilot more information and make the aircraft more flyable when it's operational. The first orbiter that's going to fly, however, is already delivered to NASA. Nothing can be done about the cockpit on that one. But there will be four of them altogether and the second, third and fourth one will have the new cockpit, as redesigned by Gregory, in place.

This is the cockpit of the first Space Shuttle Orbiter. Gregory is to redesign the cockpit for use in the next three shuttles (Gregory — Fig. 4)

Space Science Update

*This article was originally published in 1980, based on interviews with
the Deputy Director of Academic Services at NASA, Dr. Curtis Graves. A
number of changes have occurred since that time and we feel we should
share this with our readers.*

*Major Isaac Gillam IV is no longer Director of Dryden's Flight Research
Center. He has been promoted to another administrative position within the
space agency.*

*Major Frederick Gregory is now Colonel Gregory. He did not turn out to
be the first African-American astronaut in space, as was originally intended, but he will be the first to pilot a space shuttle. This is expected to
occur in 1984. Lt. Col. Guy Bluford became the first Black American to be
sent into space. He was launched on August 30, 1983. To the list of Black
American astronauts being trained for future space flights, we should add
Lt. Col. Bolden and Dr. Ronald E. McNair, a laser physicist. (Dr. McNair
was one of the seven astronauts who died in the* Challenger *explosion—Ed.)*

The Editor of the Journal of African Civilizations *attended the launch of
Lt. Col. Bluford, at the invitation of NASA. He is featured below with
Colonel Gregory, at the Kennedy Space Center in Florida, on the day before
the launch.*

Colonel Gregory, who is to pilot a space shuttle in 1984, meets the Editor of Journal of African
Civilizations *at the Kennedy Space Center, Cape Canaveral, Florida.*

ISAAC GILLAM IV

The highest ranking black operations officer at NASA is Isaac Gillam IV, Director of Dryden's Flight Research Center at Edwards Air Force Base in California. It is there under the direction of Gillam that the performance of the Space Shuttle, the critical approach and landing tests, have been carried out. When testing is complete, American astronauts will take to space again. They will enter it in a huge 150,000 pound shuttle. (see Fig. 1).

Shuttle lands after first test under the direction of Gillam.   Gillam Fig. 1

Gillam was responsible for integrating the efforts of nearly a thousand space personnel from various agencies and stations pooling their efforts to get the Space Shuttle airborne. His complex "oversee" role included checking the safety problems involved in transporting the shuttle aboard the 747 over populated territory to its final launching pad at Cape Kennedy in Florida, for its stability and control in flight, for its safe landing from outer space within a specified ten-mile strip in the Mojave Desert.

Born in Little Rock, Arkansas, Gillam received a degree in mathematics from Howard University. While at Howard he was designated a Distinguished Military Student and commissioned in the U.S. Air Force upon graduation. He came to NASA in 1966 from Strategic Air Command where he commanded a missile crew in an underground silo. His technical background combined with administrative skills led to his promotion in 1973 to Program Manager of the Small Launch Vehicle and International Project. He headed two of NASA's most important missile-launch programs, Delta and Scout. Under his direction, NASA put into orbit satellites for RCA, Comstat and Western Union, as well as companies in France, Germany, Italy, Indonesia, Canada and Japan. His role in the foreign satellite launch program earned him the Distinguished Service Medal, NASA's highest award.

During his role as Director of Shuttle Operations, which he became in 1976, Gillam had to coordinate the workings of scientists from a wide complex involved in the first phase of the Space Shuttle Program — men from Dryden, Rockwell International, American Airlines, Boeing and the John Kennedy Space Centers.

ISAAC GILLAM IV
Director, Dryden Flight Research Center

ROBERT E. SHURNEY

Robert Shurney is an aeronautical engineer. He has a degree in physics from A. & I. State University, Nashville, Tennessee. He has been working at the Marshall Space Flight Center as a Research Engineer for nearly 20 years and has gained recognition for his work as a test conductor.

As a scientific engineer, his expertise has been in the area of designing utility kinds of devices for space laboratories, especially Skylab. One of his notable contributions is his design and testing of commodes used aboard the Skylab. When the astronauts were up for long periods of time, they used eating utensils as well as commodes (refuse disposal units) that Shurney designed.

He has tested these things in weightless conditions in a KC-135 aircraft which NASA uses to fly "weightlessness" missions. For 30 seconds you get the feeling of weightlessness in this unique plane because it flies a parabolic curve and then falls for 30 seconds and in that 30 second period of time you are weightless. Shurney actually tested his space commode in this weightless environment to make sure it did what it was supposed to do. He was the first person to test it before NASA took it aboard the Skylab mission. He has probably had more time aboard the weightless airplane than even the astronauts, as many as 300 — 400 hours of weightlessness.

Shurney conducting a test in a KC-135 Zero 9 Aircraft (Laser Study of Ice Crystals.)
(Note test crew beginning to float in weightless condition).   Shurney — Fig. 1

Shurney has also been instrumental in designing the commodes used aboard the Space Shuttle but he did not have the major design responsibilities he had on the Skylab mission, where he designed the whole thing himself. The Shuttle's commode systems store the solid refuse materials on the bottom and the liquid material in tubes because they would float away and contaminate the whole cabin. Shurney has also been on test missions, examining a variety of other equipment intended for the Space Shuttle, such as the Solar Array Blanket Tube below:—

Bob Shurney — (aboard the KC-135 Zero 9 Aircraft) testing the Solar Array Blanket Tube to be used in Space Shuttle Flights. Shurney Fig. 2 —

Shurney designed the tires used on the moon buggy. NASA needed a tire that would fit three requirements. First, it would have to be extraordinarily lightweight since the payload on the moonrocket had to be as light as possible for our rockets to hurl aloft so many experimental instruments plus the men aboard. Two, it would have to hold the weight of the astronaut and the laboratory of instruments he would carry around with him. Third, the moon-buggy tire would need to have a good traction, as good as that of the rubber tire we use on Earth, even though it would be a lot lighter. The moon's surface is very dusty and there is the problem too of driving in a one third gravity environment. Shurney designed an aluminum tire that has metal plates on the inside and something like a wire mesh on the outside. This wire is a very stiff wire that holds the weight of the vehicle and gives it very good traction. Shurney came up with the tire design within the weight parameters and strength parameters they needed for moon mobility.

Tires designed by shurney on Moon Buggy "FALCON."   Shurney — Fig. 3

PATRICIA COWINGS

Dr. Patricia Cowings received her doctorate in Psychology at the University of California at Davis in 1973. She has done post-doctoral studies in Aerospace Medicine, Bioastronautics, Psychophysiological and Biological Problems of long duration manned space flight and Human Vestibular Physiology. She has had wide experience in several aspects of space medicine research and was Principal Investigator for an experiment conducted on board Space Lab Center in Houston, Texas.

Her research is in two or three areas. In one area she looks at physiological problems that astronauts have when they are flying in space. What she does is that she simulates on the ground the same emotional feelings they would experience in states of weightlessness out in space and in this simulation she makes them sick. She causes them to throw up or be sick in other ways while measuring their vital signs.

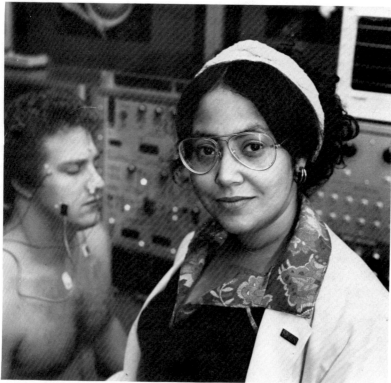

Dr. Cowings checks test subject for motion sickness before testing Astronauts.

Cowings — Fig. 1

What's she's doing is trying to determine what physiological changes occur right before the sickness which causes it. Once she determines what those are, then she prescribes a therapy which enables you to psyche yourself into not being sick. For instance, if there is an increased rate in your blood pressure that causes the throwing up or if it is the spinning and the inner ear motion that causes the sickness she tells you how to keep your head erect or move your ear to one side or to do whatever it is to counteract that which makes you ill, and so she designs the therapy for the astronauts so that they will be able to control their involuntary systems and no longer become ill because of weightlessness.

Part of what she is doing has to do with biorhythm and what we normally call yoga because what she does is she measures their biorhythm to see what effect it might have on their ability to function under pressure situations and she's able to measure this in a very exact way with a device which she has designed for body measurements.

She has also designed a therapy to exercise the veins in their legs so that when they return back to earth the pressure will not be as great as it would be, had they done this exercise. When people are exposed to weightlessness in space for long periods of time and then they return to the Earth's gravity, the lower parts of their body tend to collect fluids because the veins and arteries in their lower extremities will lose the tautness they had when they were walking in one G (that is, our gravity environment) all their life. So what she has done is design an exercise, a therapy, which enables you (even out there) to exercise those veins or even stretch those veins so that they will remain as taut as they were when you were on earth. That may involve, for instance, having a person tied down to a treadmill. You might be tied down with springs around your waist to the floor which would simulate gravity and then you would walk on this treadmill (see Fig. 2) put the same amount of pressure on your body as you would normally have if you were in one gravity which is what we have on earth — One G. So she has designed this exercise and it's an individual thing. She has to know the individual needs of the astronauts in order to take very precise measurements of their bodies so that she can guage how much exercise and therapy they'll need while they're in weightlessness in order to survive the pressures of coming back.

(see overleaf)

Basic medical testing for women astronaut candidates...Marsha Ivins, NASA engineer, is shown during treadmill testing in the Cardio-Pulmonary Lab at the Johnson Space Center, Houston, Texas. Body sensors, attached to Ivins' torso, transmit vital statistics such as heart rate and blood pressure.

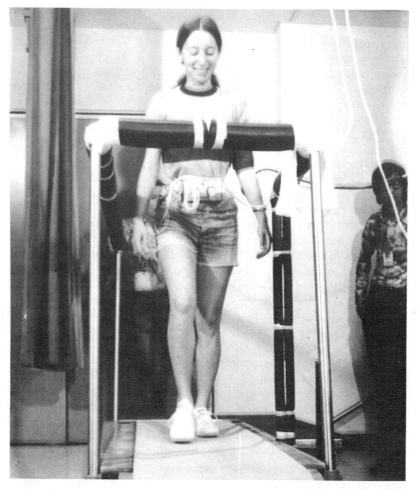

She's also developing methods of psychologically dealing with your heart rate, your heart beat and your blood pressure. She trains you in therapy to make your blood pressure go up or down. She shows you how to do this by psyching you into making your blood pressure rise or fall. If she finds that the person's blood pressure going up is what causes them to get sick, then she wants to maintain a low blood pressure and if she finds that it is the going down that gets them sick she wants to maintain a high blood pressure. She shows you how to compensate for the blood pressure changes that you may experience in your weightlessness. The same thing applies to heart rate. If what is causing you to become sick is your heart rapidly pounding she shows you how to relax to slow your heart rate down so that your heart never races in a distressful situation in space.

CHRISTINE DARDEN

Christine Darden is an Aerospace Engineer in the High-Speed Aerodynamics Division at NASA's Langley Research Center in Hampton, Virginia. Before coming to Langley in 1967, she was a mathematics instructor at Virginia State College and did aerosol physics research. She received her Master of Science degree in mathematics at the same college and is now doing her doctorate in the Department of Mechanical Engineering in the School of Engineering and Applied Science at George Washington University.

She is the leading NASA researcher in supersonic and hypersonic aircraft with expertise in the area of reducing sonic boom. She has designed wind tunnel models of airplanes with which she simulates supersonic flight and is working on the modification of planes to see whether she can alter the effects of sonic boom. Sonic boom has become a matter of great popular and scientific interest in recent years.

But how is sonic boom really caused and how can this problem be solved to make our future generations of aircraft fly more quietly without these explosive bursts of sound?

The wing of a plane cuts through the air just like a boat cuts through water. When a plane goes through the air it makes a wave. When that wave touches the ground it creates a shock and if it is touching the ground faster than the speed of sound the air pressure behind the wave is so drastically different that a sonic boom is caused as a result of the difference in front of the wave and behind the wave.

What Christine Darden is doing is manipulating the wing and the shape of the airplane so that something destroys the sharpness of the wave that hits the ground. So the sonic boom sound goes off into the atmosphere, away from the ground. One of the experiments she's working on is a means of sending the sonic boom back up instead of down, so that the air that touches the bottom of the wing would be crinkled in some kind of way. There would be something there to destroy the shape of it so that the actual air that hits the ground would be so much in disarray that it would significantly reduce the sound you get on the ground.

Modifying the wing is just one of the things she's working on. She's also trying to blunt the nose of aircraft. Planes have a tendency to get more needle-nosed as they get faster. She is taking the point out of the nose. What she is doing in effect is smoothing out the flow of air that goes above and below the wings of aircrafts. Blunting the nose causes the air that flows away from the plane to wrinkle and in wrinkling you bring about a lessening in sonic boom effect. NASA is going beyond supersonic aircraft. We're into the hypersonic, which is two or three times the speed of sound and there will be planes that eventually will fly hypersonically — about two or three thousand miles an hour.

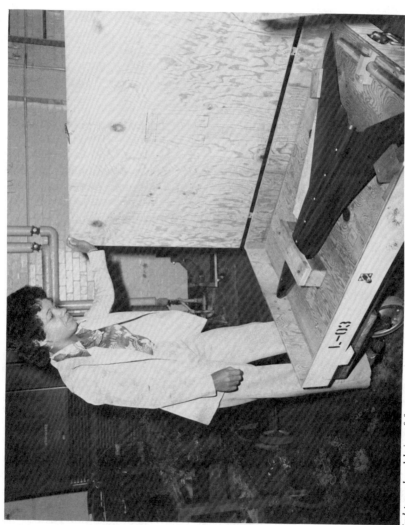

Darden uncrates a wind-tunnel model aircraft for supersonic testing at Langley, Va.

Darden — Fig. 1

The American Congress has passed a law forbidding any aircraft except military aircraft to fly above the continental United States supersonically. The Concorde had to go out into the Atlantic before it could fly supersonically. The reason for that was that when we started flying planes above the speed of sound there were sonic booms all over the place and sonic booms were very frightening. People lobbied Congress to stop the flight of aircraft above the continental United States supersonically to the point where we have to be careful not to call our space craft "aircraft." What Darden is interested in doing is eliminating the negative effect of flying supersonically. Obviously we are not going to find ways to fly slower, we want to fly faster and faster. Right now we can fly to Europe in four hours on a commercial Concorde. We'd like to be able to do it in an hour or fly to Australia in 45 minutes. That will be possible towards the end of the century. It will be possible because of the Christine Dardens who will design mechanisms to alleviate the sonic boom factor.

Darden collects computer data during a wind tunnel test of supersonic aircraft.
Darden Fig. 2

BLACKSPACE

James G. Spady

Summary: In this brief essay, James Spady investigates the role Dr. George Carruthers, Dr. Elmer Imes and other Blacks have played in the emerging multi-discipline of the space sciences. He criticises the lack of interest by black historiographers in this significant field and demonstrates the widespread implications of the breakthroughs achieved by these scientists.

In a review of historical literature one is appalled by the absence of serious attention given to space science by the growing body of American historians (Black and White). Moreover, with the exception of works on men like George Washington Carver, Benjamin Banneker, Charles Drew etc., there is virtually nothing in the historical record worthy of serious attention. Most Black graduate scholars are in the social sciences or humanities and with the exception of Dr. Kenneth Manning of the Massachusetts Institute of Technology, I know of no other Black who has specialized in the History of Science on a doctoral level.[1]

The word science does not refer to a particular class of facts, but to the method of investigating them. It does not mean knowledge, but knowledge obtained by solid principles, and in a specific way, i.e., crystallization of ideas, methodology and language. The failure of Social scientists and humanists to be conversant with new knowledge developing in the physical, natural and space sciences can be a great loss to the refinement and deepening of their disciplines.

Dr. George R. Carruthers, a Black Astrophysicist, has made a major contribution to the area of Space Astronomy. His Apollo 16 Far Ultraviolet Camera/Spectrograph is perhaps *the* most significant single contribution in recent years relating to our knowledge of the world's physical structure. (see Fig. I)

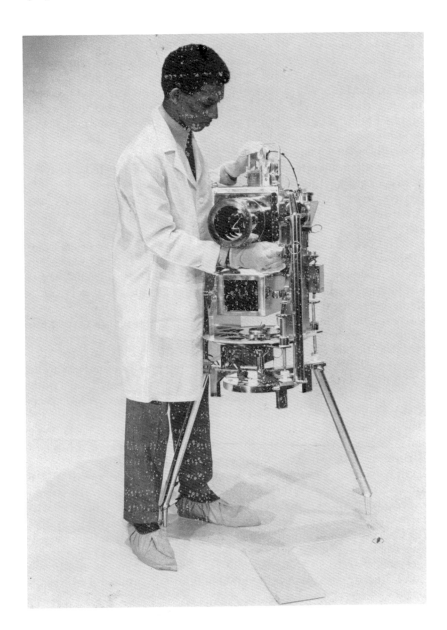

SPADY — FIG I

LUNAR SURFACE ULTRAVIOLET CAMERA/SPECTOGRAPH
For the first time, space explorers were able to study and record planetary and astronomical phenomena from the moon with a special gold-plated camera, based on concepts developed by Dr. George Carruthers.

Born in Cincinatti, Ohio, on 1 October 1939, George Carruthers evinced an early interest in science fiction, astronomy and rocket construction.[2] Although his parents encouraged this interest in the sciences, (his father was a civil engineer) most of his teachers found his futuristic thinking to be "out there in space". He attended Englewood High School in Chicago. While participating in science fairs at predominantly white schools, he was met with racial jeers. The bias was decidedly against a man of color.

George demonstrated great discipline at an early age. His knowledge of physics and mathematics did not come easy. Added to his insatiable desire to learn more about the physical structure of other planets, was Carruthers' interest in the physical construction of mechanisms to be used in outer space.

In the Fall of 1957, Carruthers entered the College of Engineering, University of Illinois, and departed in June, 1964. During that seven-year period he earned his B.S. '61, M.S. '62, Ph.D. 1964 in the area of aeronautical and astronautical engineering. His thesis was on experimental investigations of atomic nitrogen recombination.

Upon graduation, Carruthers was awarded the highly prestigious National Science Foundation's Fellowship to join the rocket astronomy group at the Naval Research Laboratory (N.R.L.) in Washington, D.C. Two years later, (1966) he became a full time research physicist at the E.O. Hulburt Center for Space Research, (N.R.L.). His first scientific publication was "An Upper Limit on the Concentration of Molecular Hydrogen in Inter-stellar Space." It was followed a year later (1968) by "Far Ultraviolet Spectroscopy and Photometry of some Early Type Stars." These two essays solidly established Carruthers as a brilliant astrophysicist destined to change our vision of the universe.

On November 11, 1969, Carruthers was granted Patent #3,478,216 for an "Image Converter For Detecting Electromagnetic Radiation Especially In Short Wave Lengths." The application had been filed as early as 27 July 1966.[3] This means at the age of 25, maybe as young as 23, Carruthers was an inventor. His first major publication was released at the age of 26. Significantly, in the very year that his patent was received, his article "Magnetically Focused Electronographic Image Converters for Space Astronomy Applications" appeared in *Applied Optics*.

In a period of 12 years, Carruthers has authored or co-authored 63 major scientific papers in such major journals and volumes as *Astrophysical Journal, Science, The Intersellar Medium* (Holland, 1974), *Apollo 16 Preliminary Science Report*, NASA SP-315 (1972), and *The Society of Photo-Optical Instrumentation Engineers' Instrumentation in Astronomy* (1973). His pioneering "Television Sensors for Ultraviolet Space Astronomy" in *Astronomical Observations with Television-Type Sensors* was published by the prestigious Institute of Astronomy and Space Science at the University of British Columbia, Canada.

Due to space and time limitations, this paper will not be a comprehensive outline of Carruthers' work. I will focus on one single breakthrough and its implications. I had the pleasure of talking with Astronaut John W. Young, Commander of the Apollo 16 flight to the moon. As an historian interested in primary sources, I asked him if he knew Carruthers. Smiling broadly, he said in that midwestern accent of his:

"I have known Dr. Carruthers for a long time. He was the Principal Investigator at the Naval Research Laboratory and had this telescope built that we used on the moon. It was the very first telescope that we have ever had operating from another celestial body. He was in charge of the whole business. I think new knowledge coming from Astronomers like him will revolutionize the way we think."[4]

In mid-May 1972 some of the first scientific results from Apollo 16 were announced from the Manned Spacecraft Center in Houston, Texas. Carruthers' camera/spectograph took ultraviolet photographs of the lunar sky.

The camera was set up in the shadow of the lunar module to photograph earth and selected celestial objects in ultraviolet light of wavelengths shorter than 1600 angstroms.

Carruthers' semiautomatic device is a combination spectrograph and camera, with an electron intensifier. A Schmidt optical system focuses an image on a potassium bromide cathode that emits electrons in proportion to the number of ultraviolet photons striking it. A 25,000 volt potential accelerates the electron toward a special photographic film. The focusing magnet surrounding the camera ensures that the electron image accurately reproduces the ultraviolet images. Thereby, a 10-20 fold reduction in exposure time results from this electronic intensification process.

In a highly illuminating essay. "Space Astronomy in the Shuttle Era" Carruthers explains the advantage of using his Far Ultraviolet Camera/Spectograph and future ones based on his prototype.

"The far ultraviolet, below the atmospheric cut off 3000 Å, and extending down to the soft x-ray range below 100Å, is of great importance to the astronomer because it allows the detection and measurement of common elements (hydrogen, oxygen, nitrogen, carbon, and many others) in their cool, unexcited condition ("Ground state" of the atom or molecule), a task which is difficult or impossible in the ground-accessible wavelength range. This allows more accurate measurements of the compositions of interstellar gas, planetary atmospheres, etc. The ultraviolet also conveys important information on solid particles ("dust") in interstellar space and elsewhere, and provides for much more accurate measurements of the energy outputs of very hot stars —

that is those stars having temperatures in the range 10,000 — 100,000° K for our sun), which emits most of their radiation in wavelengths below 3000A°...

"In the infrared, the improvement of sensitivity afforded by space observations, and the elimination of terrestrial atmospheric emissions and absorptions, will allow greatly improved measurements of the cool states of cosmic material — dense concentrations of interstellar gas and dust, stars in the process of formation, and planetary atmospheres."[5]

ELMER SAMUEL IMES: PIONEER BLACK PHYSICIST

Another distinguished Black Astro and Industrial Physicist is Dr. Elmer Samuel Imes. Dr. Imes is better known among black historians and literary critics as the husband of Nello Larsen of the "passing" novelist genre and the brother of Rev. William Imes.[6] Born in Memphis, Tennessee, on 12 October 1883, Imes received his Ph.D. in Physics at the University of Michigan (1918). (It is important to note that the first American Black to receive a Ph.D. was Edward A. Bouchet, Yale University, 1876 (Physics).) At that time Dr. H.M. Randall had attained high prestige in the University Physics Department. Imes later directed the graduate laboratory. We have an observer's account of Imes during this period:

"It was the writer's privilege to become acquainted with Professor Imes in his graduate student days at the University of Michigan, where his research laboratory was a mecca for those who sought an atmosphere of philosophic soundness and levelheaded practicalness. Gifted, moreover, with a poetic disposition, he was widely read in literature, and a discriminating and ardent appreciator of music. He had a delightful sense of humor and a skill in repartee, which he always used, however, with the kindliness and consideration so characteristic of his sensitive nature."[7]

There are the words of the distinguished research physicist/ engineer, W.F.G. Swann, director of the Bartol Research Foundation of the Franklin Institute, Swarthmore, Pa. One may recall that it was Swann to whom Albert Einstein addressed his refusal to publish "Anything about Ehrenhaft's work."[8]

While the theory of relativity was largely the work of one man, Albert Einstein, the quantum theory was developed principally over a period of thirty years through the efforts of many scientists. Max Planck in

1900 proposed that the energies of any harmonic oscillator, such as the atoms of a black body radiator, are restricted to certain values, each of which is an integral (whole number) multiple of a basic, minimum value. In 1905 Einstein posited that the radiation itself is also quartized according to the same formula, and he used the new theory of photo-electric effect. Rutherford discovered the nuclear atom in 1911. Bohr used the quantum theory to explain both atomic structure and atomic spectra.

It was left to a Black scientist born in the United States, Elmer S. Imes, to establish definitively that the quantum theory could be extended to include rotational states of molecules. His doctoral dissertation, one of two known publications by Imes, appeared in the *Astrophysical Journal,* 1919. "Measurements of the Near Infrared Absorption Spectra of Some Diatomic Molecules" initiated the field of high-resolution spectral studies. This alone earned for Imes a lasting place in both theoretical and industrial physics.

As early as 1931 Arnold Sommerfeld, Professor of Theoretical Physics at the University of Munchen in Germany stated: "Rotationssch-Wingungspektren wurden, in Linien aufgelost, mitgro Ber Prazision im Laboratium der universitat Ann Arbor nach den von Randall aus-gearbeiteten Methoden untersucht. Die ersten wichtigen Resultate erhielt Imes' bei HF, HCl, H Br."[9]

Forty-two years later Professor S.J. Cyvin, Institute of Theoretical Chemistry, University of Tronheim, Norway, says flatly:

"The infrared spectrum of hydrogen fluoride polymers is reported probably for the first time by Imes."[10]

Finally, a few years ago I read Frederick S. Simmons article on "Infrared Spectroscopic Study of Hydrogen-Fluorine Flames" done for the Advanced Research Projects Agency, Department of Defense. I was struck by this American Engineer's allusion to Imes' importance in his own area of research. I immediately wrote to Simmons to get his assessment with regard to Imes' work on Aeronautics and Astronautical Space studies. He replied:

"In regards to Dr. Imes' thesis work on HF vibration-rotation, it certainly does qualify as a pioneer effort. The consequences of his work are important today in two areas of technical concern; thermal radiation from rocket engines using fluorine compounds as oxidizers, and radiation from chemical lasers based on hydrogenfluorine reactions."[11]

In examining the works of these two Black physicists, George R. Carruthers and Elmer Samuel Imes, we have demonstrated their roles in developing and expanding Space Sciences.

It is beyond the scope of this paper to deal more fully with the role other Blacks have played. Just for further exploration we are obliged to mention others under consideration in an expanded version of this paper now-in-progress.

Dr. Vance H. Marchbanks, Jr. was Project Head Physician prior to Project Mercury (the first U.S. Space Shot). He was responsible for collecting medical information on the astronauts before, during and after their flight. While with United Aircraft Corp. as Chief of Environmental Health Services, Marchbanks assisted in the designing of space suits and monitoring systems for the Apollo moon shot. Dr. Julian Earls is presently Chief of the Office of Environmental Health at NASA, Lewis Research Center in Cleveland, Ohio. Mrs. Isabella J. Cole, Aerospace Technologist and Data Analyst, helped define the Goddard Space Center's Definitive Orbit Determination System. Cole also assisted in implementing a system called Sigpac where she managed to have the Rights in Data Clause written into all NASA software contracts, Finally, Robert A. Gordon, an Astrodynamicist with NASA (Greenbelt) authored "An Analytical terative Algorithm for the Prediction of Special Satellite Orbit Points with The Brouwer Orbit Theory." His groundbreaking work in developing a notational system for Black Music promises to be of equal importance.

In conclusion, Dr. George R. Carruthers, like all Space Scientists, is looking toward the future on other planets. His massive telescope will be used when the now delayed Space Shuttle takes off. By the time this essay appears Carruthers will be Head, Space Optical Measurements Branch, Naval Research Lab. He is currently serving on the National Academy of Sciences' panel on Ultraviolet, Optical and Infrared Astronomy Study of "Priorities in Astronomy for the 1980's." Most recently he was co-investigator for far-ultraviolet observations of Comet Kohoutek carried out from Skylab and in a sounding rocket flight. His camera/spectra is to be used in studying the North America Nebula and life on Mars.[12]

Acknowledgements

I am indebted to Dr. George R. Carruthers for his assistance and background data on very short notice; Dr. William Lloyd Imes for some biographical data on his brother Elmer Samuel Imes; The Math-Physics Library Staff at Rittenhouse, University of Penna.; The Archival Center, Naval Research Lab, Washington, D.C. and the Research Staff, Franklin Institute, Philadelphia, Pa. Finally, the Black engineer-physicists at Cornell University, Roody Rosales and M. Zarif.

NOTES

1. Professor Kenneth Manning is presently writing a biography of the noted Black Cytologist, Dr. Ernest E. Just.

2. Interview with George R. Carruthers, August, 1976 and January, 1980. Other biographical data can be found in,"Earth's Eye On The Moon" *Ebony*, Apr. 1963, p. 61-63, Hattie Carwell, *Blacks in Science: Astrophysicist to Zoologist*, N.Y. Exposition Press, 1977 p. 13-14.

3. C.R. Gibbs, *The Afro American Inventor*, Washington, D.C., 1975, p. 90. An interesting and generally accurate compendium.

4. Interview with Col. John W. Young, Co-Astronaut, Apollo 16, Phila., Pa., August 1976.

5. George R. Carruthers, "Space Astronomy in the Shuttle Era," National Technical Association Journal, 2, January 1978.

6. See, James G. Spady, "William Lloyd Imes: Crusader for Justice" *Black History Museum Umum Newsletter*, Vol. 6 #1-2, 1977.

7. W.F.G. Swann, "Elmer Samuel Imes," *Science*, December 26, 1941, p. 600-601.

8. Correspondence: Albert Einstein to W.F.G. Swann, April 7, 1941.

9. Arnold Sommerfeld, *Atombau und Spektrollinien*, Friedr. Vieweg and Sohn, Braunschweig, 1931, p. 608.

10. S.J. Cyvin et al, "Vibrational Analysis of Polymeric Hydrogen Fluoride Cyclic, (HF *Zietschrift fur Natur forschurg teil a physik, physikair sche, Chemie, Kosmophy*, U. 28, p. 1787, 1973.

11. F.S. Simmons, Correspondence with author, 15 March 1974.

12. "A Far-Ultraviolet Study of The North American Nebula," *Sky and Telescope*, January, 1980.

DR. LLOYD QUARTERMAN—NUCLEAR SCIENTIST

An interview with Ivan Van Sertima

Summary: In the Fall of 1979, while lecturing in Chicago, I was introduced to the nuclear scientist, Dr. Lloyd Quarterman, who had been awarded a certificate of appreciation by the U.S. Secretary of War for "work essential to the production of the Atomic Bomb, thereby contributing to the successful conclusion of World War II." I found, on meeting this remarkable gentleman, that his work in this field was only the beginning of his achievements, though he spoke of all he had done with great modesty and restraint. He had worked with some of the world's greatest scientists, including Einstein, when he was at Columbia University, New York. He went on to the Argonne National Laboratory in Illinois to monitor the delicate mixing of highly reactive and toxic chemical agents, many of which were radioactive, to manipulate chemicals in the development of entirely new compounds, and to devise what, in technical terms, is known as "the diamond window". He also initiated work on "synthetic blood" fifteen years ago, work which, had he been allowed to complete it, might have been one of America's major medical accomplishments.

I have always noted, in the manner and expression of great thinkers, not only creative scientists but artists, a certain child-like and naive excitement, even wonder, at the flowers blooming in the cultivated gardens of their own minds. It is hard to convey the electric vitality of a man who speaks of his work and his ideas with this intensity and excitement. It grips and persuades you, even when he is moving on ground that is difficult to follow. Quarterman is ailing and is paralyzed in the right arm but the vibration in his voice was like a blast of wind, rocking the sensitive needle on the tape-recorder. As he spoke, the shock of his voice and his occasional laughter seemed to contradict his illness and I began to see before me, not an aging scientist, but the champion footballer flying over the fields of St Augustine's College. This college in Raleigh, North Carolina, departed from 102 years of tradition in 1971 to grant Lloyd Quarterman an Honorary Doctorate in Science for a lifetime of achievement.

Dr. Quarterman is author and co-author of dozens of original scientific papers. He is a member of the most distinguished scientific bodies — The Society of Applied Spectroscopy (in which he held national office) the Society of Sigma Xi, the Scientific Research Society of America, the American Chemical Society and the American Association for the Advancement of Science. But these associations and his many duties over the years did not divorce him from a commitment to his people. He is also a Member of the National Association for the Advancement of Colored Peoples and he has gone out into the Chicago Public Schools to encourage and assist black students who are interested in pursuing careers in science.

Mr. Edward Willett, who introduced me to Dr. Quarterman, taped our conversations and I have decided to publish fragments from these, linked by a brief commentary.

VAN SERTIMA: The atom, I understand, was split right here in Chicago. But that, I presume — those secret beginnings — you cannot talk about.

QUARTERMAN: Wait a minute. You are talking about two different things. We split the atom in the East. We were working there on an Atomic Bomb. But the world's first nuclear reactor, which used the atom-splitting process in a peaceful way, was set up here in Chicago. It was under an Italian scientist, Enrico Fermi. In 1948 I did all my quantum mechanics under him.

VAN SERTIMA: You are one of the few surviving scientists who worked on the Manhattan Project — the code-name for Atom Bomb research. But there were other black scientists, I suppose...

QUARTERMAN: Yes, there were six of us.

Due to his oath of secrecy, Dr. Quarterman could not discuss in any further detail what he had contributed to the development of the Bomb and his later work on uranium, which laid the foundation for the establishment of a new nuclear research facility. We therefore avoided this subject and went on to talk about his work at the Argonne National Laboratory, which he joined on July 1, 1946.

He worked as an inorganic nuclear scientist and he worked mainly with radioactive materials. The main thing Argonne was built for was to work with radioactive materials. He worked "compounding things" as well as "creating new compounds". He worked with a team of scientists who helped develop nuclear reactors. At Argonne they made the first reactor for the *Nautilus,* the atomic powered submarine. Practically all the development in nuclear reactors started at Argonne, the first not only in this nation but the entire world.

Dr. Quarterman spoke of the difficulty and delicacy of his assignment "to monitor things, to make sure that they were properly mixed, that they weren't too radioactive, and to discuss ways of handling them...Thirty years of this is a long time and in thirty years you learn a

Quarterman — Fig. 1

lot of things. The trafficking and the monitoring of radioactivity takes time and training technicians to handle the stuff safely, takes time. I worked thirty years at Argonne and in all that time nobody ever got radioactive sickness or radioactive damage out there. We must have done our job well."

Besides this, he worked as an inorganic chemist and his inorganic chemistry was focussed on fluorides. He was a fluoride chemist, in addition to being a radioactive chemist. He made great discoveries but they were not his alone, he insists. He was in a group and his group did some astonishing things. They led the world in fluoride chemistry. For a period of time they were the greatest fluoride chemists on earth. When Quarterman was going to school there were no "compounds" of zeon or argon or krypton. These were known as the "noble" gases, since they were thought to stand sovereign and alone, reacting with nothing. But Quarterman and his team made them react with the fluorine atoms. They made zeon tetrafluoride — zeon difluoride — zeon hexafluoride. They led the world in this and, on top of that, Quarterman took zeon difluoride and incorporated it in other experiments, making a whole series of new compounds.

Apart from being a fluoride chemist and a radioactive chemist, Dr. Quarterman is a spectroscopist. A spectroscopist is like a man peering into the depths of the universe with a dozen eyes or windows. With these marvellously revealing scopes, he can look through solutions or through various spectra or spheres into the living interaction or vibration of chemical or molecular or gaseous species. He can study the composition of elements in our universe that are either invisible or elusive or obscure to us. Sometimes he needs to make a new kind of eye or a new kind of window in order to observe and determine these things with greater precision. It is for this reason that Quarterman devised a new window, which came to be known as "the diamond window".

QUARTERMAN: I made a diamond cell. The windows were of diamonds. It was a very small window — one eighth of an inch. The reason why they were one eighth of an inch was because I couldn't get the money to buy bigger windows. These small diamonds cost one thousand dollars apiece and I needed two for a window. Now the reasons I wanted this diamond-window cell is that I wanted to study something in a solution that was too corrosive for other types of windows. Something so corrosive that it would eat up glass or any other kind of container if one tried to use it as a window.

VAN SERTIMA: And what is that?

United States of America

WAR DEPARTMENT

ARMY SERVICE FORCES ~ CORPS OF ENGINEERS

Manhattan District

This is to Certify that

LLOYD ALBERT QUARTERMAN
Columbia University

has participated in work essential to the production of the Atomic Bomb, thereby contributing to the successful conclusion of World War II. This certificate is awarded in appreciation of effective service.

6 August 1945

Washington, D. C.

Henry L. Stimson
Secretary of War

Quarterman — Fig. 2

QUARTERMAN: Hydrogen fluoride. This happens to be one of the world's simplest compounds. It is made up of two atoms — hydrogen, which is number one atom, and fluorine, the seventh element in the atomic table. It has one bond...But as a molecule it is complex, in that the study of it requires the understanding of many types of interbonding. It is the world's greatest solvent. All metals known to man dissolve in hydrogen fluoride. Even platinum forms several platinum fluorides and there are silver fluorides, gold fluorides. But diamond happens to be the one thing that dissolves extremely slow, slower than any other element.

VAN SERTIMA: What could you study by using this window?

QUARTERMAN: If you want to study the X-ray, the UV (Ultraviolet) region, the Raman spectrum of a compound, it is wonderful to dissolve the compound in HF (hydrogen fluoride) and make a cell and shine your electro-magnetic beam through the solution and look at the vibrations of the molecules in the solution, and from these vibrations you can understand the structures.

VAN SERTIMA: Can you actually see molecules vibrating in the solution?

QUARTERMAN: Yes. If you shine an ultra-violet beam or an X-ray beam through a solution, you can pick up vibrations of the molecules in the solution. Every molecule has a different vibration. Imagine a molecule with two balls. If the two balls are the same size, they can vibrate up and down because they're joined together. Now that's just a simple molecule. We only have one molecule that is like this and that is the helium molecule. That's the only molecule that has two atoms. All the others have more, many more. Now you take a third atom. It will come in on the side and look like a triangle. If you take this tri-molecule and it has a big ball up here and a little ball down there and a little ball on the side, that thing is going to vibrate differently from three of them of the same size. But I was not just looking at molecules. I was also involved in the invention of molecules.

VAN SERTIMA: Can you play around with molecules the way biochemists are playing around now with genes?

QUARTERMAN: That's my specialty. That's what the game is all about. I can pull off an atom down here and put another atom on here and this would give me different vibrations. Inventing molecules is making new compounds. Making zeon difluroide, which we talked about earlier, is an example of this.

VAN SERTIMA: Around what time did you invent the diamond window?

QUARTERMAN: The diamond window was invented around 1967. It developed over a long period of time, because we tried all different kinds of windows and this was the window that worked. By the way I don't call it an invention but "a first discovery trial" because no one else did it before.

VAN SERTIMA: I have also heard of your early research probes into the development of "synthetic blood" I have been reading a newspaper report on this. It has come into the news because the Japanese used some form of synthetic blood on an American about a month ago and this has generated a lot of interest in the matter. I know that this is something that has not yet been perfected, so I was wondering in what sense, perhaps, the Japanese process might differ from the one you were working on...

QUARTERMAN: I want to say that my process never got off the ground. I ran into socio-political problems. They said that they didn't have a budget for it. I presented papers fifteen years ago on this and I have copies of those papers presented to my superiors. But they threw it on the shelf...

Our interview, however, did not end on a sour note, although Dr. Quarterman seemed grieved at the loss of the opportunity to work on this project, which he felt might have saved thousands of lives. His great excitement could not be dimmed by any disappointment. It was the excitement of the man of science who may suffer, but who will always rise above, the limitations of his place and time. "We are in an age of discovery," says Quarterman, with an almost boyish enthusiasm, "we live in the world of the unknown. That's the only place to live."

AFRICAN-AMERICAN CONTRIBUTIONS TO INFORMATION TECHNOLOGY

Kirstie Gentleman

Summary: If you can imagine a planet with more computers than people, your thoughts are at the right place at the right time. That global change occurred during 1982, according to a report in a Bell Laboratories magazine. Bell Labs is a private research and development organization where employees solve technical problems and advance scientific concepts in ways that make computers and other technology more useful to people for communications. In 1982, close to a thousand African-Americans worked at Bell Labs. Ten were asked what they considered their most important technical contributions.

Brian G. Jackson builds computers and instructs them to do extraordinary tasks. To help make manufacture of smaller and less expensive computers possible, he gave one computer the vision and thought-processes needed to position minute circular marks on two pieces of material precisely above one another, and the ability to do this in less than a second. The speed, miniscule scale and precision go far beyond what a person could see and do, even with the aid of a microscope.

Courtland Robinson supervises the search for materials to keep dust, moisture and other contaminants from affecting the performance of miniature electronic memories and other computer and telecommunications equipment parts. In chemistry experiments leading to better protective coatings, simplified electronic devices were covered with materials of different formulas. These were tested in ovens where heat and humidity are so extreme that operating for a single day is almost as wearing as working a whole year under normal conditions. Hundreds of coatings were tested and new guidelines were developed, based on the few formulas that worked best.

Jesse E. Russell, Sr. showed how the first commercial computer-on-a-chip could do more and more cheaply when applied to telecommunications than a series of simple electronic components. To prove this point, he designed devices to enter and retrieve information. He also designed circuitry to control extra memory for the computer chip. He dreamed up the idea of drafting instructions on a small computer, then dumping the edited version into the tiny computer's memory.

Robert L. Engram solved a technical obsolescence problem (the danger of machines becoming outdated) in the field of electronic system design. Looking

*ahead to future improvements in memory chips, he built a "growable memory"
system, including extra address and control wires so that when memory chips
with more capacity became available, they simply plugged in. Instructions for
address and control logic could be changed when necessary without too much
expense because Engram used computer-on-a-chip technology to direct the logic
tasks.*

Earl E. Jones *was part of a team that first demonstrated how small computers
could manage databases for large computers shared by many people. Jones devised physical arrangements and programmed instructions that made a small
computer control access to data files of a large computer. Now he is a leader in
Engineering Design and Development (an organization split off from Bell Labs
for a new Bell corporation) in advancing networking capabilities for information
exchange between computers of varying kinds.*

William R. Northover *has advanced understanding of the ability of glass to
guide light. In a technology called lightwave communications, information coded
on pulses of laser light is transported through the core of hair-thin strands of
glass. Northover showed how to make glass that would guide light as far as ten
miles before the code needed to be regenerated. The chemical composition of the
glass fiber core was changed gradually while it was fabricated. Also, Northover
determined critical dimensions to control while glass is pulled like taffy, from
tube into fiber form, during the next step in manufacture.*

Thomas C. Cannon, Jr. *wrote mathematical equations that described the
mechanical response of a cable when pulled, bent, or subjected to other forms of
physical force. His mathematics were used to evaluate a new cable structure designed for glass fiber lightguides, and to develop procedures for installing this
cable. He supervised the design of the mechanical parts and tools used to join
lightguide cable segments. He went down manholes and did cable connections
himself under Chicago streets when the Bell System first installed a lightwave
communications system.*

Alfred C. Richardson *wrote a book about submarine cable mechanics and
recommended laying procedures while on board the Bell System's cable ship. He
used this knowledge in overseeing cable manufacture for undersea lightguide.
He invented an alarm that uses a laser to detect damaging twists in glass fiber as
it is spun from a bobbin into casing for undersea protection.*

Earl D. Shaw *is coinventor of a laser important in demonstrating optical
energy can be tuned within wavelengths. This is useful for air pollution analysis
and other molecular measurements. Now he is trying to invent a tunable laser
using an accelerator like those used for cancer treatment. It ejects electrons almost at the speed of light into a magnet the length of a handball court. The
magnetic field sets the electrons spiraling. These forces should cause the electrons to emit light. Mirroring it back and forth within the electron beam should
produce the tuning of energy that Shaw and others want for scientific studies of
solid materials.*

James E. West is most broadly known as coinventor of foil electrets, the electrical equivalent to a permanent magnet. These are used to convert sound into electrical signals in hearing aids, portable tape recorders, lapel microphones, telephones and smart information terminals. He has used foil electret microphones to advance understanding of directional sound perception and blood pressure. The work that interests him most is studying the invisible and unknown electromagnetic events within the foil.

Solutions to problems spread quickly through worldwide grapevines within scientific and engineering communities. Technologists hook up to sophisticated information networks that use computers for collecting, sorting, storing and delivering facts.

Non-technical scholars of contemporary history have considerably less access to knowledge. Competitive private industry safeguards documents on who did what, when and why. However, being informed on how things work is important to everyone who must live with the results of the new technology.

Many changes linked to the introduction of new technology are being debated now in public policy forums. At a time when access to information dominates the global economy, the nation's most broadly-owned corporation—the Bell System—is expanding the scope of its business. The intended change is from a government-regulated phone service to a market-driven source of information-handling and management services and products. Recently, the Bell System's holding company, AT&T, agreed to divest itself of state-regulated operating units, but retain existing national organizations, including Bell Laboratories.

Much of the technology considered crucial to the Bell System's market expansion originates at these laboratories. Possibly the world's largest private research and development organization, Bell Labs has a staff of over 23,000 and has always maintained pride in its reputation for excellence.

About one of every twenty Bell Labs scientists, engineers and other technologists is African-American. Members of this community are involved in advancing all areas of technology considered key to progress in new growth markets. Some of these people are opening new doors to knowledge, while others concentrate on how it is applied.

Brian G. Jackson

Brian Jackson has personally built a computer and taught it to see more than a human. Now he's training it to coordinate visual alignments with extreme precision in less than a second. This work is in the Advanced Large Scale Integration Development Laboratory at Murray Hill, New Jersey. It has attracted international attention.

Murray Hill is the birthplace of the transistor—the first device made to control

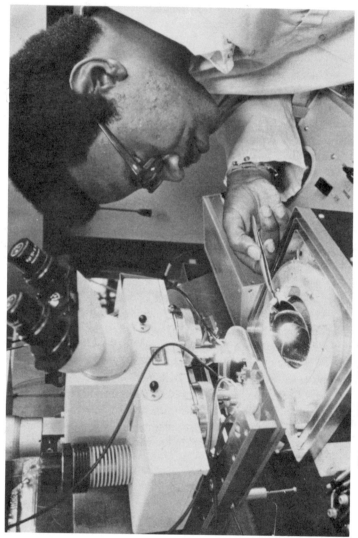

This x-ray lithographic printer is used to copy complex patterns for microelectronic circuits precisely onto a crystalline wafer. Brian Jackson (placing a wafer on the machine) is involved in exploratory design of a replacement tool. The new computer-aided system would make more finely detailed patterns.

the conduct of electrons within solid materials (the basic principle of microelectronics). It's a mecca for electronic engineers from around the world, and many visitors have seen Jackson's experimental setup. It could help give birth to a generation of even smaller computers and electronic memories.

Every major semiconductor manufacturer wants a better tool to inscribe circuit designs on crystalline wafers. These designs are highly intricate and multilayered, while so minute that they can only be seen through a microscope. Photolithography was useful for creating patterns on wafers, as long as manufacturers were satisfied with having a few hundred design elements within an area the size of a postage stamp. Today, manufacturers think in terms of thousands of components within such a space, and look forward to increasing that to a million. This very large scale of miniaturization is not possible using white light as a pen, becuase the lightray would be broader than elements of the design. A far more subtle pen is needed.

In the current state-of-the-art, the three most advanced inscription tools are deep ultra-violet rays (shortest lightwave), x-rays (next to light on the electromagnetic spectrum), and streams of electrons, called E-beams (which can be more narrowly focused than light).

Jackson's project could make the best solution a process combining E-beams and x-rays. E-beams would be used first to pattern a gold-coated thin plastic disc, so it would allow x-rays to pass through in some places but not others. This mask would be used as a stencil for x-ray reproduction of the pattern on the wafer. Drawing with an E-beam is slow. Creating two hundred circuit drawings on a three-inch mask, a line at a time, can take a full workday. However, x-ray projection of this picture onto a crystal wafer can be completed in minutes.

Jackson's computer automatically positions the mask in the correct place over the wafer for x-ray inscription of circuit designs. This step is presently done by a person looking through a microscope. A computer can do it more accurately, and a lot faster.

In the computer system, a laser is aimed at the mask and wafer. Light reflected back from concentric circle registry marks, called Frensel lenses, is relayed by a system of mirrors to a television camera. A unit Jackson created, called a "frame grabber", captures a picture of light intensity, representing the relative position of circles in the mask and wafer.

The image of varying light intensity is converted into a description written in a language of "ones" and "zeroes" (a digital code called binary mathematics). These digital bits of information are sent to Jackson's computer which uses mathematical equations to determine the geometric center of each image. The computer checks its records on previous use of the mask to see if there are any deviations in the desired distance between these centers. It then makes any necessary adjustment of the wafer holder.

Microelectronic memories fabricated on a crystalline wafer will be sliced apart along intersecting "highways." Each rectangular chip, smaller than a postage stamp, can store 64 thousand bits of information.

Once Jackson had shown that a computer could perform envisioned thought-processes with required accuracy, he began making decisions that would save time. What chores should be done by wired logic and when would mathematics be more economical? What language would be most efficient for the math? He recently decided to have the frame-grabber start the conversion to digital code only at points in the picture where data would be useful to the computer. This may reduce overall alignment time seventy percent.

Courtland Robinson

Courtland Robinson is responsible for a unique method of studying materials used to protect microelectronic devices from dust, moisture and other contaminants. He supervises the search for better materials for encapsulating, or providing protective cover, for devices. This work is done in the Film and Hybrid Technology Laboratory at Allentown, Pennsylvania.

An experimental procedure called "accelerated life testing" is commonly used during development of new microelectronic devices. Devices are tested under conditions of stress accelerated to such extremes that a day becomes almost as wearing as a year. The experiments Robinson supervises are unique because they use special test circuits, much simpler in design than real devices. The special designs avoid collecting data irrelevant to the problems being studied.

The test circuits are coated with a polymer material and then placed in a very hot and humid oven (temperatures as high as 85 percent humidity). Operations for six weeks in these stressful conditions are equal to normal performance for as long as forty years.

During the accelerated life test, the circuit is subjected to other forms of stress. It is forced to perform digital logic tasks with varying power voltages and at different speeds. Raising power levels and speeds increases heat-loss (a by-product of energetic electron maneuvers within the crystal). Robinson monitors what changes occur, if any, in the dependability of the circuit during these stress-tests.

His group has used this procedure to screen hundreds of coating materials. Only a handful have worked well. These results have enabled the researchers to better define coating properties and to formulate new guidelines for making them.

This knowledge about materials is applied by Western Electric to make memory chips and other microelectronic devices for use by the Bell System. It is also passed on to scientists at Bell Labs and engineers at Western Electric who synthesize new materials, as well as to companies supplying chemicals to the Bell System.

Robinson, who has a doctorate in Materials Science and Engineering from the University of Utah, shares his personal knowledge with students in science. He is an adjunct professor in the chemistry department of Lehigh University, Pennsylvania.

Jesse E. Russell Sr.

Jesse Russell, who now heads a system engineering department, spent his first year as a Bell Labs employee at Stanford University. While earning a master's degree in electrical engineering, he studied the computer-on-a-chip invented by Intel, a semiconductor manufacturer located in California. When Russell returned to his Bell Labs base at Columbus, Ohio, in 1973, he soon found opportunity to apply this knowledge innovatively.

His coworkers were beginning design of a system to monitor frequency of phone call connections. This network-management tool was being created with a series of microelectronic components that could each perform no more than a hundred logic functions.

Russell said more could be done, and more cheaply, with a microprocessor. He proceeded with an exploratory design, creating a ''smart'' data terminal, to prove his point. His use of Intel's first commericial microprocessor gave him both physical design and instruction writing problems to solve. This chip only performed central processing tasks. Russell had to design circuitry to control auxiliary memory chips as well as devices used to enter and retrieve information for the tiny computer. He gave the microprocessor instructions to collect data from switching machines and to deliver this information to a large computer.

The limited experience in microprocessor applications complicated writing of these instructions. Russell came up with the idea of drafting them on a small computer, then dumping the edited version into the microprocessor's memory. This type of electronic workbench is now quite common, but at that time Russell only heard of one other person doing anything similar.

When Intel came out with an improved microprocessor, Russell's coworkers modified the terminal design to use it. Russell's final contribution to that terminal was to show how the Intel device could be replaced by a Bell Labs-designed microprocessor, without changing any other hardware.

While Western Electric began manufacturing this data terminal for network management, Russell moved on to another type of engineering challenge. In 1978 he became supervisor of a group being formed in Whippany, N.J. to develop computer tools for network managers' use in designing special service circuits. Russell had to determine the mix of people needed to produce useful tools quickly. He determined that the task would involve mathemathics, computer sci-

Jesse E. Russell, Sr.

ence and electrical engineering. He recruited people who had acquired knowledge through experience in the communications industry, as well as recent university graduates.

This group formed the nucleus of the department he now heads, and the tools they've produced are being rapidly put into Bell System service.

Jesse Russell (left) and John Formica of Bell Labs in Columbus, Ohio, solve a problem during development of EADAS (Engineering and Administrative Data Acquisition System).

Robert L. Engram

Rapid advances in microelectronics pose a challenge for computer system designers. Components they choose as most practical at the start of a design project may be technically obsolete before the system is put to use. In 1975 Robert Engram came up with an innovative solution—a growable memory system.

He had begun designing a memory system using a microelectronic device that could store a thousand bits (1K) of information. Before he completed a paper study of system requirements, a four-thousand bit (4K) chip became more practical. He had to scrap initial design concepts and start over.

This time he took a more forward looking approach. He explored hopes of chip designers at Murray Hill and Allentown. They told him about miniaturization techniques that might enable them to give the same chip size a 16-thousand bit (16K) storage capacity.

He laid out a modular design, allotting space needed for enough 4K devices to give him a total of 16 million words in memory. However, he also included extra address and control wires so that 16K devices could be substituted when available. These became practical shortly after Engram left the project. Plugging them into his growable system was simple. Later, the system proved flexible enough to incorporate another leap to a 64K device.

This flexibility was possible because Engram chose space-saving digital logic for circuit controls and storage addresses. He also gave the system unprecedented flexibility by using a microprocessor to direct memory operations. Changing the written instructions for microprocessor operations has been easier than physically rearranging wired logic.

Engram's concept of modular economies—pay for current needs, add more when affordable—underlies design of a digital processing unit now being introduced to accommodate communications service growth and to make advanced service capabilities affordable even in rural areas. Engram is among hundreds of people involved in this work. The processor's Maintenance Development Department, which he heads near Chicago, is in charge of incorporating future technologies.

Earl E. Jones

Earl Jones heads the Data Network Exploratory Architecture Department at Holmdel, New Jersey. This team of digital technology developers is making major contributions to the Advanced Communications Service that the Bell System plans to introduce this year. The service will simplify interactions among different kinds of computers, terminals, networks and data bases.

Jones' contributions can be traced back to his role ten years ago on a team, breaking ground in distributing processing responsibilities. That team demonstrated how small computers could handle database management for large computers shared by numerous people.

Jones' part of this project was physical arrangements and programmed instructions that made a small computer control access to files for one of the largest computers generally used (IBM's 370). The small computer told database machinery when to turn off and on, and where on a disc memory to start reading data. The project's success was described in the Association of Computing Machinery journal.

This paper is still used by computer researchers and developers who want to improve on the technical solutions. The system economies worked well when about five people were using the computers, but bogged down as users increased to a hundred or more. Capacity is a persistent problem. Giving small computers sufficient intelligence for filing activities tips the economic balance back in favor of large computers doing the file tasks. Computers-on-a-chip and programming shorthand may swing the balance.

William R. Northover

Bill Northover, a chemist, has advanced understanding of glass. During the last eight years, he has concentrated glass fiber structures that determine their ability to guide light carrying digitally-coded information. The speed of light (much faster than wire conducts electricity) gives fiber lightguides tremendous capacity for carrying information. Northover is reducing practical limits to full use of this capacity.

To guide light, fiber must contain glass of two different compositions. An outer cladding, mostly silicon, and an inner core, usually of gradually varying composition. The cladding and core are deliberately mismatched in light-bending characteristics (refractive index). When light is injected into the fiber core, some reflects against the inner cladding wall which prevents light from leaking outside. Other light travels straight down the center of the core, arriving at the destination before the reflected light. Although the time difference is minuscule (millionths of a second), it limits how closely bits of information can be packed into lightguides (or in other words, limits transmission speed).

Since time lag increases with the distance light travels, signal regenerators are spaced along lightguide links in communications systems. The regenerators eliminate accumulated time lag by converting the light signal to an electrical form, then back to a densely packed stream of light pulses. But each regeneration adds to communications cost.

Last year, Northover and colleagues in the materials research laboratory at Murray Hill made experimental fibers that almost tripled spacing between regenerators (to ten miles). They reduced time lag at its source, the fiber composition. The experimental fibers were fabricated with a more graduated increase in refractive index difference between core and cladding.

Glass fiber lightguides have many applications: cancer detection, surgical proce-dures, computer science, television broadcasting and military defense. But the most widespread application now is in telecommunications.

The fabrication process (developed at Bell Labs and used internationally) be-gins with a tube of glass. The tube is rotated on a lathe and a very hot torch passed over it. At the same time, gases are injected through the end of the tube. The gases form particle deposits on the inner wall of the tube, and the heat fuses these into a thin layer of glass. Many layers are formed. Finally, the tube is collapsed into a solid rod, melted at the tip, and drawn like taffy into fiber strands. From the original four-foot rod comes six miles of fiber.

In making the experimental fibers, the most important variable for Northover to control was the precise amount of germanium in the vapor each time the torch passed along the tube. Also, control of dimensions was critical during the pulling of the tube into fiber strands.

Northover has increased knowledge about glass properties for twenty-five years at Bell Labs. He initially worked on low-melting glasses in search of coating suited to lengthen performance-life of early transistors. He also experimented with glasses that could conduct current under controlled conditions (semiconductors), and searched for others that would amplify light (lasers).

Thomas C. Cannon Jr.

Tom Cannon's first two Bell Labs assignments, national defense system projects, involved him in making mathematical models of mechanical systems and studying cable design principles. Both gave him experience that proved useful when he was reassigned from military work at Whippany to the transmission media laboratory adjoining Western Electric's cable-manufacturing plant in Atlanta, Georgia.

Cannon soon contributed to understanding of a new type of cable. He wrote mathematical equations that theoretically described the mechanical response of the cable when subjected to physical force. He compared results of his equations to laboratory test results. They agreed.

Cannon's equations, which allowed accurate predictions of stress applied in cable installation procedures, were particularly important because the new cable contained glass fibers. The fibers were strong, but could stretch only a little. The equations were applied during the cable design and manufacture, and also in planning installation procedures. They answered fundamental questions such as: If the cable is pulled, will it twist and stretch? Will this break fibers inside? If not now, when?

Soon after this, Cannon became a leader in decisions about procedures and tools for connecting segments of lightguide cable, both in the factory and field. In 1976, when the Bell System put its first lightwave communications system into experimental service under Chicago streets, all the mechanical parts and tools used to connect cable during installation were designed and built by a group Cannon supervised. He personally went down manholes and did splicing. He now supervises development of connector and splicing tools for a variety of transmission media and applications, including lightguide building wiring.

Lightguide cable is small, lightweight, unaffected by static or other electromagnetic forces, and uses a digital coding system compatible with computer language. It fits beside existing cable in ducts under city streets, and could provide means to get phone service into remote areas of Africa or South America where geography makes copper wire or radio waves impractical.

Alfred C. Richardson

Al Richardson's cable engineering career began on board the Bell System's Cable Ship Long Lines. He wrote a book about *Submarine Cable Mechanics And Recommended Laying Procedures*, while doing mechanical engineering to modify cable-laying equipment and the ship itself. These changes were required because the transatlantic cable laid in 1976 was physically larger than any cable before it.

Richardson currently spends most of his time translating paper designs into manufacture at a very small Bell Labs facility in Portsmouth, New Hampshire. It is adjacent to the Simplex Wire and Cable manufacturing plant where cable for a trial of proposed undersea lightguide is being fabricated.

The undersea installation procedure is more strenuous than any on land, and the bottom of the ocean is more stressful than any terrestrial territory. A special cable structure demands highly-sensitive engineering.

First, the fiber is spun off a bobbin into extremely soft plastic extruded into a molten state as a cylinder. The entire cylinder is drawn into nylon tubing to hold the glass in place and buffer it from the next layer. Steel is wound in a helix around the tube as it is sheathed in copper. Then an outer sheathing of polyethelene insulation is applied.

Getting this manufacturing process to operate at affordable speed has been tricky. Various guides and alarms had to be added to the machinery particularly for the finicky phase of spinning the glass off the bobbin.

Richardson is responsible for an innovative alarm that detects twists in the glass (which could lead to breaks). A laser is aligned with the end of the bobbin. Any change in the graphic design created by a pattern on the bobbin's flat end, sets off an alarm and remedial action begins.

As the manufacturing design nears completion, Richardson says it's time to update the book on cable mechanics and laying procedures.

Earl D. Shaw

Earl Shaw is already cited in history books among forerunners in laser technology. He's coinventor of the spin-flip Raman laser, an important demonstration of lighwave tunability used for air pollution and other molecular measurements.

A fixed wavelength has limited use, just as a radio that worked at only one frequency would. So the desire to build tunable lasers at all wavelengths has motivated scientists since the invention of the first laser. Tuning lasers (that is, changing optical energy wavelength) requires changes in electronic behavior of molecules. This type of research necessitates expensive tools, and is unlikely to be done by an isolated inventor with no financial backing. Shaw was invited to join a Bell Labs experimental group in 1969 by Kumar Patel, whose inventions included the carbon dioxide laser, the most efficient light amplifier in existence.

The CO_2 laser emits the kind of infrared light that radiates from fireplaces. Shaw's experimental setup steered this light with mirrors to a synthetic Indium Antimonide crystal kept in a thermos chilled below −250 degrees Centigrade. At particular CO_2 laser power levels, the crystal emitted a lightbeam at a longer wavelength. It could be precisely adjusted with a magnetic field, from 11 to 13 microns in length. This light tuning system became known as the spin-flip Raman laser. While other scientists worked on showing this wavelength range could be broadened, Shaw discovered he could stimulate light near the 100 micron wavelength.

The possibility of a light source tunable throughout the hundred micron region of the electromagnetic spectrum has remained Shaw's goal. He's now trying to create one, using technology referred to as free-electron lasing. If he succeeds it is likely to have as much significance for scientific studies of solid materials as any laser yet invented.

Nucleatronics, a Massachusetts supplier of x-ray units for cancer treatment, is building a similar accelerator to Shaw's specifications. This accelerator will eject electrons, traveling almost at the speed of light, into a magnet as long as a handball court. The magnet will cause the electrons to spiral. Theoretically, Shaw knows that electrons traveling in a specific helical path at 20 million electron-volt energy give off light in a forward direction at the 100 micron length. Mirrors feeding this light back and forth within the electron beam should result in lasing.

Shaw is continuing to collaborate with Patel, now executive director of Bell Labs physics division. They hope to have the free electron laser working before 1983.

James E. West

Jim West has had global impact as an experimental physicist. He is most broadly known as coinventor of foil electrets (the electrical equivalent to a permanent magnet) used to convert sound into electrical signals in hearing aids, portable tape recorders and lapel microphones. Foil electrets are also used increasingly for smart information terminals, such as the phone-with-a-memory that the Bell System introduced last December to international markets.

The *Guiness Book of World Records* pictures West working in the world's quietest room (the Murray Hill anechoic chamber) where he has used foil electret microphones to advance understanding of directional sound perception. For these studies, he has also sat motionless for hours in concert halls and jazz clubs, so that microphones molded into his ears could collect data.

Occasionally West can be found at Cornell University medical hospital in New York City, where he's collaborating in blood pressure monitoring research. The

The Acoustical Research Anechoic Chamber. (The World's Quietest Room) Bell Labs, Murray Hill, New Jersey. James E. West is making adjustments on a directional microphone (Toridal Electret Microphone) in preparation to determine its directional characteristics.

West, between an electron microscope and computer terminal, in his Murray Hill laboratory.

foil electret transducer (a piece of electrically-charged plastic, as thin as a sheet of paper, metallized on one side with the other against a thick metal plate) is strapped to the arm of patients with high-blood pressure to give them digital readouts on subtle changes in the rhythmic flow of blood through their arteries.

Most often West is swivelling between an electron microscope and computer terminal in his Murray Hill laboratory, exploring invisible and sometimes unknown electromagnetic events. He uses the microscope as an accelerator, to inject charges into traps within polymer films, such as teflon. He probes this material with electrical voltage, heat and light to see what comes out. His computer is programmed to manipulate the microscope, and to translate the results into graphs and mathematical equations the technically literate can readily interpret (as descriptions of charge-storage lifecycles and charge-transport paths).

His most recent paper describes what happened when he punched sample electrets with an extremely brief and very high-energy laser pulse. It shocked charges into revealing the depth they were trapped within the material. This experimental technique could help answer many questions about electronic behavior of polymer materials.

TEACHERS' GUIDE

Ivan Van Sertima

This guide is intended to help teachers who may attempt to introduce a general survey course on African and African-American science. Students should first be made aware of the very early beginnings of science in Africa—the domestication of fire 1,400,000 years ago in Chesowanja, near Lake Baringo in Kenya (see *New York Times*, front-page story, November 14, 1981), the cultivation of grain and cereals at Wadi Tushka (Nubia) and Wadi Kubbaniya (Egypt) about 17,000 years ago (see "An Ancient Harvest on the Nile" by Fred Wendorf et al. in this book), cattle-domestication about 15,000 years ago (see "African Cattle Bones Stir Scientific Debate" by Bayard Webster in this book), and mining, as early as 42,000 years ago, in southern Africa (see "Africa: The Birthplace of Iron Mining" by Tendal Mutunhu in *Negro History Bulletin*, vol. 44, no. 1, January-March 1981). There are several short news reports on scientific discoveries in ancient Africa, too numerous to mention, but we would like to draw special attention to "Toolmaking Tools" in *Scientific American* (January 1982, page 78) which reports on the first known working of wood in the Koobi Fora region of Kenya, east of Lake Turkana, and "View from Space of Sahara's Past" (front-page story in the *New York Times*, November 26, 1982).

Some teachers may want to dwell on the finds of the earliest man in Africa but while this is of great significance since it establishes that all men have African ancestors, it is not particularly helpful in the study of advanced technologies. The student should be acquainted with the evidence for an African origin of some of the earliest and most technologically sophisticated of ancient civilizations, particularly the Egyptian. Teachers who need the most recent and concisely written essays on this subject should secure a copy of the *Journal of African Civilizations*, vol. 4, no. 2 (November 1982). The essays of C.A. Diop and Bruce Williams are landmarks in the field of modern Egyptology, and provide in brief, highly readable, and persuasive form, replete with illustrations, the best refutation of conventional assumptions of the ancient Egyptian as Caucasoid or Asiatic or a blend of the two.

This is a crucial preliminary to the study of Egyptian technology and its impact on European technology through the Greeks. The essays on Egyptian mathematics and pyramid-building (Beatrice Lumpkin) on physics (John Pappademos) on medicine (Frederick Newsome and Charles Finch) should be read very closely. Both teachers and students should master the essentials in these essays, which are brilliantly compressed and present, in capsule form, the discoveries diffused over a hundred texts. Further readings are suggested at the end of articles. These articles provide excellent bibliographies but students are warned that the Afrocentric perspective is missing in most of the sources from which these facts are culled. That perspective must be consolidated first before they can read further afield with a critical alertness and discrimination.

The study of African science should then proceed to an examination of African science below the Sahara. This is the most comprehensive section of the book and students will find summaries and introductions to astronomy, architecture, agriculture (not just the very early Egypto-Nubian but the Saharan and Sudanic agricultural complexes) metallurgy, mathematical systems and medicine, navigation, communication and writing systems. We had hoped for a detailed essay on African herbal medicine and on drum-scripts of Africa but our search for experts in these fields turned up materials too late for inclusion.

The African-American section should provide no difficulty to the general reader. John Clarke has provided a good bibliographical guide for those who want to do further reading while Robert Hayden has done what is probably the best introductory essay on the subject. Kirstie Gentleman's article on information technology may be too technical for some students but the summary should help. My essays on the nuclear scientist, Lloyd Quarterman, one of the six blacks who worked on the atomic bomb, and on some of the black space scientists at NASA (in collaboration with Curtis Graves) were specially written for the layman and the photographs add a dimension of interest to subjects which have become a perennial fascination to the youth of today.

This is the order in which this book should be studied. Students should be called upon to note details—where a technique or artifact was found, by whom (when known) to note its function, its age, its implications, and its influence (where necessary). They should be taught the value of supporting their claims with hard evidence rather than by hollow boasts. Much of this knowledge is not only new but revolutionary. Revolutionary in the sense that it runs counter to many conventional assumptions about the lack of inventiveness among blacks, of the poverty of their past, the primitiveness of their ancestors, the paucity of their contribution to civilization. This book and the information it contains shatters all of these assumptions. Students should come away from a study of it with a new eye, a different vision and perspective of the African past and the modern black contribution. They must walk through the labyrinth of these essays, using its authors as their lights and guides, until they emerge from the end of the long dark tunnel of Eurocentric myth.

Ivan Van Sertima

BIBLIOGRAPHICAL GUIDE

John Henrik Clarke

The important contribution of African people to science and inventions is not new. In fact it is part of a very old story—as old as thinking man. Africans were the first inventors and the first scientists. In his booklet, "The African Contribution," Part one, the writer John M. Weatherwax says, in essence,

> Early Africans made hooks to catch fish, spears to hunt with, stone knives to cut with, the bolo with which to catch birds and animals, the blowgun, the hammer, the stone axe, canoes and paddles, bags and buckets, poles for carrying things, bows and arrows. This was a period in the early history of mankind called the old stone age. African inventions were already the start of man's use of power. Africans gave mankind the first machine. It was the fire stick. Knives and hammers and axes were the first tools. It is the making of tools that sets man apart from and in a sense above all living creatures. Africans started mankind along the tool-making path. From the blow-gun of ancient Africa, there followed, in later ages, many devices based on the same principle. Some of those are: the bellows, bamboo air pumps, the rifle, the pistol, the revolver, the automatic, the machine gun—and even those industrial guns that puff grains. African hunters many times cut up game. There still exist, from the Old Stone Age, drawings of animal bones, hearts and other organs. These early drawings are a part of man's early beginnings in the field of anatomy.

It must be understood that the Africans who were brought to the Americas and The Caribbean Islands, against their will, did not arrive culturally and technologically empty-handed. Some of them had been craftsmen and thinkers in Africa.

In this selected Bibliography of books, pamphlets and articles on African-Americans in Science and Invention, I am calling attention mainly to materials that are not difficult to obtain.

BIBLIOGRAPHY

"The Colored Inventor," by Henry Baker. Crisis Publishing Company, New York, NY, 1913. One of the early books on the subject.

"Great Negroes Past and Present," by Russell L. Adams. Third Edition. Afro-Am Publishing Company, Inc., Chicago, Ill., 1969. Chapter Four "Blacks in Science and Industry," is clearly written and a good introduction to the subject.

"The African Contribution," by John M. Weatherwax, Part One. Publisher: Aquarian Spiritual Center Bookshop, Los Angeles, CA., 1964. Very good on the African origins of Western technology.

"Black Pioneers of Science and Invention," by Louis Haber. Harcourt, Brace and World, Inc., New York, NY, 1970. One of the best of the recent books on the subject. The bibliography is extensive and most useful for teachers of this subject.

"The Hidden Contributors: Black Scientists and Inventors in America," by Aaron E. Klein. Doubleday and Co., New York, NY, 1971. A good general book that is also about some little known aspects of Black contributions to science and inventions.

"Eight Black American Inventors," by Robert C. Hayden. Addison-Wesley Co., Reading, Massachusetts, 1972.

"Seven Black American Scientists," by Robert C. Hayden. Addison-Wesley Co., Reading, Massachusetts, 1970.

"Black Inventors of America," by McKinley Burt, Jr. National Book Company, Portland, Oregon, 1969. The best illustrated book on the subject.

"Harlem: What Teachers, Parents, and Children Should Know About Our Community." Prepared by Beryle Banfield, for The Anniversary Bulletin Committee of P.S. 175, Manhattan, New York, NY, 1965. Excellent for teachers.

"Negroes For Medicine: Report of A Macy Conference," by Lee Cogan. The John Hopkins Press, Baltimore, MD, 1968.

"Charles Richard Drew. Pioneer in Blood Research," by Richard Hardwick. Charles Scribner's Sons. One of the most readable books about Charles Richard Drew.

"Negroes in Science: Natural Science Doctorates 1876-1969," by James M. Jay. Balamp Publishing Co., Detroit, Michigan, 1971.

"Benjamin Banneker: The Man Who Saved Washington," by Claude Lewis. McGraw-Hill Co., New York, NY, 1970.

"Your Most Humble Servant: The Amazing Story of Benjamin Banneker," by Sherley Graham, Julian Messner Co., New York, NY 1949.

"The Life of Benjamin Banneker," by Silvio A. Bedini. Charles Scribner's Sons. New York, NY, 1972. The definitive biography of the first American Black man of science.

"George Washington Carver," by Anne Terry White. Scholastic Book Services. A good introduction to the life of George Washington Carver for readers of early school age and adults who have no previous knowledge of this remarkable Black man of science.

"George Washington: An American Biography," by Rackhamp Holt, Doubleday and Co., New York, NY, 1943. One of the first extensive biographies of George Washington Carver.

"Black Americans in Science and in Engineering: Contributions of Past and Present," edited by Eugene Winslow. Afro-Am Publishing Co., Chicago, Ill., 1974. A well written introduction to the subject.

"Blacks in the Field of Science," proceedings of the 47th Annual Convention, National Technical Association, Inc., Nashville, Tennessee, July, 1975.

"Black Innovators," by Dr. Irene Diggs. Institute of Positive Education, Chicago, Ill., 1975. This is the best short book on the subject that I have so far seen written.

"1964 Freedom Calendar." The Museum of Negro History and Art. Chicago, Ill., 1964. Illustrated by Bernard Goss. Editor, Gerard N. Lew.

"Craftsmanship a Tradition in Black America," illustrated by Jessy Pinkney; historical consultant, Dr. Broadus N. Butler. Published by RCA, New York, NY, 1974.

"Science: Man's Greatest Adventure." Published by The Superintendent of Documents, U.S. Government Printing Office, Washington, D.C., 1972.

"Lewis Howard Latimer: A Black Inventor." Published by Thomas A. Edison Foundation, Detroit, Michigan, 1973.

The following books by M.A. Harris were published by Negro History Associates, 1407 Linden Blvd., Brooklyn, NY:

"The Story of Lewis Latimer," 1964

"Black Inventors: The Revolutionary Period 1770-1790," 1964

"Early American Inventors, 18th and 19th Centuries," 1964

"Granville T. Woods Memorial: Collector's Edition," 1974

"Legacy For All: A Record of Achievements by Black American Scientists." Published by Western Electric. New York and Chicago, Illinois, 1973.

BIOGRAPHICAL NOTES ON CONTRIBUTORS

ADAMS III, Hunter Havelin

Formerly on staff (1969-1970) at the University of Chicago in the Chemistry Department, where he was in charge of operations of the mass spectrometer and also assisted graduate students in their research.

Since 1970 he has been at the Argonne National Laboratory at the ZGS Atomic Accelerator. There he has been advancing the state of the art of proton beam detection and diagnostic equipment, such as proportional wire counters.

He is currently researching the impact magnetic fields may have had on the rise of civilizations. Has written science-related articles for *Ebony Jr.*

ASANTE, Molefi and Kariamu

Mr. Molefi Asante is Professor, Department of Communication, State University of New York, Buffalo. He is the author of twenty books and over 70 articles and serves as the editor of the *Journal of Black Studies*.

Ms. Kariamu Asante is Fulbright Professor, University of Zimbabwe, and founder of The National Dance Company of Zimbabwe. She is a choreographer and dance historian whose work appears in several journals and magazines; *Essence, Black World, Africa*.

CLARKE, John Henrik

Editor, writer, historian. His books include: *William Styron's Nat Turner: Ten Black Writers Respond* (1968), *Malcolm X, The Man and His Time* (1969), *Harlem U.S.A.* (1971), *Marcus Garvey and the Vision of Africa* (1974). Research Director of the First African Heritage Exposition; Associate Editor, *Freedomways Magazine*. Professor of African History and former Chairman, Black and Puerto Rican Studies Department, Hunter College, New York. On Editorial Board of the Journal of African Civilizations.

FINCH, Charles S. (M.D.)

Charles S. Finch, M.D. is a board-certified family physician, who was educated at Yale University and Jefferson Medical College. He is a former instructor of African History and Mathematics at the Commonwealth School in Boston and was the founder and chairman of the Raleigh Afro-American Life Focus Project in Raleigh, North Carolina. Dr. Finch was also an Epidemiologist for the Center for Disease Control and a Clincal Preceptor at the Duke-Watts Family Medicine

Center in Durham. He is currently Assistant Professor of community medicine and family practice at the Moorhouse School of Medicine in Atlanta, Georgia. Dr. Finch is the author of a general bibliographical guide to Afro-Eygptian and Afro-American studies, which is to be published shortly.

GENTLEMAN, Kirstie Lynn

Kirstie Gentleman is Director of Communicare, a creative resource center for individuals and organizations involved in communications. She is also a freelance writer and consultant on information program planning and spokesperson training. Initially educated as a dancer, she lectured at Carleton University in Canada on fostering creativity in children. She has worked in New York and New Jersey for 15 years as a news reporter, advertising copywriter and public relations manager.

Miss Gentleman has specialized in corporate information programs, relating science and technology to social and economic issues. She collaborated in Bell Labs research on programmed instructions, and coordinated television and radio coverage of the 1978 Nobel Prize in Physics. In 1980, she was photojournalist for a cross-cultural communications research team studying African roots of music and dance in Brazil.

GRAVES, Curtis M.

Chief of Community and Education Services Branch of the National Aeronautics and Space Administration in Washington, D.C. He is responsible for the creation and maintenance of healthy communication and relationships with educational communities nationwide. Before coming to NASA, he was Managing Associate and Director of Continuing Education for the National Civil Service League in Washington. He also served six years as a member of the Texas House of Representatives.

HAYDEN, Robert C.

Educator and Historian. Author of *Nine Black American Doctors* (1976), *Eight Black American Inventors* (1972), *Seven Black American Scientists* (1970) and *Blacks In America: Episodes in U.S. History* (1968). His *Nine Black American Doctors* was selected as one of the outstanding books for 1976 by a joint committee of the National Science Teachers Association and the Children's Book Council.

He has written and researched many articles on black history for both newspaper and television and is Regional Editor of *The Western Journal of Black Studies*.

He is on the faculty of the African American Studies Program at Northeastern University, Boston, and is presently engaged in educational research and development at the Education Development Center, Newton, Massachusetts, where he is a Project Director of the Ethnic Heritage Studies Program for Boston Youth.

JOHNSON, Willard R.

Professor of Political Science at the Massachusetts Institute of Technology. He is a specialist in African Development and is currently writing a book on African-Arab Relations. On the Board of Directors of the African Heritage Studies Association and the Journal of African Civilizations Ltd.

LYNCH, B.M.

Professor of Anthropology, Center for Archaeological Investigations, Southern Illinois University at Carbondale.

LUMPKIN, Beatrice

An Associate Professor of Mathematics at Malcolm X College in Chicago, Professor Lumpkin has written on the Afro-Asian foundations of mathematics for *Freedomways*, the *Mathematics Teacher*, *Science and Society* and *Historia Mathematica*. She has also written two major articles for Vol. 2, Nos. 1 & 2 of the *Journal of African Civilizations*—"The Pyramids—Ancient Showcase of Science and Technology" and "Africa in the Mainstream of Mathematics History." She is author of a children's book, *Young Genius in Old Egypt*.

MALLOY, Stewart C.

Masters Degree in Biological Oceanography from Dalhousie University, Halifax, Nova Scotia. Member of American Society of Limnology and Oceanography. His publications include "Bacteria induced shell disease of lobsters" and "Kinetic patterns of microbial amino acid uptake and mineralization in marine waters" (with Frank Barvenik). He is presently employed at Brookhaven National Laboratory as an Oceanographic Associate studying nutrients in seawater as affected by energy related activities.

NEWSOME, Frederick (M.D.)

Attending physician in medicine at Montefiore and Harlem Hospitals, New York. A specialist in internal medicine and hematology, he is a Diplomate of the

American Board of Internal Medicine. He is also a hieroglyphic scholar. He is presently a Lecturer in the Department of Medicine at the University of Jos, Nigeria.

PAPPADEMOS, John

John Pappademos is an Associate Professor at the University of Illinois' Chicago Circle campus, where he has been teaching and doing research in theoretical nuclear physics since the campus opened in 1965. Prior to that time he taught at the University of Illinois' Chicago Undergraduate Division at Navy Pier since 1957. He received his Ph.D. in 1964 from the University of Chicago. Recently his research interests have shifted to the social aspects of physics, including its philosophy and history. In 1981 he was a Visiting Professor in Greece, at the University of Crete.

ROBBINS, L.H.

A Professor of Anthropology, Michigan State University.

RYAN, Laurie

Student of Princeton University, majoring in mechanical and aerospace engineering. An amateur astronomer, she has studied physics and astrophysics while at Princeton.

SHORE, Debra

Managing Editor of the *Brown Alumni Monthly* for the past four years. Worked for several years at the Johns Hopkins Magazine before coming to Brown.

SPADY, James

James G. Spady is an historian, economist and lecturer based in Philadelphia, Pennsylvania. He is the author of an article "Cheikh Anta Diop and Freddie L. Thomas: Two Philosophical Perspectives on Pristine Black History" published in the *J.A.C.* (Vol. 1, No. 1) which is part of a larger study of Umum Black Historiography. Other recent publications by Spady include: "Tri-Muse: The Historiography of Joel A. Rogers, Druscilla Dundee Houston, and William Leo Hansberry" in the special 1970 issue of *Yardbird* edited by John Williams.

VAN SERTIMA, Ivan

Literary critic, linguist and anthropologist. Did field work in East Africa while doing studies in Linguistics and Anthropology at the University of London (School of Oriental and African Studies). Compiler of a *Swahili Dictionary of Legal Terms* (Tanzania, 1967). Press and Broadcasting Officer to the Guyana Information Services (1957-59). Broadcast weekly from Britain to Africa and the Caribbean (1960-70). Published *Caribbean Writers* (London, 1968). Author of major literary reviews. Honored by Nobel Committee of the Swedish Academy by being asked to nominate candidates for the Nobel Prize in Literature (1976-80)

Author of *They Came Before Columbus: The African Presence in Ancient America* (Random House, 1977). Associate Professor, Africana Studies, Rutgers University. Editor and Founder of *Journal of African Civilizations*.

WINTERS, Clyde-Ahmad

Graduate in history and anthropology, University of Illinois at Urbana. Specialist in African history and the history of Islam. His most important publications include: "The Influence of the Mande Scripts on Ancient American Writing Systems" (*Bull. de L'IFAN*, 1977), *African Colonists in the New World* (self-published, Chicago, 1978), and "Mao and Mohammed: Islam in the People's Republic of China" (*Asian Research Service*, Hong Kong, 1979). Director of the Uthman Dan Fodio Institute, Chicago. On Editorial Advisory Board of the *Journal of African Civilizations*.

ZASLAVSKY, Claudia

Professor Claudia Zaslavsky has been a mathematics teacher and curriculum specialist in New York State Schools for many years. She was an Assistant Professor of Mathematics Education at the College of New Rochelle. Her interest in Afro-American and African culture led to an investigation of mathematical development in Africa, an area completely neglected by historians of mathematics. Her travels in Africa and Europe and her interviews with African specialists in their own countries led to the first major work in this field: *Africa Counts: Number and Pattern in African Culture.*

Professor Zaslavsky has published in many mathematics and education journals and has conducted courses for teachers in the interdisciplinary and multicultural approach to the teaching of mathematics. Her book *Africa Counts* is now available in paperback from Lawrence Hill & Co.

ORDER FORM FOR BOOKS

Journal of African Civilizations

Books now available:

☐ African Presence in Early Europe $15.00
☐ African Presence in Early Asia (reprinted May) $15.00
☐ Great Black Leaders: Ancient and Modern (reprinted May) . $20.00
☐ Blacks in Science: Ancient and Modern (reprinted April) . . $15.00
☐ Black Women in Antiquity (reprinted April) $12.50
☐ Nile Valley Civilizations $15.00
☐ Great African Thinkers $15.00
☐ African Presence in Early America (to be reprinted November) $15.00
☐ Egypt Revisited $20.00

Forthcoming new issues:

1990 Annual ☐ African Presence in the Art of the Americas . $15.00
1991 Annual ☐ The Moors (Summer, 1991) $15.00

Name _____

Address _____

City/State/Zip _____

Checks and money orders should be made out to
"Journal of African Civilizations" and sent to:

Ivan Van Sertima (Editor)
Journal of African Civilizations
African Studies Department
Beck Hall
Rutger University
New Brunswick, New Jersey 08903

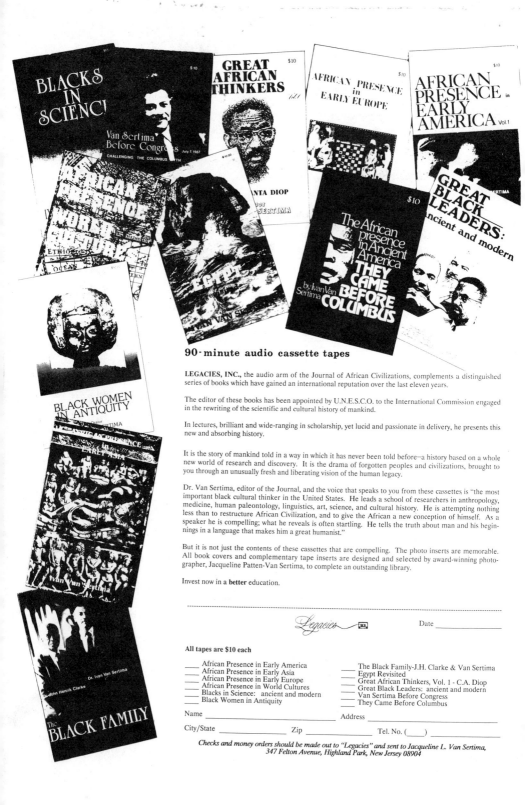

90-minute audio cassette tapes

LEGACIES, INC., the audio arm of the Journal of African Civilizations, complements a distinguished series of books which have gained an international reputation over the last eleven years.

The editor of these books has been appointed by U.N.E.S.C.O. to the International Commission engaged in the rewriting of the scientific and cultural history of mankind.

In lectures, brilliant and wide-ranging in scholarship, yet lucid and passionate in delivery, he presents this new and absorbing history.

It is the story of mankind told in a way in which it has never been told before—a history based on a whole new world of research and discovery. It is the drama of forgotten peoples and civilizations, brought to you through an unusually fresh and liberating vision of the human legacy.

Dr. Van Sertima, editor of the Journal, and the voice that speaks to you from these cassettes is "the most important black cultural thinker in the United States. He leads a school of researchers in anthropology, medicine, human paleontology, linguistics, art, science, and cultural history. He is attempting nothing less than to restructure African Civilization, and to give the African a new conception of himself. As a speaker he is compelling; what he reveals is often startling. He tells the truth about man and his beginnings in a language that makes him a great humanist."

But it is not just the contents of these cassettes that are compelling. The photo inserts are memorable. All book covers and complementary tape inserts are designed and selected by award-winning photographer, Jacqueline Patten-Van Sertima, to complete an outstanding library.

Invest now in a **better** education.

Legacies [💿]   Date _____

All tapes are $10 each

____ African Presence in Early America
____ African Presence in Early Asia
____ African Presence in Early Europe
____ African Presence in World Cultures
____ Blacks in Science: ancient and modern
____ Black Women in Antiquity

____ The Black Family-J.H. Clarke & Van Sertima
____ Egypt Revisited
____ Great African Thinkers, Vol. 1 - C.A. Diop
____ Great Black Leaders: ancient and modern
____ Van Sertima Before Congress
____ They Came Before Columbus

Name _____   Address _____

City/State _____ Zip _____   Tel. No. (____) _____

Checks and money orders should be made out to "Legacies" and sent to Jacqueline L. Van Sertima,
347 Felton Avenue, Highland Park, New Jersey 08904